중학 문법+쓰기

클리어.

Level 3

중학 문법+쓰기

클리어.

Level 3

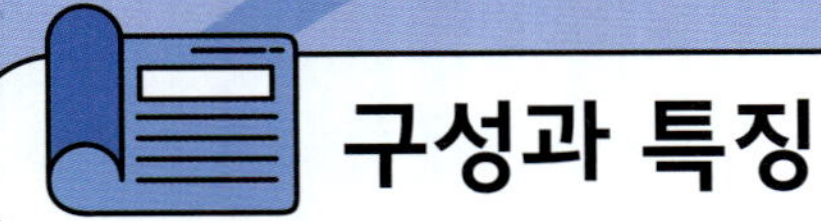

구성과 특징

영작 기본 훈련 단계

문법을 쓰기로 연결하는 체계적인 연습을 할 수 있습니다.
기본적인 형태 연습에서 완전한 문장 쓰기까지의 과정을 통해 영작 실력을 쌓을 수 있습니다.

1  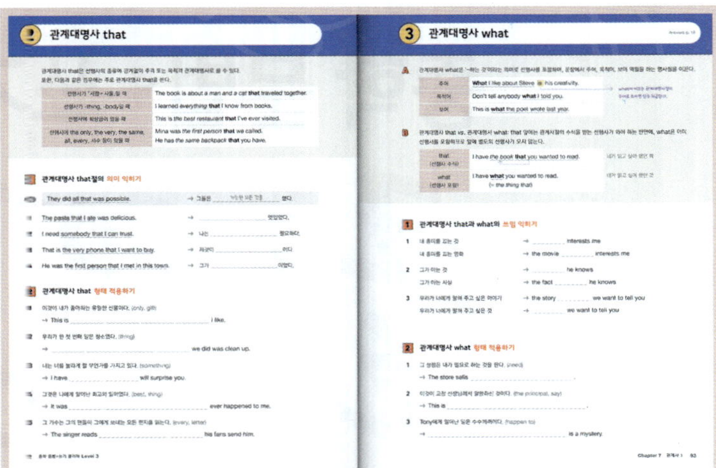

문법 설명 + 기본 형태 학습

세분화된 문법 요목으로 문법 개념을 더 쉽게 이해하고, 기본 형태 학습으로 바로 연습하여 더 쉽게 쓸 수 있습니다.

문장을 쓰기 위한 문법을 학습한 후

바로 해보는 기본 형태 학습

2   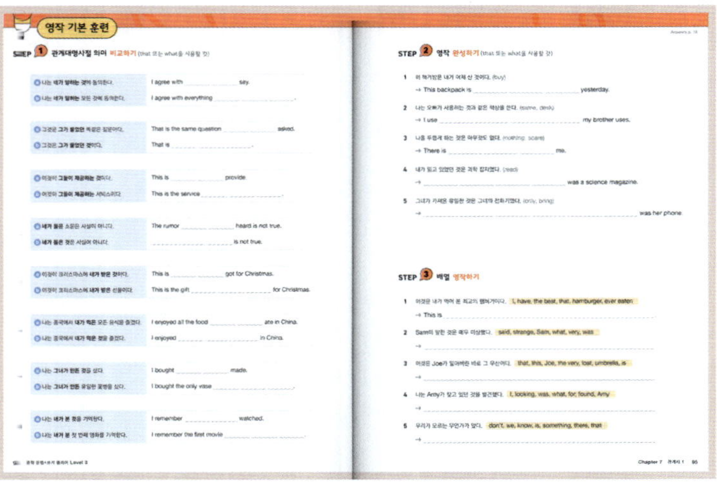

3단계 영작 기본 훈련

개념을 이해하며 쓰는 〈비교·확장하기 ▶ 영작 완성하기 ▶ 배열 영작하기〉의 3 STEP 훈련을 통해 영작의 기본기를 강화할 수 있습니다.

3

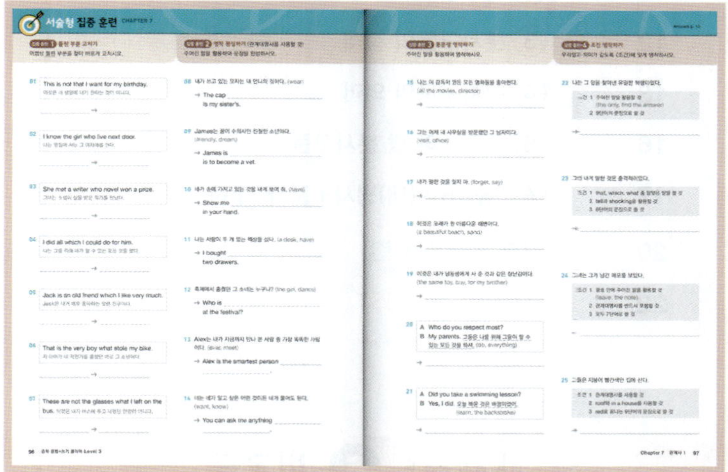

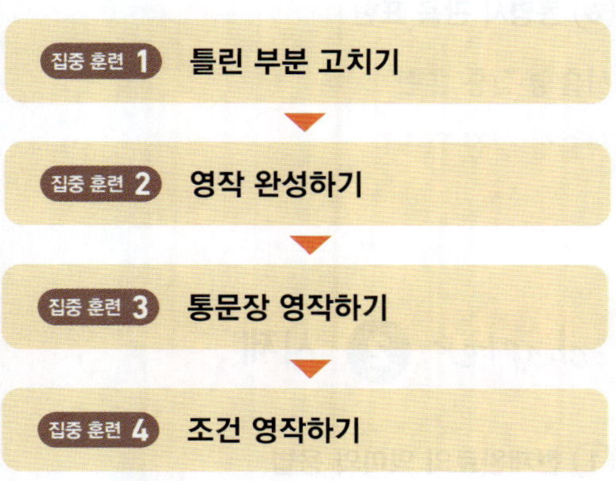

4가지 빈출 유형 서술형 집중 훈련

챕터별 4단계 집중 훈련을 통해 서술형 빈출 유형을 집중적으로 확실히 연습할 수 있습니다.

- 집중 훈련 **1** 틀린 부분 고치기
- 집중 훈련 **2** 영작 완성하기
- 집중 훈련 **3** 통문장 영작하기
- 집중 훈련 **4** 조건 영작하기

4

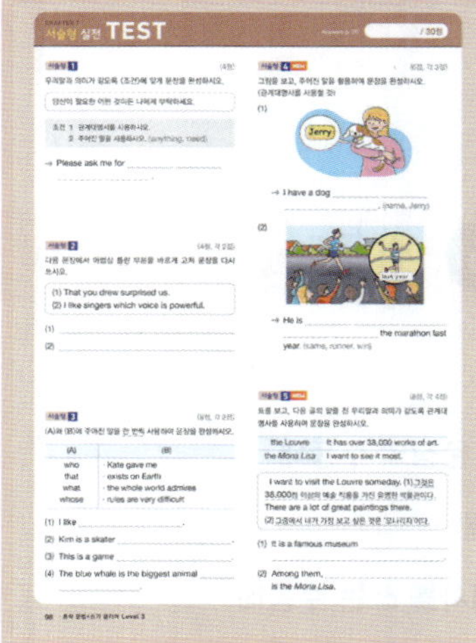

실전 유형으로 서술형 실전 TEST

체계적인 영작 훈련을 통해 쌓은 실력을 실전 유형에 적용해 보는 단계입니다.
학교 내신 시험에 출제되는 조건형·단락형·그림 서술형 문제 등 최신 서술형 유형을 골고루 배치하여 실전에 대비할 수 있습니다.

학교 내신 시험에 출제되는
다양한 유형의 문제를 풀어보며 챕터 완벽 마무리!

목차

chapter ❶ to부정사와 동명사

① to부정사의 역할 1 — 8
② to부정사의 역할 2 — 9
③ to부정사 구문 1 — 12
④ to부정사 구문 2 — 13
⑤ to부정사와 동명사 — 16
⑥ 동명사 관용 표현 — 17
서술형 집중 훈련 — 20
서술형 실전 TEST — 22

chapter ❷ 시제

① 현재완료의 의미와 용법 — 24
② 현재완료의 형태와 현재완료진행 — 25
③ 과거완료의 의미와 형태 — 28
서술형 집중 훈련 — 32
서술형 실전 TEST — 34

chapter ❸ 조동사

① can, may — 36
② must, have to — 37
③ 여러 가지 조동사 — 40
④ 조동사＋have＋p.p. — 41
서술형 집중 훈련 — 44
서술형 실전 TEST — 46

chapter ❹ 분사와 분사구문

① 분사의 종류와 쓰임 — 48
② 감정을 나타내는 분사 — 49
③ 분사구문의 형태 — 52
④ 분사구문의 의미 — 53
⑤ 주의해야 할 분사구문 — 56
⑥ 「with＋(대)명사＋분사」 구문 — 57
서술형 집중 훈련 — 60
서술형 실전 TEST — 62

chapter ❺ 비교급

① 원급/비교급 비교 — 64
② 원급과 비교급을 이용한 표현 — 65
③ 최상급 비교 — 68
④ 원급과 비교급을 이용한 최상급 의미 표현 — 69
서술형 집중 훈련 — 72
서술형 실전 TEST — 74

chapter ❻ 수동태

① 수동태의 형태 — 76
② 4형식과 5형식 문장의 수동태 — 77
③ 구동사의 수동태 — 80
④ by 이외의 전치사를 쓰는 수동태 — 81
서술형 집중 훈련 — 84
서술형 실전 TEST — 86

chapter **7** 관계사 1

1. 관계대명사의 역할과 종류   88
2. 관계대명사 that   92
3. 관계대명사 what   93

서술형 집중 훈련   96

서술형 실전 TEST   98

chapter **8** 관계사 2

1. 관계대명사의 생략   100
2. 관계대명사의 계속적 용법   101
3. 관계부사 1 | when, where   104
4. 관계부사 2 | why, how   105

서술형 집중 훈련   108

서술형 실전 TEST   110

chapter **9** 접속사

1. 시간·이유를 나타내는 접속사   112
2. 조건·양보를 나타내는 접속사   113
3. 상관접속사   116
4. 기타 접속사   117
5. 의문사가 있는 간접의문문   120
6. 의문사가 없는 간접의문문   121

서술형 집중 훈련   124

서술형 실전 TEST   126

chapter **10** 가정법

1. 가정법 과거   128
2. 가정법 과거 *vs.* 직설법 현재   129
3. 가정법 과거완료   132
4. 가정법 과거완료 *vs.* 직설법 과거   133
5. I wish 가정법   136
6. as if 가정법   137

서술형 집중 훈련   140

서술형 실전 TEST   142

chapter **11** 일치 및 특수구문

1. 수 일치   144
2. 시제 일치   145
3. 강조 구문   148
4. 부정 구문   149

서술형 집중 훈련   152

서술형 실전 TEST   154

to부정사와 동명사

1 to부정사의 역할 ①

2 to부정사의 역할 ②

3 to부정사 구문 ①

4 to부정사 구문 ②

5 to부정사와 동명사

6 동명사 관용 표현

A **명사적 용법**: to부정사는 문장 안에서 주어, 목적어, 보어 역할을 하며, '~하는 것, ~하기'로 해석한다.

주어	**To ride a roller coaster** is exciting. → **It** is exciting **to ride a roller coaster**. (It = to ride a roller coaster) 　　가주어　　　　　　　　　　진주어
목적어	I want **to ride a roller coaster**.
보어	My plan is **to ride a roller coaster in Disneyland**.

TIP to부정사(구)가 주어 역할을 하는 경우, 보통 주어 자리에 가주어 it을 쓰고 진주어인 to부정사(구)는 뒤로 보낸다.

B **to부정사의 의미상 주어**: to부정사의 행위자를 나타내며, to부정사 앞에 「for/of+목적격」의 형태로 쓴다.

for+목적격	대부분의 형용사(easy, important, possible, natural 등) 뒤에 올 경우
	It is *dangerous* **for kids** **to ride** bikes on the road.
of+목적격	사람의 성격, 태도를 나타내는 형용사(nice, mean, polite 등) 뒤에 올 경우
	It was *foolish* **of him** **to spend** all that money on video games.

① to부정사의 명사적 용법 익히기

	보기	find	finish	see

1 저녁노을을 보는 것은 멋졌다.　　　　　　→ __________ __________ the sunset was wonderful.

2 그의 목표는 그것을 3월까지 끝내는 것이다.　→ His goal is __________ __________ it by March.

3 John은 새 직장을 곧 찾기를 희망한다.　　　→ John hopes __________ __________ a new job soon.

② to부정사의 의미상 주어 형태 익히기

1 네가 네 가족을 그리워하는 것은 당연하다. (miss)

→ It is natural __________ you __________ __________ your family.

2 그가 3개월 안에 프랑스어를 배우는 것은 불가능했다. (learn)

→ It was impossible __________ him __________ __________ French in three months.

3 그들이 밤늦게 우리를 방문한 것은 무례했다. (visit)

→ It was rude __________ them __________ __________ us late at night.

 **2** to부정사의 역할 2

A   **형용사적 용법**: to부정사는 명사나 대명사를 뒤에서 꾸며 주는 역할을 하며, '~할, ~하는'으로 해석한다.

| (대)명사+to부정사 | There are *many places* **to visit** in the U.S. |
| (대)명사+to부정사+전치사 | I need *a chair* **to sit on**. (← sit **on** a chair) |

> **주의**   수식 받는 명사나 대명사가 전치사의 목적어이면 to부정사 뒤에는 반드시 전치사를 써야 한다.
> I need someone **to talk to**. (○) (← talk **to** someone)
> I need someone to talk. (×)

B   **부사적 용법**: to부정사는 동사, 형용사, 또는 문장 전체를 수식하는 부사 역할을 할 수 있다.

목적	~하기 위해	I went to the bookstore (**in order〔so as〕**) **to buy a book**.
결과	(~해서) …되다	The boy grew up **to be a scientist**.
감정의 원인	~해서	We were shocked **to hear the news**.
판단의 근거	~하다니	He must be a genius **to write such amazing stories**.
형용사 수식	~하기에	The building is easy **to find**.

> **TIP**   to부정사의 부정은 to부정사 앞에 not을 붙여 나타낸다.
> I studied hard **in order not to fail** the test again.

---

1 to부정사의 형용사적 용법 익히기

1   우리는 마실 것을 원한다. (drink)   → We want something ________ ________.

2   그들은 팔 과자를 조금 구웠다. (sell)   → They baked some cookies ________ ________.

3   나는 쓸 펜이 필요하다. (write)   → I need a pen ________ ________ ________.

4   그는 살 집을 찾고 있다. (live)   → He is looking for a house ________ ________ ________.

---

2 to부정사의 부사적 용법 의미 익히기

e.g.   I was surprised to get a good grade.   → 나는 ____좋은 성적을 받아서____ 놀랐다.

1   His speech was difficult to understand.   → 그의 연설은 ________________ 어려웠다.

2   I was careless to post that picture online.   → 내가 온라인에 ________________ 부주의했다.

3   I took a taxi in order not to be late.   → 나는 ________________ 택시를 탔다.

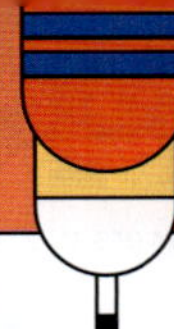

영작 기본 훈련

STEP 1 to부정사 확장하기

A to부정사의 의미상 주어로 확장하기

1
ⓐ 남을 **탓하기는** 쉽다. (blame)
It is easy __________ __________ others.

ⓑ **너희가** 남을 **탓하기는** 쉽다.
It is easy __________ __________ __________ __________ others.

2
ⓐ 그렇게 **말하는 것은** 현명하지 않다. (say)
It isn't wise __________ __________ that.

ⓑ **그가** 그렇게 **말하는 것은** 현명하지 않다.
It isn't wise __________ __________ __________ __________ that.

3
ⓐ 여기서 길을 **건너는 것은** 안전하다. (cross)
It is safe __________ __________ the street here.

ⓑ **우리가** 여기서 길을 **건너는 것은** 안전하다.
It is safe __________ __________ __________ __________ the street here.

B to부정사로 의미 확장하기

1
ⓐ 우리는 행복했다.
We were happy.　　　　　　　(finish)

ⓑ 우리는 시험을 **끝내서 행복했다.**
We were __________________________ the exam.

2
ⓐ 그는 스페인에 갔다.
He went to Spain.　　　　　　(learn)

ⓑ 그는 스페인어를 **배우기 위해 스페인에 갔다.**
He __________________________ Spanish.

3
ⓐ 우리는 빵을 좀 살 것이다.
We will buy some bread.　　　　(make)

ⓑ 우리는 샌드위치를 **만들 빵을** 좀 살 것이다.
We will buy __________________________ sandwiches.

4
ⓐ 그녀는 친절한 것이 틀림없다.
She must be kind.　　　　　　(help)

ⓑ 매일 그를 **돕다니** 그녀는 **친절한 것임이 틀림없다.**
She __________________________ him every day.

5
ⓐ 그 소년은 자랐다.
The boy grew up.　　　　　　(be)

ⓑ 그 소년은 **자라서** 작가가 **되었다.**
The boy __________________________ a writer.

STEP 2 영작 완성하기

1 우리 학교는 축제를 열기로 결정했다. (decide, hold)

→ Our school ___________ ___________ ___________ a festival.

2 네가 허락을 요청한 것은 매우 예의 바른 것이었다. (ask)

→ It was very polite ___________ ___________ ___________ ___________ for permission.

3 그녀는 잠에서 깨어 방이 어두워진 것을 알았다. (wake up, find)

→ She ___________ ___________ ___________ ___________ the room in darkness.

4 선생님께서 우리에게 쓸 주제를 주셨다. (write about, a topic)

→ The teacher gave us ___________ ___________ ___________ ___________ ___________.

5 나는 그 사고에 대해 듣고 충격 받았다. (hear, shocked)

→ I was ___________ ___________ ___________ about the accident.

STEP 3 배열 영작하기

1 나는 셀카를 찍기 위해 내 스마트폰을 자주 사용한다. to, use, take selfies, my smartphone

→ I often ___________________________________.

2 James는 다시는 학교에 늦지 않기로 약속하였다. not, late for, promised, to, school, be

→ James ___________________________________ again.

3 우리는 그 콘서트에 가게 되어 신이 났다. the concert, were, excited, to, we, go to

→ ___________________________________

4 이 앱은 사용하기 쉽다. easy, is, to, this app, use

→ ___________________________________

5 그녀는 그 경주를 마친 첫 번째 사람이었다. finish, the first person, the race, was, she, to

→ ___________________________________

too+형용사/부사+to부정사: …하기에 너무 ~한/하게, 너무 ~해서 …할 수 없는

(→ so+형용사/부사+that+주어+can't+동사원형)

> Lily is **too** young **to watch** the horror movie.
> → Lily is **so** young **that** she **can't watch** the horror movie.

TIP 「too+형용사/부사+to부정사」 구문에는 부정어가 없지만, too가 '너무 (지나치게)'라는 부정의 의미를 가진다.

문장의 주어와 to부정사의 행위자가 다를 때 의미상 주어를 쓴다.

주의 to부정사의 의미상 주어가 있는 경우엔 의미상 주어 가 that절의 주어가 된다.

> The problem was **too** difficult **for me** to solve.
> → The problem was **so** difficult **that I couldn't solve** it.
>   ①   ②   ③

① to부정사의 의미상 주어가 있는지 확인
② 시제 일치시키기
③ 문장의 주어가 to부정사의 목적어인 경우 that절에 반드시 목적어 쓰기

---

1 「too+형용사/부사+to부정사」 **형태 익히기**

e.g. 닿기에 너무 키가 작은 (reach) → ___too___ short ___to___ ___reach___

1 점심 식사를 하기에 너무 배부른 (have) → _________ full _________ _________ lunch

2 내가 잡기에 너무 빠른 (catch) → _________ fast _________ _________ _________

3 그가 재킷을 입기에 너무 더운 (wear) → _________ hot _________ _________ _________ _________ a jacket

---

2 「too+형용사/부사+to부정사」 **형태 적용하기**

1 그녀는 오늘 밤에 숙제를 끝내기에는 너무 피곤하다. (finish)

→ She is __________ tired __________ __________ her homework tonight.

2 그 사진은 그가 블로그에 올리기에는 너무 크다. (upload)

→ The photo is __________ large __________ __________ __________ __________ to his blog.

3 그는 너무 무서워서 그 롤러코스터를 탈 수 없었다. (ride)

→ He was __________ scared __________ __________ the roller coaster.

4 그 상자는 그녀가 들어 올리기에 너무 무겁다. (lift)

→ The box is __________ heavy __________ __________ __________ __________.

4 to부정사 구문 2

A 형용사/부사＋**enough**＋to부정사: …할 만큼 충분히 ~한/하게
(→ so＋형용사/부사＋that＋주어＋can＋동사원형)

> The businessman is rich **enough to buy** a yacht.
> → The businessman is **so** rich **that** he **can buy** a yacht.

> **주의** to부정사의 의미상 주어가 있는 경우엔 의미상 주어가 that절의 주어가 된다.
> The ceiling is low **enough for me to reach**.
> → The ceiling is so low **that I can reach** it.

B **seem**＋**to부정사**: ~해 보이다, ~인 것 같다(→ It seems (that)＋주어＋동사 ~)

> Ken **seems to know** a lot about music.
>
> **It seems (that)** Ken **knows** a lot about music.
> 　　　　　　　주어　시제 일치(seems이므로 현재시제로 씀)

1 「형용사/부사＋enough＋to부정사」 형태 적용하기

1 그 책가방은 내 모든 책을 가지고 다닐 만큼 충분히 크다. (carry)

→ The backpack is big ＿＿＿＿＿ ＿＿＿＿＿ ＿＿＿＿＿ all of my books.

2 그 방의 조명은 내가 책을 읽을 수 있을 만큼 충분히 밝았다. (read)

→ The light in the room was bright ＿＿＿＿＿ for me ＿＿＿＿＿ ＿＿＿＿＿ a book.

3 그녀의 목소리는 관중을 놀라게 할 만큼 충분히 아름다웠다. (surprise)

→ Her voice was beautiful ＿＿＿＿＿ ＿＿＿＿＿ ＿＿＿＿＿ the audience.

2 「seem+to부정사」 형태 적용하기

1 그는 학교에 있는 모든 사람들을 아는 것 같다. (know)

→ He ＿＿＿＿＿ ＿＿＿＿＿ ＿＿＿＿＿ everyone at school.

2 내 노트북 컴퓨터가 제대로 작동하는 것 같지 않다. (work)

→ My laptop computer doesn't ＿＿＿＿＿ ＿＿＿＿＿ ＿＿＿＿＿ right.

3 그 아이들은 생일 파티를 즐기는 것 같았다. (enjoy)

→ The children ＿＿＿＿＿ ＿＿＿＿＿ ＿＿＿＿＿ the birthday party.

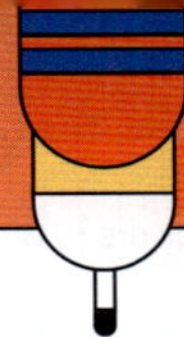

영작 기본 훈련

STEP 1 to부정사 구문 비교하기

---

e.g.

tall
be
wear

ⓐ 그녀는 패션 모델이 **될 만큼 충분히 키가 크다.**
→ She is ___tall___ ___enough___ ___to___ ___be___ a fashion model.

ⓑ 그녀는 자신의 예전 옷을 **입기에 너무 키가 크다.**
→ She is ___too___ ___tall___ ___to___ ___wear___ her old clothes.

1

small
fit
hold

ⓐ 그 상자는 장난감을 모두 **담기에는 너무 작다.**
→ The box is __________ __________ __________ __________ all the toys.

ⓑ 그 상자는 침대 밑에 **들어맞을 만큼 충분히 작다.**
→ The box is __________ __________ __________ __________ under the bed.

2

old
try
go

ⓐ 그녀는 새로운 것들을 **시도하기에 너무 나이 든** 것은 아니다.
→ She isn't __________ __________ __________ __________ new things.

ⓑ 그녀는 거기에 혼자 **갈 만큼 충분히 나이 든** 것은 아니다.
→ She isn't __________ __________ __________ __________ there alone.

3

warm
wear
play

ⓐ 우리가 밖에서 **놀 만큼** 날씨가 **충분히 따뜻하다.**
→ The weather is __________ __________ for us __________ __________ outside.

ⓑ 내가 목도리를 **하기에** 날씨가 **너무 따뜻하다.**
→ The weather is __________ __________ for me __________ __________ a scarf.

4

big
wear

ⓐ 이 셔츠는 **내가 입기에 너무 크다.**
→ This shirt is __________ __________ __________ __________ __________ __________ .

ⓑ 이 셔츠는 **네가 입을 수 있을 만큼 충분히 크다.**
→ This shirt is __________ __________ __________ __________ __________ __________ .

5

low
hide
jump

ⓐ 이 담은 **개들이 뛰어넘을 만큼 충분히 낮다.**
→ This wall is __________ __________ __________ __________ __________ over.

ⓑ 이 담은 **내가 뒤에 숨기에는 너무 낮다.**
→ This wall is __________ __________ __________ __________ __________ behind.

STEP **2** 영작 **완성하기**

1 그의 설명은 초보자들에게 도움이 될 만큼 충분히 간단했다. (simple, help)

→ His explanation was __________ __________ __________ __________ beginners.

2 그들은 너무 지쳐서 더 이상 걸을 수 없었다. (exhausted, walk)

→ They were __________ __________ __________ __________ anymore.

3 이 장소는 백 명의 사람들을 수용할 만큼 충분히 크다. (large, hold)

→ This place is __________ __________ __________ __________ 100 people.

4 Toby는 그의 이웃들과 잘 지내는 것 같다. (seem, get along well)

→ Toby __________ __________ __________ __________ __________ with his neighbors.

5 우리가 초인종 소리를 듣기에는 음악이 너무 시끄러웠다. (too loud, hear)

→ The music was __________ __________ __________ __________ __________ __________
the doorbell.

STEP **3** 문장 **전환하기** (to부정사를 사용할 것)

1 I am so busy that I can't hang out with my friends.

→ ____

2 It seems that Joan is worried about the test.

→ ____

3 These letters are so small that I can't read them.

→ ____

4 This wooden knife is so safe that children can use it.

→ ____

5 It seems that they have fun at school.

→ ____

5 to부정사와 동명사

A to부정사를 목적어로 쓰는 동사 *vs.* 동명사를 목적어로 쓰는 동사

to부정사를 목적어로 쓰는 동사	want, wish, agree, decide, expect, hope, need, plan, promise 등	We *plan* **to visit** Hawaii on vacation.
동명사를 목적어로 쓰는 동사	enjoy, finish, keep, mind, avoid, practice, quit, stop, give up 등	He *avoids* **trying** new things.

cf. stop은 동명사를 목적어로 쓰는 동사로, 뒤에 to부정사가 오면 부사적 용법 중 목적(~하기 위해)의 의미를 나타낸다.

She **stopped talking** to her neighbor.　그녀는 이웃과 **이야기하는 것을 멈췄다.**
She **stopped to talk** to her neighbor.　그녀는 이웃과 **이야기하기 위해 멈췄다.**

B to부정사와 동명사를 모두 목적어로 쓰는 동사

	동명사	(과거에) ~한 것을 기억하다	I *remember* **meeting** Tom last year.
remember+	to부정사	(미래에) ~할 것을 기억하다	I will *remember* **to meet** Tom tomorrow.
forget+	동명사	(과거에) ~한 것을 잊다	I *forgot* **bringing** my umbrella.
	to부정사	(미래에) ~할 것을 잊다	I *forgot* **to bring** my umbrella.

1 목적어의 형태 구분하여 쓰기

1　eat　They avoid ________________ fast food.

2　open　I don't mind ________________ the window.

3　drive　The man quit ________________ at the age of 75.

4　meet　They agreed ________________ on Sunday.

2 목적어의 의미 구분하여 쓰기

1　그는 물을 마시는 것을 멈췄다. (drink)

→ He stopped ________________ water.

2　그녀는 그에게 문자 메시지를 보내는 것을 잊었다. (send)

→ She forgot ________________ him a text message.

3　나는 오늘 아침에 내 개에게 먹이 준 것을 기억한다. (feed)

→ I remember ________________ my dog this morning.

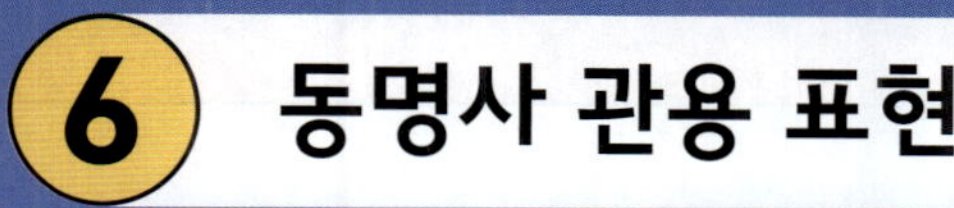 6 동명사 관용 표현

동명사를 사용한 관용 표현으로 다양한 의미를 나타낼 수 있다.

be used to -ing	~하는 데(것에) 익숙하다	be worth -ing	~할 가치가 있다
cannot(can't) help -ing	~하지 않을 수 없다	feel like -ing	~하고 싶다
look forward to -ing	~하기를 고대하다	on -ing	~하자마자
Would you mind -ing ...?	~해 주시겠어요?	There is no -ing	~하는 것은 불가능하다

I'm used to being the center of attention.
I can't help singing when I take a shower.
They **look forward to going** to the concert.

1 동명사 관용 표현 익히기

	보기	arrive	eat	jog	laugh	meet

1 학교에 도착하자마자 → on ___________ at school

2 당신을 다시 만날 것을 고대하다 → look forward to ___________ you again

3 매일 조깅하는 것에 익숙하다 → be used to ___________ every day

4 웃지 않을 수 없다 → can't help ___________

5 매운 음식을 먹고 싶다 → feel like ___________ spicy food

2 동명사 관용 표현 적용하기

1 그 문학 수업은 들을 가치가 있다. (take)

→ The literature class is ___________ ___________.

2 저와 자리를 바꿔 주시겠습니까? (change)

→ Would you ___________ ___________ seats with me?

3 다음에 무슨 일이 일어날지 아는 것은 불가능하다. (know)

→ There is ___________ ___________ what will happen next.

4 나는 경주를 마쳤을 때 울고 싶었다. (cry)

→ I ___________ ___________ ___________ when I finished the race.

영작 기본 훈련

STEP 1 to부정사 또는 동명사로 의미 **확장하기**

1
- ⓐ 나는 뉴욕을 방문했다.
  I visited New York.
- ⓑ 나는 뉴욕을 **방문한 것을 기억한다.**
  I __________ __________ New York.

2
- ⓐ 그는 재택근무를 한다.
  He works from home.
- ⓑ 그는 재택근무를 **하는 데 익숙하다.**
  He __________ __________ __________ __________ from home.

3
- ⓐ 나는 매일 저녁 컴퓨터 게임을 한다.
  I play computer games every evening.
- ⓑ 나는 컴퓨터 게임을 **하고 싶다.**
  I feel __________ __________ computer games.

4
- ⓐ 너는 이 호수에서 낚시할 수 없다.
  You can't fish in this lake.
- ⓑ 이 호수에서 **낚시하는 것은 불가능하다.**
  There __________ __________ __________ in this lake.

5
- ⓐ 그들은 밤에 외출하지 않는다.
  They don't go out at night.
- ⓑ 그들은 밤에 **외출하는 것을 피한다.**
  They __________ __________ out at night.

6
- ⓐ 우리는 새로운 자동차를 원한다.
  We want a new car.
- ⓑ 우리는 새로운 자동차를 **살 계획이다.**
  We __________ __________ __________ a new car.

7
- ⓐ 그녀는 그 소포를 보내지 않았다.
  She didn't send the package.
- ⓑ 그녀는 그 소포를 **보낼 것을 잊었다.**
  She __________ __________ __________ the package.

8
- ⓐ 그는 이집트로 여행 가기로 결정했다.
  He decided to travel to Egypt.
- ⓑ 그는 이집트로 **여행 가기를 고대한다.**
  He __________ __________ __________ __________ to Egypt.

STEP **2** 영작 **완성하기**

1 여기서 저를 기다려 주시겠어요? (mind, wait)

→ Would ___________ ___________ ___________ for me here?

2 그는 그 소식을 듣자마자 방을 뛰쳐나갔다. (hear, the news)

→ ___________ ___________ ___________ ___________, he ran out of the room.

3 그 문제는 신중하게 고려할 가치가 있다. (consider, carefully)

→ The matter is ___________ ___________ ___________.

4 그들은 오후 5시까지 공항에 도착할 것으로 예상했다. (expect, arrive)

→ They ___________ ___________ ___________ at the airport by 5 p.m.

5 나는 이번 여름에 이탈리아를 방문하기를 고대하고 있다. (visit)

→ I'm ___________ ___________ ___________ ___________ Italy this summer.

STEP **3** 배열 **영작하기**

1 Carol은 커피 마시는 것을 포기하기로 결심했다. drinking, to, coffee, give up, decided

→ Carol ____.

2 우리는 그의 생각을 비웃지 않을 수 없었다. couldn't, we, laughing, help, at his idea

→ ____

3 그는 약속 날짜를 바꾼 것을 잊었다. forgot, the date, of his appointment, he, changing

→ ____

4 이 구역에 주차하는 것은 불가능하다. no, there, in this area, parking, is

→ ____

5 나는 밤늦게까지 깨어 있는 것에 익숙하다. staying up late, am, I, to, at night, used

→ ____

집중 훈련 1 틀린 부분 고치기
어법이나 의미가 틀린 부분을 찾아 바르게 고치시오.

집중 훈련 2 영작 완성하기
주어진 말을 활용하여 문장을 완성하시오.

01 The girl was enough smart to solve the math problem.
그 소녀는 그 수학 문제를 풀 만큼 충분히 똑똑했다.

__________ → __________

02 There are no benches to sit around here.
이곳 주변에는 앉을 벤치가 없다.

__________ → __________

03 They stopped to play basketball when we arrived.
우리가 도착했을 때 그들은 농구 하는 것을 멈췄다.

__________ → __________

04 The dog seem to likes children.
그 개는 아이들을 좋아하는 것 같다.

__________ → __________

05 It wasn't easy for we to follow his lecture.
우리가 그의 강의를 따라가기는 쉽지 않았다.

__________ → __________

06 He avoided to answer my calls for a week.
그는 일주일 동안 내 전화를 받는 것을 피했다.

__________ → __________

07 She couldn't help cry during the movie.
그녀는 영화 보는 동안 울지 않을 수 없었다.

__________ → __________

08 그는 집을 칠하는 것을 어제 끝냈다. (paint, his house)

→ __________________________ yesterday.

09 저희 사진 한 장 찍어 주시겠어요? (would, take, mind)

→ __________________________ a picture of us?

10 나는 그를 볼 때마다 미소 짓지 않을 수 없다. (help, smile)

→ Whenever I see him, __________________.

11 나는 처음에는 안경을 쓰는 것에 익숙하지 않았다. (wear, glasses)

→ __________________________ at first.

12 나는 누구와도 이야기하고 싶지 않았다. (feel, talk)

→ __________________________ with anyone.

13 그 길은 트럭들이 지나가기에는 너무 좁다. (too, narrow, trucks, pass through)

→ The road is ____________________________________.

14 그들은 그들 사이에 비밀이 있는 것처럼 보였다. (seem, have a secret)

→ They __________________________ between them.

집중 훈련 3 통문장 영작하기
주어진 말을 활용하여 영작하시오.

15 그 박물관은 두 번 방문할 가치가 있다. (visit, twice)

→ ______________________________

16 그는 문을 잠그는 것을 잊었다. (lock, the door)

→ ______________________________

17 이 보드게임은 아이들이 할 수 있을 만큼 충분히 쉽다.
(board game, kids, play)

→ ______________________________

18 나는 내 스마트폰을 교실에 두고 온 것이 기억난다.
(leave, smartphone, in the classroom)

→ ______________________________

19 너를 실망시키지 않기 위해 나는 최선을 다할 것이다.
(do my best, disappoint)

→ ______________________________

20
A I passed the audition!
B 나는 좋은 소식을 듣게 되어서 기뻐.
    (pleased, the good news)

→ ______________________________

21
A I do volunteer work for the homeless
    every weekend.
B 네가 어려운 사람들을 도와주다니 착하구나.
    (it, nice, help, people in need)

→ ______________________________

집중 훈련 4 조건 영작하기
우리말과 의미가 같도록 〈조건〉에 맞게 영작하시오.

22 그녀가 그를 설득하는 것은 어려울 것이다.

조건 **1** 가주어 it을 사용할 것
      2 필요한 경우 적절한 전치사를 사용할 것
      3 〈보기〉의 단어를 사용할 것

보기 will   difficult   persuade

→ ______________________________

23 그 미술관은 우리가 하루 안에 전부 보기에는 너무 크다.

조건 **1** 「too ~ to부정사」 구문을 사용할 것
      2 to부정사의 의미상 주어를 포함할 것
      3 주어진 대화를 활용할 것

A The gallery is big.
B We can't see all in one day.

→ ______________________________

24 사람들은 소셜 미디어에서 그들의 생각들을 나누는 데 익숙하다.

조건 **1** 주어진 말을 활용할 것
          (used, share, ideas, on social media)
      2 10단어의 문장으로 쓸 것

→ ______________________________

25 그녀는 자라서 훌륭한 예술가가 되었다.

조건 **1** grow up, a great artist를 활용할 것
      2 모두 8단어의 문장으로 쓸 것

→ ______________________________

서술형 **1**　　　　　　(4점, 각 2점)

우리말과 의미가 같도록 어법상 <u>틀린</u> 부분을 바르게 고쳐 문장을 다시 쓰시오.

> (1) Sam forgot buying some milk on the way home.
> (Sam은 집에 오는 길에 우유 사는 것을 잊었다.)
> (2) It was rude for you to ask that question.
> (네가 그런 질문을 하다니 무례했다.)

(1) ___________________________________

(2) ___________________________________

서술형 **2**　　　　　　(4점)

그림을 보고, 우리말과 의미가 같도록 주어진 말을 사용하여 문장을 완성하시오.

나는 돌봐야 할 세 마리의 개가 있다. (take care of)

→　I have ___________________________.

서술형 **3**　　　　　　(6점, 각 3점)

다음 글의 밑줄 친 우리말과 의미가 같도록 주어진 말을 사용하여 영작하시오. (to부정사를 사용할 것)

> To be a K-pop star is Minjae's dream.
> (1) <u>그는 가수가 될 만큼 충분히 잘 노래 부른다.</u> (well, become, a singer) He decided to take part in an audition to make his dream come true. It's his turn next. (2) <u>그는 무대에서 신나 보인다.</u>
> (excited, on the stage)

(1) He sings ___________________________.

(2) He ___________________________.

서술형 **4**　　　　　　(6점, 각 3점)

두 문장의 의미가 같도록 문장을 완성하시오.

(1) We were too afraid to look down.

　　→ We were so ___________________________
　　___________________________.

(2) The boy is smart enough to read that difficult book.

　　→ The boy is so ___________________________
　　___________________________.

서술형 **5**　　　　　　(4점)

우리말과 의미가 같도록 주어진 말을 활용하여 영작하시오.

> 나는 휴가 가기를 고대하고 있다.

→ ___________________________

(look, go on vacation)

서술형 **6** NEW　　　　　　(6점, 각 2점)

가족 여행 중인 친구가 Diana에게 쓴 이메일을 보고, 〈조건〉에 맞게 문장을 완성하시오.

> 조건　1　to부정사 또는 동명사를 사용하시오.
> 　　　2　주어진 말을 활용하시오.
> 　　　　(1) watch a game
> 　　　　(2) us, buy tickets
> 　　　　(3) see

> Dear Diana,
> 　We arrived in London last weekend. We're having fun here. Yesterday, we went to a soccer stadium (1) ___________________.
> It was not easy (2) ___________________,
> but we finally got them. The game was worth (3) ___________________. We had a great time.

시제

1 현재완료의 의미와 용법

2 현재완료의 형태와 현재완료진행

3 과거완료의 의미와 형태

A 현재완료: 「have/has+p.p.」의 형태로, 과거에 일어난 일이 현재까지 영향을 미칠 때 쓴다.

현재완료
과거 ——— 현재

| 현재완료 | Mr. White **has taught** English since 2010. | (현재 계속 가르치고 있음) |
| 과거 | Mr. White **taught** English in 2010. | (현재 가르치는지는 모름) |

TIP yesterday, ago, when, last 등 특정 과거 시점을 나타내는 말은 현재완료와 함께 쓸 수 없다.

B 현재완료의 용법

함께 자주 쓰이는 표현

계속	~해 왔다	My uncle **has lived** here *since* 2020.	since, for, how long 등
경험	~한 적이 있다	**Have** you *ever* **seen** a shooting star?	before, ever, never 등
완료	막/이미 ~했다	We **have** *already* **finished** our project.	already, just, yet 등
결과	~해 버렸다	I **have lost** my passport.	

---

1 현재완료 **형태 익히기**

1 나는 3년 동안 John을 알고 지내 왔다. (know)
→ I ___________ ___________ John for three years.

2 그는 전에 스카이다이빙을 해 본 적이 있다. (try)
→ He ___________ ___________ skydiving before.

3 그녀는 이미 그 도시를 떠났다. (leave)
→ She ___________ already ___________ the city.

4 그들은 호주로 가 버렸다. (go)
→ They ___________ ___________ to Australia.

5 그는 어제부터 아프다. (be)
→ He ___________ ___________ sick since yesterday.

---

2 현재완료 **의미 익히기**

e.g. I have seen this movie twice.
→ 나는 이 영화를 두 번 ____본 적이 있다____.

1 I have studied Spanish since last year.
→ 나는 작년부터 스페인어를 ___________________.

2 She has spent all her money.
→ 그녀는 자신의 돈을 모두 ___________________.

3 The actor has just arrived at the airport.
→ 그 배우는 공항에 ___________________.

4 Have you ever eaten Thai food?
→ 너는 태국 음식을 ___________________?

2 현재완료의 형태와 현재완료진행

A 현재완료의 부정문과 의문문

| 부정문 | have/has+not(never)+p.p. | We **have not(haven't) seen** each other since 2023. |
| 의문문 | Have/Has+주어+p.p. ~? | **Have** you **talked** to Karen recently? |

B **현재완료진행**: 「have/has been+-ing」의 형태로, 과거에 시작된 일이 현재까지 계속 진행되고 있음을 나타낸다.

They **have been walking** in the park for an hour.
She **has been playing** mobile games for hours.

---

1 현재완료 부정문과 의문문 형태 익히기

1 경기가
- 이미 시작했다. (start) → The game __________ already __________.
- 아직 시작하지 않았다. → The game __________ __________ yet.
- 벌써 시작했니? → __________ the game already __________?

2 Amy는
- 전에 해외에 가 본 적이 있다. (be) → Amy __________ __________ abroad before.
- 해외에 가 본 적이 없다. → Amy __________ __________ __________ abroad.
- 해외에 가 본 적이 있니? → __________ Amy ever __________ abroad?

3 너는
- 이미 지불했다. (pay) → You __________ already __________.
- 아직 지불하지 않았다. → You __________ __________ __________ yet.
- 벌써 지불했니? → __________ you already __________?

---

2 현재완료진행 형태 적용하기

1 그는 한 시간 동안 기타를 연주하고 있다. (play)

→ He __________ __________ __________ the guitar for an hour.

2 그들은 두 시간 동안 저녁을 요리하고 있다. (cook)

→ They __________ __________ __________ dinner for two hours.

3 지난주부터 계속 눈이 오고 있다. (snow)

→ It __________ __________ __________ since last week.

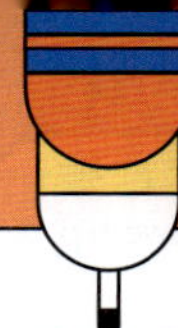

STEP 1 과거·과거진행과 현재완료·현재완료진행 비교하기

1 finish
- ⓐ 우리는 30분 전에 저녁 식사를 **끝냈다**.   We __________ dinner half an hour ago.
- ⓑ 우리는 막 저녁 식사를 **끝냈다**.   We __________ just __________ dinner.

2 clear
- ⓐ 그녀는 오늘 아침 식탁을 **치우지 않았다**.   She __________ __________ the table this morning.
- ⓑ 그녀는 아직 식탁을 **치우지 않았다**.   She __________ __________ the table yet.

3 meet
- ⓐ 너는 지난 주말에 Jane을 **만났니**?   __________ you __________ Jane last weekend?
- ⓑ 너는 전에 Jane을 **만난 적이 있니**?   __________ you __________ Jane before?

4 come
- ⓐ 그는 어제 회의에 **오지 않았다**.   He __________ __________ to the meeting yesterday.
- ⓑ 그는 아직 회의에 **오지 않았다**.   He __________ __________ to the meeting yet.

5 watch
- ⓐ 나는 그때 TV를 **보고 있었다**.   I __________ __________ TV at that time.
- ⓑ 나는 그때부터 TV를 **보고 있다**.   I __________ __________ __________ TV since then.

6 work
- ⓐ Tim은 2022년에 교사로 **일했다**.   Tim __________ as a teacher in 2022.
- ⓑ Tim은 2022년부터 교사로 **일해왔다**.   Tim __________ __________ as a teacher since 2022.

7 play
- ⓐ 우리는 9시에 테니스를 **치고 있었다**.   We __________ __________ tennis at 9 o'clock.
- ⓑ 우리는 한 시간 동안 테니스를 **치고 있다**.   We __________ __________ __________ tennis for an hour.

8 see
- ⓐ 너는 어제 Mike를 **봤니**?   __________ you __________ Mike yesterday?
- ⓑ 너는 최근에 Mike를 **본 적이 있니**?   __________ you __________ Mike lately?

STEP 2 문장 전환하기 (완료시제를 사용할 것)

> **e.g.** He was very busy two hours ago. He is still very busy. (be)
> → He _has been very busy for two hours_________________________.

1 He moved to the countryside two years ago. He still lives in the countryside. (live)

→ He ____.

2 Jane left her umbrella at home. She doesn't have it now. (leave)

→ Jane ____.

3 The wind was very strong last night. It is still very strong. (be)

→ ____.

4 They started waiting for her an hour ago. They are still waiting for her. (wait)

→ ____.

STEP 3 배열 영작하기

1 나는 Jack으로부터 문자 메시지를 방금 받았다. a text message, just, have, I, received

→ ____ from Jack.

2 Maggie는 월요일 이후로 내게 전화하지 않고 있다. since, called, not, Monday, me, has

→ Maggie ____.

3 우리는 한 시간 동안 같은 노래를 듣고 있는 중이다. the same song, we, been, have, listening to

→ ____ for one hour.

4 Dave는 이전에는 학교에 결석한 적이 결코 없다. before, never, been, has, absent from school

→ Dave ____.

5 그들은 어린 시절부터 서로 알고 지내 왔다. each other, since, have, childhood, known, they

→ ____.

A 과거완료는 「had+p.p.」의 형태로, 과거의 특정 시점을 기준으로 그 이전에 일어난 일이 기준이 되는 그 시점까지 영향을 미칠 때 쓴다.

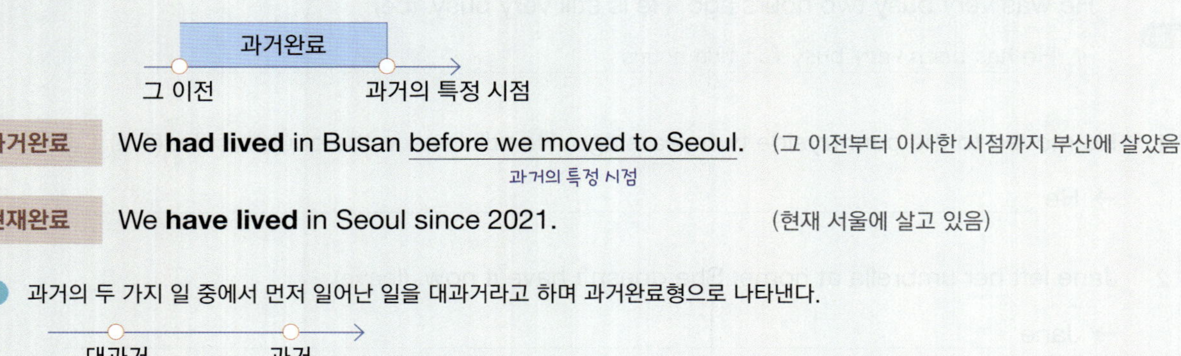

| 과거완료 | We **had lived** in Busan before we moved to Seoul. | (그 이전부터 이사한 시점까지 부산에 살았음) |
| 현재완료 | We **have lived** in Seoul since 2021. | (현재 서울에 살고 있음) |

TIP 과거의 두 가지 일 중에서 먼저 일어난 일을 대과거라고 하며 과거완료형으로 나타낸다.

Alex **lost** the notebook that I **had lent** him.

B 과거완료의 부정문과 의문문

| 부정문 | had+not(never)+p.p | I **had never been** to Europe until I went to school there. |
| 의문문 | Had+주어+p.p. ~? | **Had** the show already **started** when you turned on the TV? |

---

1 과거완료 형태 익히기

1	work	Steve ______________ ____________ as an actor Steve는 배우로 일했었다	until he quit. 그가 그만둘 때까지
2	prepare	We ____________ ____________ everything for the party 우리는 파티를 위한 모든 것을 준비해 두었다	before he arrived. 그가 도착하기 전에
3	travel	Susan ____________ ____________ ____________ by train Susan은 기차로 여행해 본 적이 없었다	until last year. 작년까지
4	take	I realized 나는 깨달았다	that my mom ____________ ____________ my umbrella with her. 엄마가 내 우산을 가지고 가셨다는 것을

2 과거완료 **형태 적용하기**

| 보기 | buy | pass | study | see | start |

1 나는 전에 그녀를 본 적이 있었기 때문에 그녀를 즉시 알아보았다.

→ I recognized her at once because I __________ __________ her before.

2 나는 네가 그 시험에 합격했다는 것을 몰랐다.

→ I didn't know that you __________ __________ the test.

3 그녀는 그 전날 샀던 책에 대해 환불을 받았다.

→ She got a refund for the book that she __________ __________ the day before.

4 Lily가 강의실에 들어갔을 때 이미 강의는 시작했었다.

→ The lecture __________ already __________ when Lily entered the room.

5 내가 그들을 만났을 때 그들은 이미 30분 동안 공부했었다.

→ They __________ already __________ for 30 minutes when I met them.

3 과거완료 부정문과 의문문 **형태 적용하기**

1 그녀는 2022년 이전에 중국에 가 본 적이 없었다. (be)

→ She __________ __________ __________ to China before 2022.

2 그 지역에서는 작년까지 비가 많이 오지 않았었다. (rain)

→ It __________ __________ __________ a lot in the area until last year.

3 그들은 지난여름 이전에 뱀을 본 적이 있었니? (see)

→ __________ __________ __________ snakes before last summer?

4 그녀는 감독이 되기 전에 선생님이었니? (be)

→ __________ __________ __________ a teacher before she became a director?

5 그 소년은 지난달까지 수영 강습을 받아 본 적이 없었다. (take)

→ The boy __________ __________ __________ swimming lessons until last month.

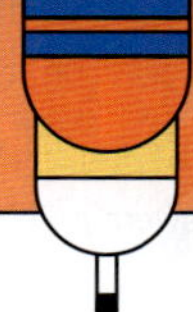

영작 기본 훈련

STEP 1 과거시제와 과거완료 의미 **비교하기**

1
ⓐ 영화는 **시작했다**. (begin)
The movie __________.

ⓑ 영화는 이미 **시작했었다**.
The movie __________ already __________.

2
ⓐ 나는 2년 전에 도쿄에 **살았다**. (live)
I __________ in Tokyo two years ago.

ⓑ 나는 2020년도에 도쿄에 2년 동안 **살았었다**.
I __________ __________ in Tokyo for two years in 2020.

3
ⓐ 나는 너를 지난 겨울에 **만났다**. (meet)
I __________ you last winter.

ⓑ 나는 전에 너를 **만난 적이 있었다**는 것을 깨달았다.
I realized that I __________ __________ you before.

4
ⓐ 그는 2023년에 파리를 **방문했다**. (visit)
He __________ Paris in 2023.

ⓑ 그는 2023년 이전에 파리를 두 번 **방문했었다**.
He __________ __________ Paris twice before 2023.

5
ⓐ 우리는 그 소식을 **듣지 못했다**. (hear)
We __________ __________ the news.

ⓑ 우리는 그 순간까지 그 소식을 **듣지 못했었다**.
We __________ __________ the news until that moment.

6
ⓐ 아빠는 아침 일찍 집을 **떠나셨다**. (leave)
My dad __________ the house early in the morning.

ⓑ 내가 일어났을 때 아빠는 이미 집을 **떠나셨었다**.
My dad __________ already __________ the house when I woke up.

7
ⓐ Sam은 그녀를 **알았다**. (know)
Sam __________ her.

ⓑ 내가 그녀를 소개하기 전부터 Sam은 그녀를 **알고 있었다**.
Sam __________ __________ her before I introduced her.

8
ⓐ 그녀는 아무 **말도 하지 않았다**. (say)
She __________ __________ anything.

ⓑ 내가 사과하기 전까지 그녀는 아무 **말도 하지 않았었다**.
She __________ __________ anything before I apologized.

STEP 2 영작 완성하기 (완료시제를 사용할 것)

1 그녀는 다리를 다쳤기 때문에 마라톤을 뛸 수 없었다. (hurt her leg)

→ She couldn't run the marathon because she ___________ ___________ ___________ ___________.

2 Toby가 도착했을 때, 우리 팀은 이미 3골을 넣었었다. (already, score)

→ When Toby arrived, our team ___________ ___________ ___________ three goals.

3 나는 거스름돈을 잘못 받았었다는 것을 알았다. (get the wrong change)

→ I found that I ___________ ___________ ___________ ___________ ___________.

4 우리가 그곳에 도착했을 때, 그들은 두 시간 동안 아무것도 먹지 않았었다. (eat, not)

→ When we got there, they ___________ ___________ ___________ anything for two hours.

5 그는 대학에 입학하기 전에 혼자 살아 본 적이 있었니? (live by himself)

→ ___________ ___________ ___________ ___________ ___________ before he entered college?

STEP 3 배열 영작하기

1 우리가 외출했을 때 비는 이미 그쳐 있었다. already stopped, had, it, raining

→ When we went out, ____.

2 그들은 밴쿠버로 이사하기 전에 10년 동안 토론토에 살았었다.

lived, they, for 10 years, before, in Toronto, they, had, moved

→ ____ to Vancouver.

3 그는 내가 그의 생일에 사 줬었던 가방을 무척 좋아했다. had, for, bought, birthday, his, I

→ He loved the bag ____.

4 우리 반은 대회 당일까지 계속해서 그 노래를 연습했었다. practiced, our class, over and over, the song, had

→ ____ until the day of the competition.

5 나는 내가 전등을 끄지 않았었다는 것을 깨닫지 못했다. hadn't, realize, I, turned off, didn't, the light, that

→ I ____.

집중 훈련 1 틀린 부분 고치기
어법상 틀린 부분을 찾아 바르게 고치시오.

집중 훈련 2 영작 완성하기 (완료시제를 사용할 것)
주어진 말을 활용하여 문장을 완성하시오.

01
> They have gone to Africa last week.
> 그들은 지난주에 아프리카에 갔다.

__________ → __________

02
> Lisa had her dog since she was three years old. Lisa는 세 살이었을 때부터 그녀의 개를 키워 왔다.

__________ → __________

03
> They have never gone to the zoo before.
> 그들은 전에 그 동물원에 가 본 적이 한 번도 없다.

__________ → __________

04
> When have you met Anna?
> 너는 언제 Anna를 만났니?

__________ → __________

05
> I use this phone since last month.
> 나는 지단달부터 이 전화기를 사용해왔다.

__________ → __________

06
> Did you ever eat sushi before?
> 너는 전에 초밥을 먹어 본 적이 있니?

__________ → __________

07
> Ellen hasn't studied Spanish before she traveled to Spain last year.
> Ellen은 작년에 스페인으로 여행 가기 전에는 스페인어를 공부한 적이 없었었다.

__________ → __________

08 그들은 휴가를 어디로 갈지 아직 결정하지 못했다.
(decide, where to go)

→ ______________________________
on vacation yet.

09 우리는 버스를 30분 동안 기다리고 있는 중이다.
(wait for)

→ ________________________ the bus
for 30 minutes.

10 우리는 그 자동차를 팔기 전에 5년 동안 그 차를 소유했었다. (own, for)

→ We __________________________
before we sold it.

11 너는 전에 학교에 지각한 적이 있니?
(ever, be late for)

→ ________________________ before?

12 그 아기는 2시부터 자고 있는 중이다. (sleep)

→ ________________________ since
2 o'clock.

13 내가 그 공지를 보기 전에는 아무도 내게 그 행사에 대해 말해 주지 않았었다. (nobody, tell, about the event)

→ ________________________ before
I saw the notice.

14 누군가 그의 자전거를 훔쳐 가 버렸다. (steal, bike)

→ Someone ______________________ .

집중 훈련 3 통문장 영작하기 (완료시제를 사용할 것)
주어진 말을 활용하여 영작하시오.

15 그들은 어린 시절부터 함께 자라왔다.
(grow up, together, childhood)

→ _________________________________

16 그가 은퇴할 때 그는 20년 동안 일해왔었다.
(work, retire, 20 years)

→ _________________________________

17 나는 자이언트판다를 본 적이 없다.
(never, see, a giant panda)

→ _________________________________

18 그녀는 이 과정을 3개월 동안 듣고 있는 중이다.
(take, course, months)

→ _________________________________

19 나는 내 신분증을 잃어버렸었기 때문에 그 건물에 들어갈 수 없었다. (enter, because, lose my ID)

→ _________________________________

20
A Hello. May I speak to Karen?
B No, I'm sorry. 그녀는 방금 외출했어요.
(just, go out)

→ _________________________________

21
A What's wrong? You look so sad.
B Emma가 다른 도시로 이사 가 버렸어.
(move, another city)
She's my best friend.

→ _________________________________

집중 훈련 4 조건 영작하기
우리말과 의미가 같도록 〈조건〉에 맞게 영작하시오.

22 Steve는 지난주부터 내게 말을 걸지 않고 있다.

조건 **1** 완료시제를 쓸 것
2 주어진 단어를 활용할 것
(not, speak to me, last week)
3 since와 for 중 알맞은 것을 쓸 것

→ _________________________________

23 Lucy는 작가가 되기 전에는 사진작가였었다.

조건 **1** 과거시제와 과거완료시제를 한 번씩 사용할 것
2 〈보기〉의 단어를 활용할 것

보기　a writer　　a photographer
be　　become　　before

→ _________________________________
____

24 너는 그랜드 캐니언에 가 본 적이 있니?

조건 **1** 7단어의 문장으로 쓸 것
2 주어진 단어들 중 필요한 것만 골라 활용할 것
(the Grand Canyon, go, be, to)

→ _________________________________

25 Sue는 두 시간째 피아노를 치고 있는 중이다.

조건 **1** 주어진 단어를 모두 사용할 것
(play the piano, for two hours)
2 필요시 형태를 변형할 것
3 모두 9단어로 쓸 것

→ _________________________________

서술형 1 (4점, 각 2점)

우리말과 의미가 같도록 어법상 틀린 부분을 바르게 고쳐 문장을 다시 쓰시오.

> (1) He visited 10 countries so far.
> (그는 지금까지 10개국을 방문했다.)
> (2) She hasn't eaten kimchi before she visited Korea. (그녀는 한국을 방문하기 전에는 김치를 먹어본 적이 없었었다.)

(1) _______________________________________

(2) _______________________________________

서술형 2 (6점, 각 3점)

완료시제를 사용하여 두 문장을 한 문장으로 쓰시오.

(1) Amy went to Canada. She isn't here now.

→ Amy ________________________________.

(2) Max came to my house last weekend. He is still staying at my house.

→ Max ________________________________.

서술형 3 (6점, 각 3점)

그림을 보고, 주어진 말을 활용하여 문장을 완성하시오. (완료시제를 사용할 것)

(1)  (2) 

(1) When I got home, _________________________________
_______________________________.
(my mother, already, prepare, dinner)

(2) The man _________________________________
_______________________ now. (run, 35 minutes)

서술형 4 (4점)

우리말과 의미가 같도록 주어진 말을 활용하여 문장을 완성하시오.

> Amy는 며칠 동안 잠을 잘 자지 못했어서 어젯밤에 지쳤다.

→ Amy ___________ ___________ last night, as she ___________ ___________ ___________ for several days. (exhausted, sleep well)

서술형 5 NEW (6점, 각 3점)

다음 문자 메시지를 보고, 밑줄 친 우리말과 의미가 같도록 〈조건〉에 맞게 영작하시오.

> Hi, Minho. (1) 나는 부산에 막 도착했어. (2) 나는 전에 이곳에 와 본 적이 없어. I'm going to stay here for a week and visit many places. I'm so excited!

> 조건 1 완료시제를 사용하시오.
> 2 주어진 말을 활용하시오.
> (1) just, arrive in
> (2) never, be, here, before

(1) _______________________________________

(2) _______________________________________

서술형 6 NEW (4점, 각 2점)

다음 기사를 읽고, (1), (2)에서 어법상 틀린 부분을 찾아 바르게 고쳐 쓰시오.

> **Mystery of the Dragon Castle**
> Have you heard of the Dragon Castle? It is a mysterious castle. (1) It amazed people for hundreds of years. (2) Last week, an old document about the castle has been found. Researchers hope this document will reveal the castle's secrets.

(1) _______________ → _______________

(2) _______________ → _______________

chapter 3

조동사

1 can, may

2 must, have to

3 여러 가지 조동사

4 조동사＋have＋p.p.

1 can, may

A can은 능력·가능, 허가, 요청 등을 나타낸다.

능력·가능	~할 수 있다 (= be able to)	I **can** play the drums well.
허가	~해도 된다 (= may)	You **can** use my computer.
요청	~해 주겠니?	**Can**(**Could**) you pick me up at the airport?
부정적 추측	~일 리가 없다	The news **cannot**(**can't**) be true.

요청의 의미일 때 could를 쓰면 can보다 더 정중한 표현이 된다.

> **TIP** 능력·가능을 나타내는 can은 be able to로 바꿔 쓸 수 있으며, be동사는 주어의 인칭과 수, 문장의 시제에 맞춰 쓴다.
> She **was able to** finish her homework. 〈과거시제〉
> He **will be able to** take a trip to Canada this summer. 〈미래시제〉

B may는 허가, 불확실한 추측을 나타낸다.

허가	~해도 된다	You **may** leave early today. **May** I hand in my report tomorrow?
불확실한 추측	~일지도 모른다	Kate **may**(**might**) come back late.

might는 may보다 실현 가능성이 더 낮은 추측을 나타낸다.

1 can과 may 형태 익히기

e.g. 차를 운전할 수 있다 → ___can(be able to)___ drive a car

1 화장실을 사용해도 된다 → ________________ use the bathroom

2 늦을지도 모른다 → ________________ be late

3 틀릴 리가 없다 → ________________ be wrong

2 can과 may 형태 적용하기

1 너는 한 번에 책 세 권을 빌릴 수 있다. (borrow)

→ You ________ ________ three books at one time.

2 그는 그 회의에 참석하지 않을지도 모른다. (attend)

→ He ________ ________ ________ the meeting.

3 그녀가 그 상황을 설명할 수 있을 것이다. (explain)

→ She ________ ________ ________ ________ ________ the situation.

2 must, have to

A   must는 강한 의무와 강한 추측을 나타낸다.

| 강한 의무 | ~해야 한다 | You **must** fasten your seat belt. |
| 강한 추측 | ~임이 틀림없다 | Tony **must** be good at math. |

> **TIP**   강한 의무를 나타내는 must는 have/has to로 바꿔 쓸 수 있으며, 주어의 인칭과 수, 문장의 시제에 맞춰 쓴다.
> She **had to** wake up early. 〈과거시제〉
> He **will have to** learn from his mistakes. 〈미래시제〉

cf.   강한 추측을 나타내는 must의 부정은 cannot(can't)(~일 리가 없다)이다.
    He **must** be a liar. (거짓말쟁이임이 틀림없다)
    ↔ He **can't** be a liar. (거짓말쟁이일 리가 없다)

B   must의 부정형 must not과 have/has to의 부정형 don't/doesn't have to는 서로 다른 의미를 가진다.

| 강한 금지 | ~하면 안 된다 | You **must not** make noise. |
| 불필요 | ~할 필요가 없다 | We **don't have to** worry. |

---

1   must와 have to 형태 익히기

1   그 소년들은 배고픈 게 틀림없다. (be)

→ The boys ___________ ___________ hungry.

2   그녀는 폭풍우 때문에 여행을 취소해야 했다. (cancel)

→ She ___________ ___________ ___________ the trip because of the storm.

3   우리는 그 대회에 온라인으로 등록해야 한다. (register)

→ We ___________ ___________ online for the competition.

2   must와 have to 부정문의 형태 익히기

1   너는 복도에서 뛰면 안 된다. (run)

→ You ___________ ___________ ___________ in the hallway.

2   그녀는 우산을 가져올 필요가 없다. (bring)

→ She ___________ ___________ ___________ ___________ an umbrella.

3   5세 미만의 어린이들은 입장료를 낼 필요가 없다. (pay)

→ Children under five ___________ ___________ ___________ ___________ the entrance fee.

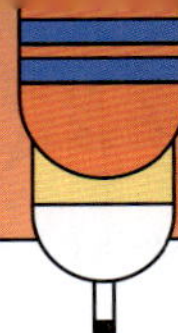

영작 기본 훈련

1 call

ⓐ Joe가 오늘 내게 **전화할지도 모른다.**
Joe ＿＿＿＿＿ ＿＿＿＿＿ me today.

ⓑ Joe는 오늘 내게 **전화해야 한다.**
Joe ＿＿＿＿＿ ＿＿＿＿＿ me today.

2 be

ⓐ 그의 이야기는 가짜**임이 틀림없다.**
His story ＿＿＿＿＿ ＿＿＿＿＿ fake.

ⓑ 그의 이야기는 가짜**일 리가 없다.**
His story ＿＿＿＿＿ ＿＿＿＿＿ fake.

3 rush

ⓐ 너는 **서두르면 안 된다.**
You ＿＿＿＿＿ ＿＿＿＿＿ ＿＿＿＿＿.

ⓑ 너는 **서두를 필요가 없다.**
You ＿＿＿＿＿ ＿＿＿＿＿ ＿＿＿＿＿ ＿＿＿＿＿.

4 know

ⓐ 그는 내 이름을 **알지도 모른다.**
He ＿＿＿＿＿ ＿＿＿＿＿ my name.

ⓑ 그는 내 이름을 **아는 게 틀림없다.**
He ＿＿＿＿＿ ＿＿＿＿＿ my name.

5 play

ⓐ 그녀는 하프를 **연주할 수 있다.**
She ＿＿＿＿＿ ＿＿＿＿＿ ＿＿＿＿＿ ＿＿＿＿＿ the harp.

ⓑ 그녀는 하프를 **연주해야 한다.**
She ＿＿＿＿＿ ＿＿＿＿＿ ＿＿＿＿＿ the harp.

6 park

ⓐ 너는 여기에 **주차해도 된다.**
You ＿＿＿＿＿ ＿＿＿＿＿ here.

ⓑ 너는 여기에 **주차해서는 안 된다.**
You ＿＿＿＿＿ ＿＿＿＿＿ here.

7 reply

ⓐ 나는 그의 이메일에 **답을 해야 했다.**
I ＿＿＿＿＿ ＿＿＿＿＿ ＿＿＿＿＿ to his email.

ⓑ 나는 그의 이메일에 **답을 해야 할 것 이다.**
I ＿＿＿＿＿ ＿＿＿＿＿ ＿＿＿＿＿ ＿＿＿＿＿ to his email.

8 find

ⓐ 그는 그 건물을 쉽게 **찾을 수 있다.**
He ＿＿＿＿＿ ＿＿＿＿＿ the building easily.

ⓑ 그는 그 건물을 쉽게 **찾을 수 있었다.**
He ＿＿＿＿＿ ＿＿＿＿＿ ＿＿＿＿＿ ＿＿＿＿＿ the building easily.

STEP **2** 영작 **완성하기** (<보기>의 조동사를 한 번씩만 쓸 것)

| 보기 | can | can't | might | must | have to |

1 나는 다음 달에 파리에 갈지도 모른다. (go to Paris)

→ I ___________ ___________ ___________ ___________ next month.

2 그녀는 물구나무를 설 수 있다. (stand on)

→ She ___________ ___________ ___________ her head.

3 나는 이번 주에 이 프로젝트를 끝내야 한다. (finish, this project)

→ I ___________ ___________ ___________ ___________ ___________ this week.

4 Alice는 그 면접 때문에 긴장한 게 틀림없다. (nervous)

→ Alice ___________ ___________ ___________ about the interview.

5 이 교과서는 네 것일 리가 없다. (yours)

→ This textbook ___________ ___________ ___________ .

STEP **3** 배열 **영작하기**

1 Karl은 수학 시험에서 A를 받을지도 모른다. `may, the math test, an A, get, on`

→ Karl ____ .

2 Amy는 그녀의 새로운 반 친구들을 만나게 되어 신이 난 게 틀림없다.

`to, her new classmates, must, excited, be, meet`

→ Amy ____ .

3 우리는 저녁 식사 예약을 할 필요가 없다. `don't, make a reservation, have to, for dinner`

→ We ____ .

4 Betty가 그것 때문에 너에게 화가 났을 리가 없다. `because of that, angry, can't, with you, be`

→ Betty ____ .

5 당신이 Dan을 학교까지 태워다 주겠어요? `drive, you, to school, Dan, could`

→ ____

3 여러 가지 조동사

A should, ought to, had better는 충고를 나타낸다.

should	~해야 한다, ~하는 게 좋겠다	You **should** exercise regularly.
ought to	~해야 한다	You **ought to** apologize to Jamie. You **ought** not **to** say that.
had better	~하는 것이 낫다	You **had better** clean your room right now. You **had better** not spend all your money.

cf. '(차라리) ~하겠다'를 의미하는 would rather는 had better와 의미가 비슷해 보이지만, had better는 '권고 또는 경고'를 나타내고 would rather는 '선호 또는 선택'을 나타낸다.

    I **would rather** go out tonight.　나는 오늘 밤에 차라리 나가겠다.

B 과거의 반복적인 일이나 습관은 used to 또는 would로, 과거의 상태는 used to로 나타낸다.

과거의 반복적인 일 또는 습관	~하곤 했다	We **used to** meet every Tuesday. = We **would** meet every Tuesday.
과거의 상태	~이었다	This city **used to** be quiet.

> **TIP**　used to는 '(과거에는) ~했으나, 지금은 그렇지 않다'라는 의미를 포함한다.
>
> There **used to** be a big tree, but now there is a building.

---

1 여러 가지 조동사 형태 익히기

1 조심스럽게 운전하는 게 낫다 (drive) → __________ __________ __________ carefully

2 지금 당장 떠나야 한다 (leave) → __________ __________ __________ right now

3 차라리 버스를 타겠다 (take) → __________ __________ __________ a bus

4 아침에 TV를 보곤 했다 (watch) → __________ __________ __________ TV in the morning

2 여러 가지 조동사 의미 익히기

e.g. He <u>used to live</u> in San Francisco. → 그는 샌프란시스코에 ____살았었다____.

1 You <u>had better tell</u> the truth. → 너는 사실을 ____________.

2 You <u>should listen to</u> her advice. → 너는 그녀의 조언을 ____________.

3 You <u>ought not to talk</u> loudly. → 너는 큰 소리로 ____________.

4 조동사＋have＋p.p.

「조동사＋have＋p.p.」는 과거의 일에 대한 추측이나 후회, 유감을 나타낸다.

may(might) have＋p.p.	~했을지도 모른다	You **may have made** a mistake on the exam.
must have＋p.p.	~했던 게 틀림없다	She **must have been** on vacation last week.
cannot(can't) have＋p.p.	~했을 리가 없다	James **cannot have written** the story.
should have＋p.p.	~했어야 했다 (그런데 안 했다)	You **should have checked** my message.

cf. 「should not(shouldn't) have＋p.p.」는 '~하지 말았어야 했다 (그런데 했다)'라는 의미를 나타낸다.

The concert was fantastic. You **shouldn't have missed** it.
콘서트는 환상적이었다. 너는 그것을 놓치지 말았어야 했다. (그런데 놓쳤다.)

1 「조동사＋have＋p.p.」 형태 익히기

1 잠들었을지도 모른다 (fall) → ___________ ___________ ___________ asleep

2 아팠던 게 틀림없다 (be) → ___________ ___________ ___________ sick

3 벌써 떠났을 리가 없다 (leave) → ___________ ___________ ___________ already

4 그 책을 읽었어야 했다 (read) → ___________ ___________ ___________ the book

5 늦잠을 자지 말았어야 했다 (oversleep) → ___________ ___________ ___________ ___________

2 「조동사＋have＋p.p.」 형태 적용하기

1 그가 그 피자 한 판을 혼자서 다 먹었을 리가 없다. (eat)

→ He ___________ ___________ ___________ the whole pizza alone.

2 나는 좌석을 더 일찍 예약했어야 했다. (book)

→ I ___________ ___________ ___________ a seat earlier.

3 Kate는 그 소식을 들었을지도 모른다. (hear)

→ Kate ___________ ___________ ___________ the news.

4 그들은 약속을 잊어버렸던 게 틀림없다. (forget)

→ They ___________ ___________ ___________ their appointment.

5 너는 직장을 그만두지 말았어야 했다. (quit)

→ You ___________ ___________ ___________ ___________ your job.

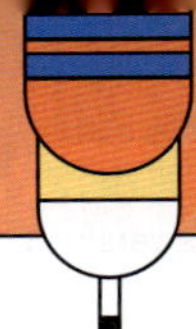

영작 기본 훈련

STEP 1 조동사 의미 **비교하기**

1
ⓐ 그는 런던으로 이사 갈지도 모른다.
He may move to London.

ⓑ 그는 런던으로 **이사 갔을지도 모른다**.
He ＿＿＿＿ ＿＿＿＿ ＿＿＿＿ to London.

2
ⓐ 그녀는 회의에 일찍 도착할 수 있다.
She can arrive at the meeting early.

ⓑ 그녀는 회의에 일찍 **도착했던 게 틀림없다**.
She ＿＿＿＿ ＿＿＿＿ ＿＿＿＿ at the meeting early.

3
ⓐ 너는 이 따뜻한 외투를 입어야 한다.
You should wear this warm coat.

ⓑ 너는 이 따뜻한 외투를 **입었어야 했다**.
You ＿＿＿＿ ＿＿＿＿ ＿＿＿＿ this warm coat.

4
ⓐ 모퉁이를 돌아서 상점이 있음이 틀림없다.
There must be a store around the corner.

ⓑ 모퉁이를 돌아서 상점이 **있었다**.
There ＿＿＿＿ ＿＿＿＿ ＿＿＿＿ a store around the corner.

5
ⓐ 그는 독일어를 말할 수 없다.
He can't speak German.

ⓑ 그가 독일어를 **말했을 리가 없다**.
He ＿＿＿＿ ＿＿＿＿ ＿＿＿＿ German.

6
ⓐ 나는 과거에 주말마다 캠핑을 가곤 했다.
I would go camping every weekend in the past.

ⓑ 나는 이번 주말에 **차라리 캠핑을 가겠다**.
I ＿＿＿＿ ＿＿＿＿ ＿＿＿＿ camping this weekend.

7
ⓐ 그녀는 오늘 밤에 가방을 쌀 지도 모른다.
She may pack her bags tonight.

ⓑ 그녀는 오늘 밤에 가방을 **싸는 것이 낫다**.
She ＿＿＿＿ ＿＿＿＿ ＿＿＿＿ her bags tonight.

8
ⓐ 너는 저 값싼 셔츠를 사면 안 된다.
You should not buy that cheap shirt.

ⓑ 너는 저 값싼 셔츠를 **사지 말았어야 했다**.
You ＿＿＿＿ ＿＿＿＿ ＿＿＿＿ ＿＿＿＿ that cheap shirt.

STEP **2** 영작 **완성하기**

1 Fred가 규칙을 어겼을 리가 없다. (break)

→ Fred ____________ ____________ ____________ the rules.

2 그들은 그 영화를 함께 보았을지도 모른다. (see)

→ They ____________ ____________ ____________ the movie together.

3 너는 선생님 말씀에 집중했어야 했다. (pay)

→ You ____________ ____________ ____________ attention to the teacher.

4 너는 시험 전에 잠을 좀 자는 편이 낫다. (get)

→ You ____________ ____________ ____________ some sleep before your test.

5 공원에는 놀이터가 있었다. (be)

→ There ____________ ____________ ____________ a playground in the park.

STEP **3** 배열 **영작하기**

1 그는 전화번호를 바꿨던 게 틀림없다.　changed, he, must, his phone number, have

→ ____

2 너는 네 친구들에게 소리 질러서는 안 된다.　your friends, shout at, not, ought, to, you

→ ____

3 너는 그 파티에 가지 않는 편이 낫다.　go, not, to the party, had, you, better

→ ____

4 그녀가 그 시험에서 떨어졌을 리가 없다.　have, cannot, she, the exam, failed

→ ____

5 그 문제는 Sam에게 너무 쉬웠을지도 모른다.　have, the problem, been, for Sam, too easy, might

→ ____

집중 훈련 1 틀린 부분 고치기
어법상 틀린 부분을 찾아 바르게 고치시오.

01
> May you recommend a good book?
> 좋은 책을 추천해 주시겠어요?

__________ → __________

02
> You have better check the weather before you leave.
> 너는 떠나기 전에 날씨를 확인하는 것이 낫다.

__________ → __________

03
> She should sleep more last night.
> 그녀는 어젯밤에 더 잤어야 했다.

__________ → __________

04
> You ought to not be rude to them.
> 너는 그들에게 무례하게 굴면 안 된다.

__________ → __________

05
> Mike have to go to bed now.
> Mike는 지금 잠자리에 들어야 한다.

__________ → __________

06
> Danny use to be healthy before the injury.
> Danny는 그 부상 전에는 건강했었다.

__________ → __________

07
> He must studied hard last weekend.
> 그는 지난 주말에 열심히 공부해야 했다.

__________ → __________

집중 훈련 2 영작 완성하기
주어진 말을 활용하여 문장을 완성하시오.

08 그는 이 수업을 들을 필요가 없다. (take, this class)

→ He ______________________.

09 나는 내일 너를 도와줄 수 있을 것이다. (able, help)

→ ______________________ tomorrow.

10 너는 달리기 전에 아무것도 먹지 않는 것이 낫다.
(better, eat, anything)

→ ______________________ before running.

11 그들은 일찍 떠났을지도 모른다. (leave)

→ ______________________ early.

12 우리는 더 큰 케이크를 샀어야 했다. (buy)

→ ______________________ a bigger cake.

13 Joe는 동물원에서 그의 지갑을 잃어버렸던 게 틀림없다.
(lose, his wallet)

→ Joe ______________________ at the zoo.

14 그가 비밀번호를 잊었을 리가 없다. (forget)

→ ______________________ the password.

집중 훈련 3 통문장 영작하기
주어진 말을 활용하여 영작하시오.

집중 훈련 4 조건 영작하기
우리말과 의미가 같도록 〈조건〉에 맞게 영작하시오.

15 너는 네 가방을 여기에 둬도 된다. (put, bag)

→ ________________

16 그는 그 대회 후에 피곤한 것임이 틀림없다.
(tired, after the competition)

→ ________________

17 그들은 매주 월요일에 도서관에 가곤 했다.
(the library, every Monday)

→ ________________

18 나는 오늘 밤에 차라리 TV를 보겠다. (watch TV)

→ ________________

19 너는 네 조부모님을 찾아뵈어야 한다. (ought, visit)

→ ________________

20
A I was late for school again.
B 너는 어젯밤에 알람을 맞췄어야 했어.
(set the alarm, last night)

→ ________________

21
A James isn't answering his phone.
B 그는 그것을 껐던 게 틀림없어.
(turn it off)

→ ________________

22 그녀는 그 요리법을 따를 필요가 없다.

조건 **1** 주어진 말을 사용할 것
(follow, the recipe)
2 줄임말을 사용할 것
3 7단어의 문장으로 쓸 것

→ ________________

23 그는 내년에 스페인어를 유창하게 말할 수 있을 것이다.

조건 **1** 주어진 말을 모두 사용할 것
(speak Spanish, fluently, next year)
2 미래시제를 사용할 것
3 10단어의 문장으로 쓸 것

→ ________________

24 네가 Jane을 봤을 리가 없다.

조건 **1** 조동사를 반드시 사용할 것
2 모두 5단어로 쓸 것

→ ________________

25 나는 그 농담을 하지 말았어야 했다.

조건 **1** make that joke를 활용할 것
2 알맞은 조동사를 추가하여 쓸 것
3 총 7단어의 문장으로 쓸 것

→ ________________

서술형 **1**   (4점, 각 2점)

빈칸에 알맞은 말을 〈보기〉에서 골라 쓰시오.

| 보기 | don't have to | must | used to |

(1) David ________________ read the newspaper,
     but now he reads the news on his phone.

(2) You ________________ bring your own lunch.
     Lunch will be provided.

서술형 **2**   (4점, 각 2점)

다음 문장에서 어법상 <u>틀린</u> 부분을 찾아 바르게 고쳐 쓰시오.

> (1) Neil had better apologizes for his mistake.
> (2) We must don't talk to others during the
>   exam.

(1) ________________ → ________________
(2) ________________ → ________________

서술형 **3**   (6점, 각 3점)

그림을 보고, 주어진 말을 사용하여 문장을 완성하시오.
(조동사를 사용할 것)

(1)   (2)

(1) Look at the tourists over there. One of them is
     holding a flag. They __________ __________
     Chinese. (be)
(2) Sally __________ __________ __________
     glasses when she was young. (wear)

서술형 **4**   (6점, 각 3점)

주어진 문장과 같은 의미가 되도록 문장을 완성하시오.
(조동사를 사용할 것)

(1) I'm sure that she didn't paint the picture.
     → She ________________________________.

(2) Maybe they took the wrong bus.
     → They ________________________________.

서술형 **5**   (4점)

우리말과 의미가 같도록 〈조건〉에 맞게 영작하시오.

> 나는 차라리 침묵을 지키겠다.

조건 1 조동사를 사용하시오.
      2 주어진 말을 사용하시오. (keep silent)

→ ____

서술형 **6** NEW   (6점, 각 3점)

다음 글을 읽고, 태우에게 할 수 있는 말을 〈조건〉에 맞게 완성
하시오.

> Last semester, Taewoo had a bad attitude.
> He often fell asleep in class. Also, he didn't
> listen to his teacher. That's why he got low
> scores on his final exams.

조건 1 「should (not) have+p.p.」를 사용하시오.
      2 윗글에 나온 표현을 활용하시오.

(1) Taewoo, you ________________________
     in class.

(2) Taewoo, you ________________________
     to your teacher.

chapter 4

분사와 분사구문

1 분사의 종류와 쓰임

2 감정을 나타내는 분사

3 분사구문의 형태

4 분사구문의 의미

5 주의해야 할 분사구문

6 「with + (대)명사 + 분사」 구문

① 분사의 종류와 쓰임

A 현재분사는 능동·진행(~하는, 하고 있는)의 의미를, 과거분사는 수동·완료(~된)의 의미를 나타낸다.

현재분사(-ing)	Wash fruit under **running** water. (흐르는 물)
	Don't wake up the **sleeping** baby. (자고 있는 아기)
과거분사(p.p.)	They found the **hidden** treasure. (숨겨진 보물)
	The **broken** window was fixed. (깨진 유리창)

B 분사는 명사를 수식하거나, 문장에서 주격 보어 또는 목적격 보어로 쓰인다.

(대)명사 수식	Look at the **sleeping** cat. <단독으로 명사 앞에서 수식>
	Look at the cat **sleeping** on the mat. <구를 이루어 명사 뒤에서 수식>
보어 역할	The boy seemed **tired**. <주격 보어>
	Max saw his friends **swimming**. <목적격 보어>

1 분사 형태 익히기

1 smile

미소 짓고 있는 소녀 → the ___________ girl

카메라를 향해 미소 짓고 있는 소녀 → the ___________ ___________ at the camera

2 steal

도난당한 시계 → the ___________ watch

어젯밤에 도난당한 시계 → the ___________ ___________ last night

3 run

달리고 있는 사람들 → the ___________ people

트랙 위를 달리고 있는 사람들 → the ___________ ___________ on the track

2 분사 형태 적용하기

1 나는 해변에서 놀고 있는 아이들의 사진을 찍었다. (play)

→ I took a picture of the kids ___________ at the beach.

2 이것들은 2000년대에 출간된 책들이다. (publish)

→ These are the books ___________ in the 2000s.

3 이 그림은 바다 위로 지고 있는 해를 보여 준다. (set)

→ This painting shows the sun ___________ over the sea.

2 감정을 나타내는 분사

분사가 수식하거나 설명하는 대상이 감정을 일으키는 원인이면 현재분사를, 감정을 느끼는 주체이면 과거분사를 쓴다.

amazing 놀라운	amazed 놀란	confusing 혼란스러운	confused 혼란스러워하는
shocking 충격적인	shocked 충격 받은	annoying 짜증스러운	annoyed 짜증 난
exciting 신나게 하는	excited 신이 난	disappointing 실망스러운	disappointed 실망한
satisfying 만족스러운	satisfied 만족한	touching 감동적인	touched 감동한
surprising 놀라운	surprised 놀란	embarrassing 당황스러운	embarrassed 당황해하는

The news was **shocking**.
People were **shocked** at the news.

The results were **disappointing**.
He was **disappointed** with the results.

1 감정을 나타내는 분사 형태 익히기

| 보기 |　　amaze　　confuse　　disappoint　　embarrass　　interest　　satisfy　　touch

1 나는 그 질문에 무척 혼란스러웠다.

→ I was very ___________ by the question.

2 그 고객은 그들의 서비스에 실망했다.

→ The customer was ___________ by their service.

3 나는 그녀의 놀라운 공연을 봐서 신이 났다.

→ I was excited to watch her ___________ performance.

4 우리는 그 음식이 만족스럽다고 생각했다.

→ We found the food ___________.

5 그는 그 당황스러운 순간을 피하고 싶었다.

→ He wanted to avoid the ___________ moment.

6 그녀는 대학에서 물리학을 공부하는 데 관심이 있다.

→ She is ___________ in studying physics at college.

7 그 책은 감동적인 이야기들로 가득 차 있다.

→ The book is full of ___________ stories.

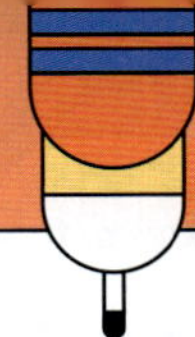

영작 기본 훈련

1 satisfy

ⓐ 우리는 그 저녁 식사에 **만족했다**.
We were ___________ with the dinner.

ⓑ 그 저녁 식사는 **만족스러웠다**.
The dinner was ___________.

2 burn

ⓐ 그 가족은 **불타고 있는** 집에서 빠져나왔다.
The family escaped from the ___________ house.

ⓑ 그들은 **불타 버린** 집에서 그 열쇠를 찾았다.
They found the key in the ___________ house.

3 surprise

ⓐ 그 연구자들은 **놀라운** 사실을 밝혀냈다.
The researchers revealed a ___________ fact.

ⓑ 모두가 그 사실에 **놀랐다**.
Everyone was ___________ by the fact.

4 touch

ⓐ 그녀의 친구에게서 온 편지는 **감동적이었다**.
The letter from her friend was ___________.

ⓑ 그녀는 그 편지에 **감동했다**.
She was ___________ by the letter.

5 shock

ⓐ 우리는 어제 **충격적인** 이야기를 들었다.
We heard a ___________ story yesterday.

ⓑ 그의 친구들 모두 **충격 받았다**.
All his friends were ___________.

6 build

ⓐ 모래성을 **쌓고 있는** 소년들을 봐라.
Look at the boys ___________ a sandcastle.

ⓑ 이것은 소년들에 의해 **만들어진** 모래성이다.
This is a sandcastle ___________ by the boys.

7 annoy

ⓐ 우리는 그의 태도에 **짜증이 났다**.
We were ___________ at his attitude.

ⓑ 아무도 그의 **짜증스러운** 태도를 좋아하지 않는다.
No one likes his ___________ attitude.

8 bore

ⓐ 그 아이는 그 영화가 **지루하다고** 생각했다.
The child thought the movie was ___________.

ⓑ **지루해진** 아이는 시끄럽게 굴기 시작했다.
The ___________ child began to make noise.

STEP **2** 배열 **영작하기**

1 그 보트는 그 두 섬을 잇는 다리 밑을 지나갔다.   the two islands, connecting, the bridge

→ The boat passed under ___________________________.

2 그 불꽃 축제는 매우 실망스러웠다.   was, the fireworks festival, disappointing, very

→ ___________________________.

3 배트맨 옷을 입고 있는 소년은 내 사촌이다.   the boy, is, wearing, my cousin, a Batman costume

→ ___________________________.

4 그녀는 큰 소음에 짜증 나 보였다.   the loud noise, she, by, annoyed, looked

→ ___________________________.

5 우리는 한 유명한 건축가에 의해 설계된 박물관을 방문했다.

  by, we, designed, the museum, a famous architect, visited

→ ___________________________.

STEP **3** 부분 **영작하기**

1 나는 중고차 한 대를 살 예정이다. (buy, use, car)

→ I'm going to ___________________________.

2 그녀는 공원에서 큰 소리로 울고 있는 아이를 보았다. (a child, cry loudly)

→ She saw ___________________________ in the park.

3 눈으로 뒤덮인 그 산은 매우 아름다웠다. (the mountain, cover with)

→ ___________________________ was very beautiful.

4 그 선수들은 새로운 규칙에 혼란스러워했다. (confuse, by, the new rules)

→ The players ___________________________.

5 사람들이 잔디 위에 누워 있는 개 한 마리를 발견했다. (a dog, lie, on the grass)

→ People found ___________________________.

3 분사구문의 형태

분사구문은 「접속사+주어+동사 ~」의 부사절을 분사를 이용해 부사구로 만든 구문이다.

As he realized his mistake,	he apologized to her.	① 부사절의 접속사 생략
he realized his mistake,	he apologized to her.	② 부사절의 주어 생략 (주절의 주어와 같은 경우)
Realizing his mistake, 그의 실수를 깨달았기 때문에	he apologized to her. 그는 그녀에게 사과했다.	③ 부사절의 동사를 현재분사(-ing)로 바꿔 씀 (주절의 시제와 같은 경우)

TIP 분사구문의 부정은 분사 앞에 not을 써서 나타낸다.
Not knowing what to do, he asked for help.　무엇을 해야할지 몰라서 그는 도움을 청했다.

1 분사구문으로 바꿔 쓰기

1 As he grew older, James became interested in history.

→ ______________________________, James became interested in history.

2 If you turn right at the corner, you will find the library.

→ ______________________________, you will find the library.

3 When I entered the park , I could smell lilacs.

→ ______________________________, I could smell lilacs.

4 As she didn't have enough money, she couldn't buy a concert ticket.

→ ______________________________, she couldn't buy a concert ticket.

2 분사구문 형태 적용하기

1 Emma는 친구들에게 손을 흔들면서 작별 인사를 했다. (wave)

→ ___________ to her friends, Emma said goodbye.

2 우리는 택시를 기다리면서 인도에 서 있었다. (wait)

→ ___________ for a taxi, we stood on the sidewalk.

3 뉴질랜드에 살 때 Joe는 여행을 많이 했다. (live)

→ ___________ in New Zealand, Joe traveled a lot.

4 요리할 시간이 없어서 그들은 음식을 좀 배달시켰다. (have)

→ ___________ no time to cook, they had some food delivered.

4 분사구문의 의미

분사구문은 시간, 이유, 조건, 동시동작 등의 다양한 의미를 나타낸다.

시간	~할 때, ~하는 동안	**Opening** the window, she saw a bird. (→ *When(As)* she opened the window, she saw a bird.)
이유	~하기 때문에	**Feeling** confused, I kept silent. (→ *As(Because/Since)* I felt confused, I kept silent.)
조건	~하면	**Turning** to the right, you'll see the new hotel. (→ *If* you turn to the right, you'll see the new hotel.)
동시동작	~하면서	**Singing** loudly, he washed the dishes. (→ *While* he was singing loudly, he washed the dishes.)

TIP 의미를 명확하게 하기 위해 분사구문 앞에 접속사를 남겨 두기도 한다.

After **meeting** Kevin at the cafe, I came back home.　카페에서 Kevin을 만난 후에 나는 집으로 돌아왔다.

1 분사구문 의미 구분하여 쓰기

e.g. Listening to music, she read a book.　　이유 / (동시동작) →　음악을 들으면서

1 Taking the bus, you will arrive earlier.　　동시동작 / 조건 →

2 Working hard, I got tired.　　이유 / 동시동작 →

3 Eating popcorn, he watched a movie.　　동시동작 / 조건 →

2 분사구문 형태 적용하기

1 그 집은 언덕 위에 있기 때문에 전망이 좋다. (stand)

→ ___________ on a hill, the house has a good view.

2 Ben은 외투를 입으면서 집을 나섰다. (put)

→ ___________ on his coat, Ben left the house.

3 몸이 좋지 않아서 나는 자리에 앉았다. (not, feel)

→ ___________ ___________ well, I sat down.

4 네가 거리를 걸으면 새로운 건물들을 많이 볼 수 있을 것이다. (walk)

→ ___________ down the street, you will see many new buildings.

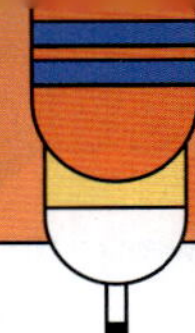

영작 기본 훈련

1 eat

- **a** 나는 항상 기분이 좋다.
  I always feel good.
- **b** **초콜릿을 먹을 때** 나는 항상 기분이 좋다.
  __________ chocolate, I always feel good.

2 walk

- **a** 나는 전화기를 잃어버렸다.
  I lost my phone.
- **b** **공원을 걷다가** 나는 전화기를 잃어버렸다.
  __________ around the park, I lost my phone.

3 see

- **a** 그 개는 짖었다.
  The dog barked.
- **b** **낯선 사람을 보자** 그 개는 짖었다.
  __________ a stranger, the dog barked.

4 give up

- **a** 너는 그것을 후회할 것이다.
  You'll regret it.
- **b** **지금 포기하면** 너는 그것을 후회할 것이다.
  __________ __________ now, you'll regret it.

5 know

- **a** 그는 그저 미소 지었다.
  He just smiled.
- **b** **뭐라고 말해야 할지 몰라** 그는 그저 미소 지었다.
  __________ __________ what to say, he just smiled.

6 feel

- **a** 그녀는 목도리를 했다.
  She wore a scarf.
- **b** **추웠기 때문에** 그녀는 목도리를 했다.
  __________ cold, she wore a scarf.

7 read

- **a** 나는 새로운 것들을 배웠다.
  I learned new things.
- **b** **이 책을 읽고서** 나는 새로운 것들을 배웠다.
  __________ this book, I learned new things.

8 listen

- **a** 나는 차를 마셨다.
  I drank tea.
- **b** **빗소리를 들으며** 나는 차를 마셨다.
  __________ to the rain, I drank tea.

STEP **2** 영작 완성하기

1 피곤해서 그녀는 평소보다 일찍 잠자리에 들었다. (be, tired)

→ ___________ ___________, she went to bed earlier than usual.

2 자신의 하루에 대해 이야기하면서 그들은 모바일 게임을 했다. (talk about their day)

→ ___________ ___________ ___________ ___________, they played mobile games.

3 그의 질문을 이해하지 못해서 그녀는 그에게 다시 말해 달라고 요청했다. (understand, question)

→ ___________ ___________ ___________ ___________, she asked him to repeat it.

4 신제품을 출시했기 때문에 그 회사는 팝업 스토어를 열었다. (launch, a new product)

→ ___________ ___________ ___________ ___________, the company opened a pop-up store.

5 결승선을 통과하면서 그 주자는 관중에게 손을 흔들었다. (cross, the finish line)

→ ___________ ___________ ___________ ___________, the runner waved at the crowd.

STEP **3** 부분 영작하기

1 해변을 걷다가 나는 예쁜 조개껍데기를 발견했다. (walk, on the beach)

→ _______________________________, I found a pretty seashell.

2 공항에 도착한 후에 나는 내 여행 가이드를 찾았다. (after, arrive, at the airport)

→ _______________________________, I looked for my tour guide.

3 하이킹하러 가고 싶지 않아서 나는 집에 머물렀다. (want, go hiking)

→ _______________________________, I stayed home.

4 그 버스를 기다리는 동안 나는 교통사고를 보았다. (while, wait for)

→ _______________________________, I saw a traffic accident.

5 모든 과정들을 마치고 나서 그녀는 수료증을 받았다. (complete, all the courses)

→ _______________________________, she received a certificate.

A **주어가 있는 분사구문**: 부사절의 주어와 주절의 주어가 다른 경우에는 부사절의 주어를 생략하지 않는다.

부사절의 주어 주절의 주어
As **the weather** was nice, **we** went on a picnic.   날씨가 좋아서 우리는 소풍을 갔다.

→ **The weather** **being nice**, we went on a picnic. 〈The weather를 생략하지 않음〉

B **수동형 분사구문**: 부사절의 동사가 수동태일 때 「being+p.p.」 형태로 쓰며, 이때 being은 주로 생략한다.

As it **is made** of colorful glass, the vase is beautiful.   색이 화려한 유리로 만들어져서 그 꽃병은 아름답다.
→ (Being) **Made** of colorful glass, the vase is beautiful.

cf. 부사절의 동사가 진행형일 때, 분사구문의 being은 보통 생략한다.
While she **was talking** to Tony, she missed your call.   그녀는 Tony와 이야기하다가 네 전화를 받지 못했다.
→ (Being) **Talking** to Tony, she missed your call.

1 주어가 있는 분사구문으로 바꿔 쓰기

1 Since it was late, we came back home. 시간이 늦어서 우리는 집으로 돌아왔다.

→ ___________ ___________ late, we came back home.

2 Because today is my birthday, I'm happy. 오늘이 내 생일이라서 나는 행복하다.

→ ___________ ___________ my birthday, I'm happy.

3 As the price was too high, they couldn't buy the house. 가격이 너무 비싸서 그들은 그 집을 살 수 없었다.

→ ___________ ___________ ___________ too high, they couldn't buy the house.

2 수동형 분사구문으로 바꿔 쓰기

1 As it was hit by a hurricane, the entire town was flooded.

→ ___________ by a hurricane, the entire town was flooded.

2 Since she was born in this town, she knows many people here.

→ ___________ in this town, she knows many people here.

3 While he was stuck inside the elevator, he shouted for help.

→ ___________ inside the elevator, he shouted for help.

4 Because this song was used in a movie, it became popular.

→ ___________ in a movie, this song became popular.

6 「with+(대)명사+분사」 구문

'~이 …한/된 채로'라는 의미로, 동시에 일어나는 동작을 나타낸다. (대)명사와 분사의 관계가 능동이면 현재분사를, 수동이면 과거분사를 쓴다.

with+(대)명사+현재분사	I jog every morning **with my dog following** me. (개가 나를 따라오면서) 능동 관계
with+(대)명사+과거분사	She was sitting **with her legs crossed**. (다리를 꼰 채로) 수동 관계

1 「with+(대)명사+분사」 구문 형태 익히기

1 run　　내 얼굴에 눈물이 흐르는 채로　　→ ___________ tears ___________ down my face

2 fold　　내 팔짱을 낀 채로　　→ ___________ my arms ___________

3 turn　　전등이 꺼진 채로　　→ ___________ the light ___________ off

4 blow　　바람이 불면서　　→ ___________ the wind ___________

5 lock　　그의 전화기가 잠긴 채로　　→ ___________ his phone ___________

6 delay　　우리의 비행편이 지연된 채로　　→ ___________ our flight ___________

2 「with+(대)명사+분사」 구문 형태 적용하기

1 나는 모자가 눈에 덮인 채 내 방으로 걸어 들어갔다. (cover)

→ I walked in ___________ my hat ___________ in snow.

2 관객들이 '앙코르'를 외치면서 그 가수는 무대를 떠났다. (shout)

→ The singer left the stage ___________ the audience ___________ "Encore."

3 창문들이 닫힌 채로 그는 잠자고 있었다. (close)

→ He was sleeping ___________ the windows ___________.

4 그들은 눈을 반짝이며 그 배우를 바라보았다. (shine)

→ They looked at the actor ___________ their eyes ___________.

5 그녀는 무릎을 구부린 채 바닥에 앉았다. (bend)

→ She sat on the floor ___________ her knees ___________.

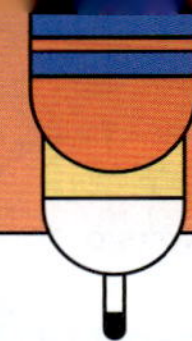

STEP 1 분사구문으로 문장 전환 · 확장하기

A 분사구문으로 전환하기

1 As it was a national holiday, many shops were closed.

→ _______________________, many shops were closed. (국경일이라서 많은 가게들이 문을 닫았다.)

2 Because a storm was coming, the farmers locked their animals inside.

→ _______________________, the farmers locked their animals inside.
(폭풍이 오고 있어서 농부들은 그들의 동물들을 안에 가두었다.)

3 When I was lost in the forest, I was scared.

→ _______________________, I was scared. (숲에서 길을 잃었을 때 나는 무서웠다.)

4 Since he was satisfied with his report, he decided to submit it.

→ _______________________, he decided to submit it. (그는 자신의 보고서에 만족해서 그것을 제출하기로 했다.)

B 「with + (대)명사 + 분사」 구문으로 확장하기

1
ⓐ 그는 벽에 기대어 있었다.　　He was leaning against the wall.　(cross)
ⓑ 그는 **팔짱을 낀 채로** 벽에 기대어 있었다.　　He was leaning against the wall ________ his arms ________.

2
ⓐ 그녀는 잠에서 깼다.　　She woke up.　(ring)
ⓑ **그녀의 전화기가 크게 울리면서** 그녀는 잠에서 깼다.　　She woke up ________ her phone ________ loudly.

3
ⓐ 그는 천천히 걸었다.　　He walked slowly.　(pour)
ⓑ **비가 쏟아지는 가운데** 그는 천천히 걸었다.　　He walked slowly ________ the rain ________ down.

4
ⓐ 그녀는 선생님을 바라보았다.　　She looked at the teacher.　(raise)
ⓑ 그녀는 **손을 든 채로** 선생님을 바라보았다.　　She looked at the teacher ________ her hand ________.

STEP **2** 영작 **완성하기**

1 팬들에게 둘러싸여 그 가수는 사인을 해 주었다. (surround, fans)

→ _____________ _____________ _____________, the singer signed autographs.

2 지역 농부들에 의해 생산되어 그 채소들은 항상 신선하다. (produce, local farmers)

→ _____________ _____________ _____________ _____________, the vegetables are always fresh.

3 너는 다리를 꼰 채로 앉으면 안 된다. (with, your legs, cross)

→ You should not sit _____________ _____________ _____________ _____________.

4 그녀는 눈을 감은 채 소파에 누워 있었다. (with, her eyes, close)

→ She was lying on the sofa _____________ _____________ _____________ _____________.

5 내일은 일요일이므로 우리는 늦게 일어나도 된다. (be, Sunday)

→ _____________ _____________ _____________, we can get up late.

STEP **3** 부분 **영작하기** (분사구문을 사용할 것)

1 간단한 영어로 쓰여져서 그 책은 읽기 쉽다. (write, in simple English)

→ _____________________________, the book is easy to read.

2 그 노래에 싫증이 나서 그는 그것을 그만 들었다. (tired of)

→ _____________________________, he stopped listening to it.

3 그녀의 개가 옆에서 잠든 채로 그녀는 책을 읽었다. (with, sleep)

→ She read a book _____________________________ next to her.

4 그는 안전벨트를 맨 채로 비행기 창밖을 내다보았다. (with, his seat belt, fasten)

→ He looked out the plane's window _____________________________.

5 정오가 되어서 해가 강하게 내리쬐고 있었다. (it, be, noon)

→ _____________________________, the sun was shining strongly.

집중 훈련 1 틀린 부분 고치기
어법상 <u>틀린</u> 부분을 찾아 바르게 고치시오.

집중 훈련 2 영작 완성하기 (분사를 사용할 것)
주어진 말을 활용하여 문장을 완성하시오.

01
I took a class teaching in English.
나는 영어로 가르치는 수업을 들었다.

_______________ → _______________

02
I found the ending of the story shocked.
나는 그 이야기의 결말이 충격적이라고 생각했다.

_______________ → _______________

03
Making of metal, the laptop is hard to break.
금속으로 만들어졌기 때문에 그 노트북은 부수기 어렵다.

_______________ → _______________

04
Turned to your left, you'll find the hospital.
왼쪽으로 돌면 너는 병원을 발견할 것이다.

_______________ → _______________

05
I'm reading a novel publishing last year.
나는 작년에 출간된 소설을 읽고 있다.

_______________ → _______________

06
Having not an umbrella, Jessica got wet in the rain.
우산이 없어서 Jessica는 비에 젖었다.

_______________ → _______________

07
Kelly focused on studying with the door closing.
Kelly는 문을 닫은 채 공부에 집중했다.

_______________ → _______________

08 우리는 James에 의해 제안된 아이디어들을 논의할 것이다. (the ideas, suggest)

→ We will discuss _______________

_______________.

09 이 신발을 파는 가게가 바로 길 건너편에 있다.
(the store, sell, these shoes)

→ _______________

is just across the street.

10 열심히 일하면서, 모두가 그 프로젝트를 제때 끝내기 위해 노력했다. (work, hard)

→ _______________, everyone tried to finish the project on time.

11 산산이 부서져서, 그 거울은 위험해 보였다.
(break, into pieces)

→ _______________, the mirror seemed dangerous.

12 설문 조사 결과들은 몇 가지 놀라운 사실들을 밝혀냈다.
(a few, surprise, facts)

→ The survey results revealed _______________

_______________.

13 노란색으로 칠해져서, 그 신호등들은 눈에 띈다.
(paint, yellow)

→ _______________, the traffic lights stand out.

14 그들은 양손을 높이 올린 채로 셀카를 찍었다.
(with, their hands, raise high)

→ They took a selfie _______________

_______________.

집중 훈련 **3** 통문장 영작하기 (분사를 사용할 것)

주어진 말을 활용하여 영작하시오.

15 이것은 유명한 사진작가에 의해 찍힌 사진이다.
(a photo, take, a famous photographer)

→ _______________________________________

16 초인종 소리를 들었을 때, 그는 문으로 달려갔다.
(hear, the doorbell, run to)

→ _______________________________________

17 짙은 안개에 가려져, 그 건물은 보이지 않았다.
(cover, a thick fog, invisible)

→ _______________________________________

18 웹사이트를 방문하면, 여러분은 더 많은 정보를 얻을 수
있습니다. (the website, get, more information)

→ _______________________________________

19 그녀는 우유를 함유하고 있는 어떤 것도 먹을 수 없다.
(eat, anything, contain)

→ _______________________________________

20
A Have you watched this movie?
B Yes. 결말이 매우 실망스러웠어.
　　　(the ending, very, disappoint)

→ _______________________________________

21
A How was the new restaurant? Was the
food good?
B It was okay. 나는 음식과 서비스에 만족했어.
　　　　　(satisfy, the food, the service)

→ _______________________________________

집중 훈련 **4** 조건 영작하기

우리말과 의미가 같도록 〈조건〉에 맞게 영작하시오.

22 Jane은 지루한 일에 지쳤다.

> 조건 **1** 분사를 사용할 것
> **2** 다음 단어들을 활용할 것
> (tire, of, bore, work)
> **3** 현재시제로 쓸 것

→ _______________________________________

23 그 도둑에 의해 운전된 자동차가 다른 자동차를 들이받았
다.

> 조건 **1** 주어진 말을 모두 활용할 것
> (drive, the thief, hit, another)
> **2** 분사를 사용할 것
> **3** 9단어의 과거시제 문장으로 쓸 것

→ _______________________________________

24 파리를 여행하는 동안, 우리는 에펠탑을 방문했다.

> 조건 **1** 분사구문으로 문장을 시작할 것
> **2** 주어진 말을 활용할 것
> (travel in Paris, visit, the Eiffel Tower)
> **3** 8단어의 문장으로 쓸 것

→ _______________________________________

25 그는 팔짱을 낀 채 그 선수들을 바라보았다.

> 조건 **1** 「with+명사+분사」 구문으로 쓸 것
> **2** 괄호 안의 단어를 활용할 것
> (the players, look at, his arms, fold)
> **3** 9단어로 쓸 것

→ _______________________________________

서술형 1 (4점)

〈보기〉와 같이 주어진 두 문장을 한 문장으로 쓰시오.

> 보기
> · The woman is my grandmother.
> · The woman is wearing a straw hat.
> → The woman wearing a straw hat is my grandmother.

· The flowers are in the living room.
· The flowers were given to me by John.

→ ______________________________ are in the living room.

서술형 2 (5점)

두 문장의 의미가 같도록 〈조건〉에 맞게 문장을 완성하시오.

> 조건 1 부사절을 분사구문으로 바꾸시오.
>   2 접속사를 생략하고 4단어로 쓰시오.

When the Earth is seen from the Moon, it looks like a ball.

→ ______________________________, the Earth looks like a ball.

서술형 3 (5점)

그림을 보고, 〈조건〉에 맞게 문장을 완성하시오.

> 조건 1 분사를 사용하시오.
>   2 주어진 말을 활용하시오. (with, cover)

→ Sally took me into the room ______________ ______________.

서술형 4 (4점, 각 2점)

다음 글을 읽고, 주어진 말을 빈칸에 알맞은 형태로 쓰시오.

> Kate finished reading a book by her favorite author yesterday. She was (1) ____________ (touch) by its ending. She will recommend this (2) ____________ (amaze) book to her friends.

서술형 5 (3점)

그림을 보고, 주어진 말을 활용하여 분사구문을 쓰시오.

→ ______________________________, I went back to sleep.
   (turn off, the alarm)

서술형 6 NEW (9점, 각 3점)

다음 일기를 읽고, 밑줄 친 (1)~(3)에서 어법상 틀린 부분을 바르게 고쳐 문장을 다시 쓰시오.

> (1) Today, on the way to school, my purse was stealing. (2) I was so shocking. After school, I got a call from the police. They said someone found my purse. (3) Heard the news, I was glad. But I when I checked my purse, there was no money in it.

(1) ______________________________

(2) ______________________________

(3) ______________________________

비교급

1 원급/비교급 비교

2 원급과 비교급을 이용한 표현

3 최상급 비교

4 원급과 비교급을 이용한 최상급 의미 표현

① 원급/비교급 비교

A 원급 비교는 비교하는 두 대상의 정도가 비슷하거나 같을 때 사용한다.

as+형용사/부사의 원급+as	…만큼 ~한/하게	Baseball is **as exciting as** basketball.
not as(so)+원급+as	…만큼 ~하지 않은/않게	An elephant is **not as(so) big as** a blue whale.

B 비교급 비교는 두 대상의 정도의 차이를 비교할 때 사용한다.

비교급+than	…보다 더 ~한/하게	This summer is **hotter than** last summer. Nate eats **more slowly than** his sister.

> **TIP** much, even, still, far, a lot은 비교급 앞에 쓰여 비교급을 강조한다. very는 원급을 강조할 때 사용한다.
> This new computer is *much* **better** than the old one. (훨씬 더 좋다)
> This new computer is *very* good.

1 원급/비교급 비교 형태 익히기

1 **fast**
치타만큼 빠르게 → ＿＿＿＿＿ ＿＿＿＿＿ ＿＿＿＿ the cheetah
치타보다 더 빠르게 → ＿＿＿＿＿ ＿＿＿＿＿ the cheetah

2 **cold**
작년만큼 추운 → ＿＿＿＿＿ ＿＿＿＿＿ ＿＿＿＿ last year
작년만큼 춥지 않은 → ＿＿＿＿＿ ＿＿＿＿＿ ＿＿＿＿＿ ＿＿＿＿ last year

3 **useful**
이 도구만큼 유용한 → ＿＿＿＿＿ ＿＿＿＿＿ ＿＿＿＿ this tool
이 도구보다 더 유용한 → ＿＿＿＿＿ ＿＿＿＿＿ this tool

4 **easy**
그 질문보다 더 쉬운 → ＿＿＿＿＿ ＿＿＿＿＿ that question
그 질문보다 훨씬 더 쉬운 → ＿＿＿＿＿ ＿＿＿＿＿ ＿＿＿＿ that question

2 원급/비교급 비교 형태 적용하기

1 자유의 여신상은 에펠탑만큼 유명하다. (famous)

→ The Statue of Liberty is ＿＿＿＿＿＿＿＿＿＿＿＿＿＿ the Eiffel Tower.

2 이 신발은 운동화만큼 편하지 않다. (comfortable)

→ These shoes are ＿＿＿＿＿＿＿＿＿＿＿＿＿＿ sneakers.

3 그들의 새 앨범은 이전 앨범보다 더 인기 있다. (popular)

→ Their new album is ＿＿＿＿＿＿＿＿＿＿＿＿＿＿ the previous one.

 **원급과 비교급을 이용한 표현**

A 원급을 이용한 표현

배수사+as+원급+as (= 배수사+비교급+than)	…보다 –배 더 ~한/하게	This rope is **four times as long as** that one. (= This rope is **four times longer than** that one.)
as+원급+as possible (= as+원급+as+주어+can)	가능한 한 ~한/하게	Tom came back **as soon as possible**. (= Tom came back **as soon as he could**.)

주어는 문장의 주어를 대명사로 쓰고, 과거시제(came)이므로 could로 쓴다.

TIP 배수를 나타낼 때 두 배는 twice로 나타내고 그 이후부터는 three times와 같이 「기수+times」로 나타낸다.

B 비교급을 이용한 표현

비교급+and+비교급	점점 더 ~한/하게	My English is getting **better and better**.
the+비교급 ~, the+비교급 …	~할수록 더 …하다	**The more** you laugh, **the happier** you get.

TIP 「비교급+and+비교급」 구문에서 비교급이 「more+원급」 형태인 경우 「more and more+원급」으로 쓴다.
I'm feeling **more and more confident** these days. (점점 더 자신감 있는)

1 원급을 이용한 표현 익히기

1 내 새 책상은 이전 책상보다 두 배 더 넓다. (wide)

→ My new desk is _________ _________ _________ _________ the old one.

2 내가 가능한 한 빨리 네 이메일에 답장을 하겠다. (soon)

→ I will reply to your email _________ _________ _________ I _________.

3 그는 가능한 한 조용히 문을 닫았다. (quietly)

→ He closed the door _________ _________ _________ _________.

2 비교급을 이용한 표현 익히기

1 네가 더 많이 읽을수록 더 잘 쓰게 될 것이다. (well)

→ The more you read, _________ _________ you will write.

2 서핑이 점점 더 인기를 얻고 있다. (popular)

→ Surfing is getting _________ _________ _________.

3 이 소설은 저 잡지보다 세 배 더 두껍다. (thick)

→ This novel is _________ _________ _________ _________ that magazine.

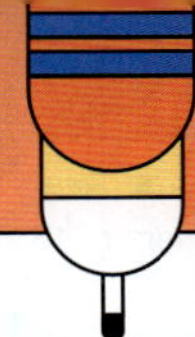

영작 기본 훈련

1 heavy

a 내 가방은 네 것**만큼** 무겁다.

My bag is ___________ ___________ ___________ yours.

b 내 가방은 네 것**보다 더** 무겁다.

My bag is ___________ ___________ yours.

2 deep

a 이 구덩이는 저 구덩이**보다 더** 깊다.

This hole is ___________ ___________ that one.

b 이 구덩이는 저 구덩이**보다 세 배 더** 깊다.

This hole is ___________ ___________ ___________ than that one.

3 fast

a 그녀는 Tom**만큼** 빨리 달렸다.

She ran ___________ ___________ ___________ Tom.

b 그녀는 **가능한 한 빨리** 달렸다.

She ran ___________ ___________ ___________ ___________.

4 large

a 내 집은 이 집**보다 더** 크다.

My house is ___________ ___________ this house.

b 이 집은 내 집**만큼** 크지 않다.

This house is not ___________ ___________ ___________ my house.

5 well

a 그는 테니스를 나**보다 더** 잘 친다.

He plays tennis ___________ ___________ I do.

b 그는 테니스를 나**보다 훨씬 더** 잘 친다.

He plays tennis ___________ ___________ ___________ I do.

6 narrow

a 이 길은 저 길**만큼** 좁다.

This road is ___________ ___________ ___________ that one.

b 이 길은 저 길**보다 두 배 더** 좁다.

This road is ___________ ___________ ___________ as that one.

7 hot

a 이번 여름은 지난여름**보다 더** 덥다.

This summer is ___________ ___________ last summer.

b 여름은 **점점 더** 더워지고 있다.

Summer is getting ___________ ___________ ___________.

8 happy

a 그는 여동생**보다 더 행복해** 보였다.

He looked ___________ ___________ his sister.

b 그의 집이 가까워질수록 그는 **더 행복해** 보였다.

The closer his home got, ___________ ___________ he looked.

STEP 2 영작 완성하기

1 그 영화는 원작 소설만큼 성공적이었다. (successful)

→ The movie was __________ __________ __________ the original novel.

2 기말시험은 중간시험보다 더 어려웠다. (difficult)

→ The final exam was __________ __________ __________ the midterm exam.

3 그 반죽은 종이만큼 얇지 않다. (thin)

→ The dough is __________ __________ __________ __________ paper.

4 나는 가능한 한 침착하게 있으려고 애썼다. (calm)

→ I tried to keep __________ __________ __________ __________.

5 네가 더 많이 소비할수록 더 적게 저축할 것이다. (much, little)

→ __________ __________ you spend, __________ __________ you will save.

STEP 3 배열 영작하기

1 빛은 소리보다 더 빠르게 이동한다. | sound, than, travels, faster |

→ Light ____________________________________.

2 실제 자동차는 이 모델보다 4배 더 크다. | as, this model, big, four times, as |

→ The real car is ___________________________.

3 시간이 돈보다 훨씬 더 중요하다. | a lot, important, money, more, than |

→ Time is ________________________________.

4 그 프로그램은 점점 더 흥미진진해지고 있다. | more, getting, is, more, interesting, and |

→ The program ___________________________.

5 가능한 한 빨리 우리의 숙제를 끝내자. | we, as, finish, can, our homework, quickly, as |

→ Let's ________________________________.

A 최상급 비교는 셋 이상을 비교하여 그중 하나의 정도가 가장 심하거나 높음을 나타낼 때 사용한다.

| the+최상급+ | in+장소/범위 | …에서 가장 ~한/하게 |
| | of+비교 대상 | |

Tony is **the most intelligent** student *in the class*.
(학급에서 **가장 똑똑한** 학생)

The math test was **the easiest** *of all the tests*.
(모든 시험들 중에서 **가장 쉬운**)

B 최상급을 이용한 표현

| one of the+최상급+복수명사 | 가장 ~한 …들 중 하나 |
| the+최상급+명사(+that)+주어
+have ever+p.p. | 지금껏 …한 것들
중에서 가장 ~한 |

She is **one of the greatest artists** in the world.
(가장 훌륭한 예술가들 중 하나)

This is **the best movie (that) I have ever seen**.
(내가 지금껏 본 것들 중에서 최고의 영화)

---

1 최상급 형태 익히기

e.g.   a big city   →   the biggest city

1   a happy moment   → ___________________________

2   a bad situation   → ___________________________

3   a popular song   → ___________________________

---

2 최상급 형태 적용하기

1   금성은 우리 태양계에서 가장 밝은 행성이다. (bright)

→ Venus is ___________ ___________ planet in our solar system.

2   Jane은 지금껏 내가 만난 사람들 중에서 가장 긍정적인 사람이다. (positive)

→ Jane is ___________ ___________ ___________ person I've ever met.

3   그는 그 셋 중에서 가장 책임감 있는 학생이다. (responsible)

→ He is ___________ ___________ ___________ student of the three.

4   John의 조언이 나에게 가장 도움이 되었다. (helpful)

→ John's advice was ___________ ___________ ___________ to me.

 4 원급과 비교급을 이용한 최상급 의미 표현

원급과 비교급을 이용해 최상급의 의미를 나타낼 수 있다.

최상급	the+최상급		가장 ~한
원급 이용	No (other)+단수명사 ~ as(so)+원급+as		(다른) 어떤 –도 …만큼 ~하지 않은
비교급 이용	No (other)+단수명사 ~ 비교급+than		(다른) 어떤 –도 …보다 더 ~하지 않은
	비교급+than any other+단수명사		다른 어떤 …보다 더 ~한

Vatican City is **the smallest country** in the world.
= **No (other) country** in the world is **as small as** Vatican City.
= **No (other) country** in the world is **smaller than** Vatican City.
= Vatican City is **smaller than any other country** in the world.

1 원급과 비교급 이용한 최상급 표현 익히기

1 Russia is the largest country in the world.

→ No other country is ＿＿＿＿ ＿＿＿＿ ＿＿＿＿ Russia.

→ No other country is ＿＿＿＿ ＿＿＿＿ Russia.

2 Mr. Parker is the wealthiest person in the city.

→ No one in the city is ＿＿＿＿ ＿＿＿＿ ＿＿＿＿ Mr. Parker.

→ No one in the city is ＿＿＿＿ ＿＿＿＿ Mr. Parker.

3 Antarctica is the coldest continent on Earth.

→ Antarctica is ＿＿＿＿ ＿＿＿＿ any other continent on Earth.

2 원급과 비교급 이용해 최상급 의미 나타내기

1 어떤 것도 가족보다 더 중요하지 않다. (important)

→ Nothing is ＿＿＿＿ ＿＿＿＿ ＿＿＿＿ family.

2 다른 어떤 스포츠도 스키를 타는 것만큼 신나지 않다. (exciting)

→ ＿＿＿＿ ＿＿＿＿ sport is ＿＿＿＿ ＿＿＿＿ ＿＿＿＿ skiing.

3 이 성당은 이 동네의 다른 어떤 건물보다 더 오래되었다. (old)

→ This cathedral is ＿＿＿＿ ＿＿＿＿ ＿＿＿＿ ＿＿＿＿ building in this town.

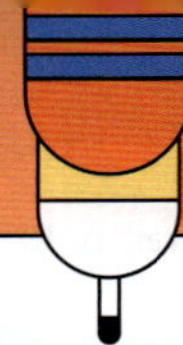

영작 기본 훈련

STEP 1 최상급 의미 **확장하기**

1

- ⓐ 나는 빠른 선수이다.
  I'm a fast player.
- ⓑ 나는 팀에서 **가장 빠른 선수**이다.
  I'm ___________________________ on the team.
- ⓒ 나는 팀에서 **가장 빠른 선수들 중 한 명**이다.
  I'm ___________________________ on the team.

2

- ⓐ 그것은 놀라운 쇼였다.
  It was an amazing show.
- ⓑ 그것은 내가 지금껏 본 것들 중 **가장 놀라운 쇼**였다.
  It was ___________________________ I've ever watched.
- ⓒ 그것은 다른 어떤 쇼**보다 더 놀라웠다**.
  It was ___________________________ any other show.

3

- ⓐ Amy는 키가 큰 소녀이다.
  Amy is a tall girl.
- ⓑ Amy는 그 반에서 **가장 키가 큰 소녀**이다.
  Amy is ___________________________ in the class.
- ⓒ 그 반의 어떤 소녀도 Amy**보다 더 키가 크지** 않다.
  No girl in the class is ___________________________ Amy.

4

- ⓐ 나의 형은 성실한 사람이다.
  My brother is a diligent person.
- ⓑ 나의 형은 우리 가족 중에서 **가장 성실한 사람**이다.
  My brother is ___________________________ in my family.
- ⓒ 우리 가족 중 어떤 사람도 나의 형**만큼 성실하지** 않다.
  No person in my family is ___________________________ my brother.

5

- ⓐ 이 그림은 환상적이다.
  This painting is fantastic.
- ⓑ 이것은 여기에서 **가장 환상적인 그림**이다.
  This is ___________________________ here.
- ⓒ 이것은 여기에서 **가장 환상적인 그림들 중 하나**이다.
  This is ___________________________ here.

6

- ⓐ 그의 연설은 감동적이었다.
  His speech was touching.
- ⓑ 그의 연설은 모든 것들 중에서 **가장 감동적이었다**.
  His speech was ___________________________ of all.
- ⓒ 그의 연설은 다른 어떤 연설**보다 더 감동적이었다**.
  His speech was ___________________________ any other speech.

STEP **2** 영작 **완성하기**

1 여름은 모든 계절들 중에서 가장 덥다. (hot, seasons)

→ Summer is __________ __________ __________ __________ __________.

2 어떤 것도 정직보다 더 가치 있지 않다. (valuable)

→ Nothing is __________ __________ __________ honesty.

3 너의 대답이 어떤 다른 대답보다 더 좋다. (good)

→ Your answer is __________ __________ __________ __________ answer.

4 <The Avengers>는 내가 지금껏 본 것들 중에서 가장 흥미진진한 영화이다. (exciting, film)

→ *The Avengers* is __________ __________ __________ __________ I've ever seen.

5 세계의 어떤 강도 아마존강만큼 길지 않다. (long)

→ __________ river in the world is __________ __________ __________ the Amazon.

STEP **3** 배열 **영작하기**

1 Owen은 그 가게에서 가장 저렴한 시계를 샀다. the store, watch, cheapest, in, the, bought

→ Owen ____.

2 컴퓨터는 역사상 가장 위대한 발명품들 중 하나이다. greatest, is, of, the, in history, inventions, one

→ The computer ____.

3 이것이 내가 지금껏 경험한 것 중에서 가장 행복한 순간이다.

I, have, the, moment, ever experienced, happiest

→ This is ____.

4 세계의 다른 어떤 바다도 사해보다 더 소금기가 있지 않다. sea, saltier, is, in the world, than, no, other

→ ________________________________ the Dead Sea.

5 다른 어떤 게임도 이 게임만큼 어렵지 않다. no, as, game, this game, difficult, other, as, is

→ ____.

집중 훈련 1 틀린 부분 고치기
어법상 틀린 부분을 찾아 바르게 고치시오.

01
It is getting more and more warm.
날이 점점 더 따뜻해지고 있다.

_________ → _________

02
This tree is as three times tall as Susan.
이 나무는 Susan보다 세 배 더 크다.

_________ → _________

03
Elephants are one of the bigger animals on Earth.
코끼리는 지구상에서 가장 큰 동물들 중 하나이다.

_________ → _________

04
She is more polite than any other girls in her class.
그녀는 학급의 다른 어떤 소녀보다 더 예의 바르다.

_________ → _________

05
The situation is very worse than it looks.
상황은 보이는 것보다 훨씬 더 안 좋다.

_________ → _________

06
The longer I waited, the angry I got.
나는 더 오래 기다릴수록 더 화가 났다.

_________ → _________

07
We should call him as quickly as can.
우리는 가능한 한 빨리 그에게 전화해야 한다.

_________ → _________

집중 훈련 2 영작 완성하기
주어진 말을 활용하여 문장을 완성하시오.

08 이 노트북은 저 태블릿 컴퓨터만큼 새 것이 아니다. (new)

→ This laptop is _________________ that tablet PC.

09 태평양은 세계에서 가장 큰 바다이다. (large, ocean)

→ The Pacific Ocean is _________________
_________________.

10 Tom은 평소보다 더 늦게 잠자리에 들었다.
(go to bed, late, usual)

→ Tom _________________.

11 네가 더 높이 올라갈수록 기온은 더 낮아진다.
(low, the temperature, become)

→ The higher you go up, _________________
_________________.

12 그것은 내가 지금껏 들어 본 것들 중 가장 믿기지 않는 이야기이다. (unbelievable, story)

→ _________________
I've ever heard.

13 다른 어떤 활동도 그 게임을 하는 것만큼 따분하지 않았다.
(boring, other, activity, as)

→ _________________
playing that game.

14 이 사무실의 누구도 Jane보다 더 바쁘지 않다.
(busy, in this office, no one)

→ _________________ than Jane.

집중 훈련 3 통문장 영작하기
주어진 말을 활용하여 영작하시오.

집중 훈련 4 조건 영작하기
우리말과 의미가 같도록 〈조건〉에 맞게 영작하시오.

15 사하라 사막은 지구상에서 가장 뜨거운 사막들 중 하나다.
(The Sahara Desert, hot, on Earth)

→ _______________________________________

16 그들의 공연은 점점 더 즐거워졌다.
(performance, become, enjoyable)

→ _______________________________________

17 이 지하철 노선은 저 지하철 노선보다 두 배 더 짧다.
(subway line, short, as, that one)

→ _______________________________________

18 그것은 그들이 지금까지 한 것들 중 가장 놀라운 발견이다.
(amazing, discovery, ever, make)

→ _______________________________________

19 이 지역의 다른 어떤 탑도 이 탑보다 높지 않다.
(tower in this area, tall, than)

→ _______________________________________

20
> **A** How was your presentation?
> **B** Terrible. I forgot some words.
> 그것은 내 인생에서 가장 당황스러운 순간이었어.
> (embarrassing, moment, in my life)

→ _______________________________________

21
> **A** What do you think about Tim?
> **B** He's nice.
> 그는 우리 학교의 다른 어떤 사람보다 더 상냥해.
> (friendly, than, person, at my school)

→ _______________________________________

22 그의 이야기는 너의 이야기만큼 무섭지는 않았다.

> 조건 **1** 원급 비교를 사용할 것
> **2** 주어진 단어를 모두 사용할 것
> (his, scary, yours)

→ _______________________________________

23 세상의 다른 어떤 새도 타조보다 더 크지는 않다.

> 조건 **1** 비교급을 사용할 것
> **2** 부정 주어로 문장을 시작할 것
> **3** 다음 주어진 말을 활용할 것
> (other, in the world, large, the ostrich)

→ _______________________________________

24 이것은 내가 지금껏 읽은 것들 중 가장 웃기는 기사이다.

> 조건 **1** 최상급을 사용할 것
> **2** 현재완료를 포함할 것
> **3** 〈보기〉의 단어를 모두 활용할 것

> 보기   funny   read   article   ever

→ _______________________________________

25 그녀가 더 오래 걸을수록 그녀는 더 느긋해졌다.

> 조건 **1** 「the+비교급 ~, the+비교급 …」을 사용할 것
> **2** 과거시제로 쓸 것
> **3** walk, become, long, relaxed의 형태를
> 바꾸어 쓸 것

→ _______________________________________

서술형 **1**   (3점)

우리말과 의미가 같도록 〈조건〉에 맞게 문장을 완성하시오.

> TV 쇼들이 점점 더 폭력적으로 되고 있다.

> 조건 **1** 비교급을 사용하시오.
>   **2** 괄호 안에 주어진 말을 활용하시오.
>   (become, violent)

→ TV shows are ___________________

 ___________________.

서술형 **2**   (6점, 각 3점)

우리말과 의미가 같도록 어법상 <u>틀린</u> 부분을 바르게 고쳐 문장을 다시 쓰시오.

> (1) This screen is not as wider as that one.
> (이 화면은 저 화면만큼 넓지 않다.)
> (2) It is one of the bestselling book of all time.
> (그것은 역대 가장 많이 팔린 책들 중 하나이다.)

(1) ___________________

(2) ___________________

서술형 **3**   (6점)

다음 세 문장의 의미가 같도록 문장을 완성하시오.

> This was the most exciting trip.
> → No other trip was ___________ as this.
> → This was more exciting ___________ trip.

서술형 **4**   (6점, 각 3점)

그림을 보고, 주어진 말을 사용하여 문장을 완성하시오.

(1)

→ Amy's chair is ___________________
Tim's. (far, comfortable)

(2)

→ This is ___________________
the three. (delicious, dessert)

서술형 **5** NEW   (9점, 각 3점)

다음 세 가지 상품에 관한 정보 표를 보고, 〈조건〉에 맞게 문장을 완성하시오.

Model	Price	Weight
Model A	$ 30	1.5 kg
Model B	$ 20	2 kg
Model C	$ 10	1 kg

> 조건 **1** 원급, 비교급, 최상급을 각각 한 번씩 사용하시오.
>   **2** 필요시 배수사를 사용하시오.
>   **3** 주어진 말을 사용하시오. (필요시 형태를 바꿀 것)

(1) Model A is ___________ ___________
 ___________ than Model C. (expensive)

(2) Model C is ___________ ___________ ___________
the three. (light)

(3) Model B is ___________ ___________ ___________
 ___________ Model C. (heavy)

chapter 6

수동태

1 수동태의 형태

2 4형식과 5형식 문장의 수동태

3 구동사의 수동태

4 by 이외의 전치사를 쓰는 수동태

A 수동태는 주어가 행위의 대상이 될 때 사용하며, 「be동사+p.p.」 형태로 쓴다.

The museum **is visited** by many tourists.

행위(visit)의 대상 → 수동태 문장에서 행위자는 「by+목적격」으로 나타내며, 행위자가
일반인이거나 언급할 필요가 없는 경우에는 생략할 수 있다.

B 수동태의 시제는 be동사를 시제에 맞게 바꿔 나타내고, 조동사가 있는 문장의 수동태는 조동사를 수동태 앞에 쓴다.

현재	am/are/is+p.p.	Dinner **is** usually **cooked** by my father.
과거	was/were+p.p.	The novel **was written** by a famous writer.
미래	will be+p.p.	The package **will be delivered** tomorrow.
진행	be동사+being+p.p.	The music festival **is being held** in Seoul.
완료	have/has been+p.p.	The cake **has** already **been eaten**.
조동사	조동사+be+p.p.	The office **should be cleaned** today.

---

1 다양한 시제의 수동태 형태 익히기

1 delay

비행편이 지연된다. → The flight ＿＿＿＿＿＿ ＿＿＿＿＿＿.

비행편이 지연되고 있다. → The flight ＿＿＿＿＿＿ ＿＿＿＿＿＿ ＿＿＿＿＿＿.

2 cancel

수업들이 취소되었다. → The classes ＿＿＿＿＿＿ ＿＿＿＿＿＿.

수업들이 취소될 것이다. → The classes ＿＿＿＿＿＿ ＿＿＿＿＿＿ ＿＿＿＿＿＿.

3 accept

그의 제안이 막 받아들여졌다. → His offer ＿＿＿＿＿＿ just ＿＿＿＿＿＿ ＿＿＿＿＿＿.

그의 제안은 받아들여지지
않을 것이다. → His offer ＿＿＿＿＿＿ ＿＿＿＿＿＿ ＿＿＿＿＿＿.

---

2 조동사가 있는 수동태 형태 익히기

1 You must make your reservation online.

→ Your reservation ＿＿＿＿＿＿ ＿＿＿＿＿＿ ＿＿＿＿＿＿ online.

2 The president may announce new plans.

→ New plans ＿＿＿＿＿＿ ＿＿＿＿＿＿ ＿＿＿＿＿＿ by the president.

3 John can lead the team.

→ The team ＿＿＿＿＿＿ ＿＿＿＿＿＿ ＿＿＿＿＿＿ by John.

A **4형식 문장의 수동태**: 간접목적어와 직접목적어를 각각 주어로 하는 두 가지 형태의 수동태가 가능하다.

> The fans **gave** him a gift.
> 수여동사 간·목 직·목
> → He **was given** a gift by the fans. <간접목적어가 주어인 수동태>
> → A gift **was given** to him by the fans. <직접목적어가 주어인 수동태>

> 간접목적어 앞에 쓰는 전치사
> · to: give, teach, tell, send, bring 등
> · for: buy, make, cook, get 등
> · of: ask 등

주의 buy, make, cook, get 등의 동사는 직접목적어만 수동태 문장의 주어로 쓴다.
He **bought** me a book. → A book **was bought** for me by him.

B **5형식 문장의 수동태**: 대부분의 경우 목적격 보어를 그대로 쓰지만, 사역·지각동사의 경우 형태를 바꿔 쓴다.

목적격 보어가 명사/형용사/분사/to부정사	목적격 보어 → 그대로	They **allowed** us **to use** the Internet for free. → We **were allowed to use** the Internet for free.
사역동사의 목적격 보어	동사원형 → to부정사	They **made** us **stay** inside. → We **were made to stay** inside.
지각동사의 목적격 보어	동사원형 → 현재분사/to부정사	We **saw** Mina **run** out of the classroom. → Mina **was seen running**(**to run**) out of the classroom.

cf. 지각동사의 목적격 보어가 분사이면 수동태 문장에서도 분사로 쓴다.
They **heard** someone **singing** outside. → Someone **was heard singing** outside (by them).

---

1 **4형식/5형식 문장을 수동태로 바꿔 쓰기**

1 Ms. Brown taught the students Spanish.

→ The students ____________ ____________ ____________ by Ms. Brown.

2 My father cooked us spaghetti and pizza.

→ Spaghetti and pizza ____________ ____________ ____________ ____________ by my father.

3 The police officer showed them those pictures.

→ They ____________ ____________ ____________ ____________ by the police officer.

4 We painted the front door green.

→ The front door ____________ ____________ ____________ by us.

5 They made Sam choose between the two plans.

→ Sam ____________ ____________ ____________ ____________ between the two plans by them.

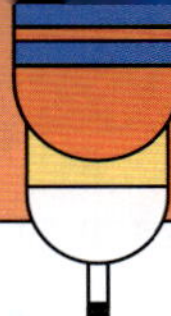

영작 기본 훈련

STEP 1 다양한 형태의 수동태 의미 **비교하기**

A 시제 및 조동사에 따른 수동태 의미 비교하기

1 find

a 그 소년은 한 시간 전에 **발견되었다.**
The boy __________ __________ one hour ago.

b 그 소년은 곧 **발견될 것이다.**
The boy __________ __________ __________ soon.

2 destroy

a 매년 열대 우림들이 **파괴된다.**
Rainforests __________ __________ every year.

b 이 순간에도 열대 우림들이 **파괴되고 있다.**
Rainforests __________ __________ __________ at this moment.

3 influence

a 아이들은 부모에게 **영향을 받는다.**
Kids __________ __________ by their parents.

b 아이들은 부모에게 **영향을 받을 수 있다.**
Kids __________ __________ __________ by their parents.

B 4형식/5형식 문장의 수동태 비교하기

1

a 그들은 그녀에게 그 소식을 전했다.
They told her the news.

b 그 소식이 **그녀에게 전해졌다.**
The news __________ __________ __________ __________.

c 그녀는 **그 소식을 들었다.**
She __________ __________ __________ __________.

2

a 의사는 그에게 체중을 줄이라고 권고했다.
The doctor advised him to lose weight.

b 그는 체중을 **줄일 것을 권고받았다.**
He __________ __________ __________ __________ weight.

3

a 그 운전사는 그 남자를 버스에서 내리게 했다.
The driver made the man get off the bus.

b 그 남자는 그 운전사에 의해 버스에서 **내리게 되었다.**
The man __________ __________ __________ __________ __________ the bus by the driver.

4

a 우리는 그 커플이 춤추고 있는 것을 보았다.
We saw the couple dancing.

b 그 커플이 **춤추고 있는 것이** 우리에게 **보였다.**
The couple __________ __________ __________ by us.

STEP **2** 영작 **완성하기**

1 나의 가족은 그들의 결혼식에 초대받을 것이다. (invite)

→ My family ＿＿＿＿＿ ＿＿＿＿＿ ＿＿＿＿＿ to their wedding.

2 이 기사는 지금까지 수백만 명의 사람들에게 읽혀 왔다. (read)

→ This article ＿＿＿＿＿ ＿＿＿＿＿ ＿＿＿＿＿ by millions of people so far.

3 나는 그의 컴퓨터를 사용해도 된다고 허락받았다. (allow, use)

→ I ＿＿＿＿＿ ＿＿＿＿＿ ＿＿＿＿＿ ＿＿＿＿＿ his computer.

4 모든 참가자들은 계약서에 서명하도록 요청받았다. (ask, sign)

→ All the participants ＿＿＿＿＿ ＿＿＿＿＿ ＿＿＿＿＿ ＿＿＿＿＿ a contract.

5 그가 그 아파트 건물에 들어가는 것이 보였다. (see, enter)

→ He ＿＿＿＿＿ ＿＿＿＿＿ ＿＿＿＿＿ that apartment building.

STEP **3** 배열 **영작하기**

1 한 소년이 지붕 위에서 도움을 요청하고 있는 소리가 들렸다. was, calling, a boy, heard, for help

→ ＿＿＿＿＿＿＿＿＿＿＿＿＿＿＿＿＿＿＿ on the roof.

2 우리는 그 행사에 대한 어떤 정보도 받지 못했다. given, no information, were, we

→ ＿＿＿＿＿＿＿＿＿＿＿＿＿＿＿＿＿＿＿ about the event.

3 그 영화는 한국인 감독에 의해 만들어질 것이다. by, will, the film, be, a Korean director, made

→ ＿＿＿＿＿＿＿＿＿＿＿＿＿＿＿＿＿＿＿

4 나는 자리를 바꾸게 되었다. I, change, to, seats, made, was

→ ＿＿＿＿＿＿＿＿＿＿＿＿＿＿＿＿＿＿＿

5 그 도둑은 경찰에게 쫓기고 있는 중이었다. being, the thief, chased, the police, was, by

→ ＿＿＿＿＿＿＿＿＿＿＿＿＿＿＿＿＿＿＿

두 단어 이상으로 이루어진 구동사를 수동태로 만들 때 동사는 「be동사+p.p.」로 바꾸고 나머지는 동사 뒤에 그대로 쓴다.

break into	~에 침입하다	turn on/off	~을 켜다/끄다
take care of	~을 돌보다	turn down	~을 거절하다
look after	~을 돌보다	put off	~을 연기하다
look down on	~을 얕보다/무시하다	cut off	~을 차단하다
look up to	~을 존경하다	deal with	~을 다루다

My neighbor **took care of** my dog.
→ My dog **was taken care of** by my neighbor.

They **put off** the meeting until December.
→ The meeting **was put off** until December.

1 구동사의 수동태 형태 익히기

1 우리가 그 문제를 다뤘다. → We dealt with the problem.

그 문제는 우리에 의해 다뤄졌다. → The problem ＿＿＿＿＿ ＿＿＿＿＿ ＿＿＿＿＿ by us.

2 그들이 전기를 차단할지도 모른다. → They may cut off the electricity.

전기가 차단될지도 모른다. → The electricity ＿＿＿＿＿ ＿＿＿＿＿ ＿＿＿＿＿ ＿＿＿＿＿.

3 그녀는 알람을 껐다. → She turned off the alarm.

그 알람은 그녀에 의해 꺼졌다. → The alarm ＿＿＿＿＿ ＿＿＿＿＿ ＿＿＿＿＿ by her.

2 구동사의 수동태 형태 적용하기

1 그 선생님은 모든 학생들에게 존경받는다. (look up to)

→ The teacher ＿＿＿＿＿ ＿＿＿＿＿ ＿＿＿＿＿ ＿＿＿＿＿ by all the students.

2 요리를 시작하기 전에 오븐이 켜져야 한다. (turn on)

→ The oven should ＿＿＿＿＿ ＿＿＿＿＿ ＿＿＿＿＿ before you start cooking.

3 그의 건의 사항들은 그 위원회에 의해 거절당했다. (turn down)

→ His proposals ＿＿＿＿＿ ＿＿＿＿＿ ＿＿＿＿＿ by the committee.

4 비 때문에 소풍은 연기되었다. (put off)

→ The picnic ＿＿＿＿＿ ＿＿＿＿＿ ＿＿＿＿＿ due to the rain.

 4 by 이외의 전치사를 쓰는 수동태

수동태 문장에서는 행위자 앞에 by를 주로 쓰지만, by 이외의 전치사를 쓰는 경우가 있다.

be filled with	~로 가득 차다	be pleased with	~에 기뻐하다
be known as	~로 알려져 있다	be covered with	~로 덮여 있다
be known to	~에게 알려져 있다	be satisfied with	~에 만족하다
be surprised at(by)	~에 놀라다	be worried about	~에 대해 걱정하다
be made of/from	~로 만들어지다	be crowded with	~로 붐비다

This chair **is made of** wood. ┄┄┄┄┄
Cheese **is made from** milk. ┄┄┄┄┄ ➔ be made of는 재료의 형태만 변하고 성질이 변하지 않는 경우에,
The road **was covered with** snow. be made from은 재료의 형태와 성질이 모두 변하는 경우에 쓴다.
He **is** also **known as** a cultural icon.

1 by 이외의 전치사를 쓰는 수동태 형태 익히기

1 know 관광 명소로 알려져 있다 ➔ be ____________ ____________ a tourist attraction

2 cover 먼지로 덮여 있다 ➔ be ____________ ____________ dust

3 worry 시험 결과에 대해 걱정하다 ➔ be ____________ ____________ the test results

4 surprise 갑작스러운 방문에 놀라다 ➔ be ____________ ____________ a sudden visit

2 by 이외의 전치사를 쓰는 수동태 문장 완성하기

보기	crowd	fill	make	know

1 그 욕조는 따뜻한 물로 가득 채워져 있었다.

➔ The bathtub ____________ ____________ ____________ warm water.

2 그 박물관은 매일 관광객들로 붐빈다.

➔ The museum ____________ ____________ ____________ tourists every day.

3 그는 그의 반에서 가장 웃기는 학생으로 알려져 있다.

➔ He ____________ ____________ ____________ the funniest student in his class.

4 그 빵은 통밀 가루로 만들어진다.

➔ The bread ____________ ____________ ____________ whole wheat flour.

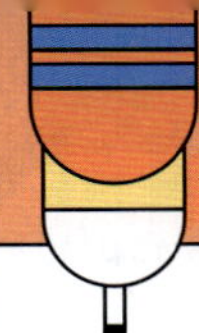

영작 기본 훈련

STEP 1 주의해야 할 수동태 의미 **비교하기**

1
ⓐ 내 고양이는 여동생에 의해 **돌봐졌다**.
My cat was ＿＿＿＿ ＿＿＿＿ by my sister.

ⓑ 내 고양이는 이제 아버지에 의해 **돌봐진다**.
My cat is ＿＿＿＿ ＿＿＿＿ ＿＿＿＿ by my father now.

2
ⓐ 가로등은 저녁 7시에 **켜진다**.
The streetlights are ＿＿＿＿ ＿＿＿＿ at 7 p.m.

ⓑ 가로등은 아침 6시에 **꺼진다**.
The streetlights are ＿＿＿＿ ＿＿＿＿ at 6 a.m.

3
ⓐ 그 의사는 환자들에게 **존경받는다**.
The doctor is ＿＿＿＿ ＿＿＿＿ ＿＿＿＿ by her patients.

ⓑ 그녀는 여러 해 전에 **무시당했다**.
She was ＿＿＿＿ ＿＿＿＿ ＿＿＿＿ several years ago.

4
ⓐ 그 코치는 경기 결과**에 기뻐했다**.
The coach was ＿＿＿＿ ＿＿＿＿ the result of the game.

ⓑ 그 코치는 선수들의 기술**에 만족했다**.
The coach was ＿＿＿＿ ＿＿＿＿ the players' skills.

5
ⓐ 그 방은 풍선**으로 가득 차 있다**.
The room is ＿＿＿＿ ＿＿＿＿ balloons.

ⓑ 그 탁자는 꽃**으로 덮여 있다**.
The table is ＿＿＿＿ ＿＿＿＿ flowers.

6
ⓐ 그는 재능 있는 예술가**로 알려져 있다**.
He is ＿＿＿＿ ＿＿＿＿ a talented artist.

ⓑ 그의 얼굴은 많은 사람들**에게 알려져 있다**.
His face is ＿＿＿＿ ＿＿＿＿ many people.

7
ⓐ 이 와인 잔은 크리스털**로 만들어진다**.
This wine glass is ＿＿＿＿ ＿＿＿＿ crystal.

ⓑ 이 와인은 여러 품종의 포도**로 만들어진다**.
This wine is ＿＿＿＿ ＿＿＿＿ various kinds of grapes.

8
ⓐ 그의 집은 어젯밤에 **침입당했다**.
His house was ＿＿＿＿ ＿＿＿＿ last night.

ⓑ 그의 집에서 하려던 파티는 **연기되었다**.
The party at his house was ＿＿＿＿ ＿＿＿＿.

STEP 2 영작 완성하기

1 그 마을 전체는 화산재로 덮여 있었다. (cover)

→ The whole town __________ __________ __________ volcanic ash.

2 우리는 그 호텔의 서비스에 만족했다. (satisfy)

→ We __________ __________ __________ the service at the hotel.

3 Tom과 Jane은 사은품에 기뻐했다. (please)

→ Tom and Jane __________ __________ __________ the free gift.

4 그 고객의 불만 사항은 신속하게 처리되었다. (deal with)

→ The complaints from the customer __________ __________ __________ quickly.

5 그의 환불 요청은 관리자에 의해 거절되었다. (turn down)

→ His request for a refund __________ __________ __________ __________ the manager.

STEP 3 배열 영작하기

1 긴 연휴를 앞두고 공항은 여행객들로 붐볐다. crowded, travelers, was, with, the airport

→ _________________________________ before the long holiday.

2 많은 소비자들이 식품 안전에 대해 걱정한다. consumers, worried, food safety, are, many, about

→ _________________________________

3 나는 그 축제 입장권의 가격에 놀랐다. the price, was, at, surprised, I, of the festival tickets

→ _________________________________

4 노숙자들은 지역 사회에 의해 돌보아진다. by, after, are, the community, the homeless, looked

→ _________________________________

5 이 가방들은 재활용된 플라스틱병으로 만들어진다. of, these bags, made, are, plastic bottles, recycled

→ _________________________________

집중 훈련 1 틀린 부분 고치기
어법상 틀린 부분을 찾아 바르게 고치시오.

집중 훈련 2 영작 완성하기
주어진 말을 활용하여 문장을 완성하시오.

01 This car will given to the winner.
이 자동차는 우승자에게 주어질 것이다.

__________ → __________

02 A nice dinner was cooked to me on my birthday.
내 생일날에 맛있는 저녁 식사가 나를 위해 요리되었다.

__________ → __________

03 She was heard cry last night.
어젯밤에 그녀가 우는 소리가 들렸다.

__________ → __________

04 His bag was filled by books.
그의 가방은 책들로 가득 차 있었다.

__________ → __________

05 The injured dog was taken care by the vet.
그 다친 개는 수의사에 의해 돌봐졌다.

__________ → __________

06 His room is painting right now by his father.
그의 방은 그의 아버지에 의해 바로 지금 칠해지고 있다.

__________ → __________

07 Some people were asked show their IDs.
몇몇 사람들은 신분증을 보여 달라고 요구받았다.

__________ → __________

08 몇몇 학생들은 수업이 끝난 후에 남게 되었다.
(make, stay)

→ Several students ________________________ after class.

09 그 책상은 Jane을 위해 그녀의 어머니에 의해 만들어졌다. (make, the desk, for)

→ _________________________________ by her mother.

10 그녀의 자동차는 지금 수리점에서 수리되고 있다. (fix)

→ ___________________________ in the repair shop now.

11 그는 회사로부터 하와이행 비행기표를 받았다.
(award, a flight ticket)

→ ___________________________ to Hawaii by the company.

12 에펠탑은 파리의 상징으로 알려져 있다.
(know, the symbol)

→ The Eiffel Tower ___________________ of Paris.

13 이 문제들은 내일 다뤄질 것이다.
(deal, these issues)

→ ___________________________ tomorrow.

14 그 벽 전체는 포스터들로 덮여 있었다.
(cover, with posters)

→ The whole wall _____________________.

집중 훈련 3 통문장 영작하기
주어진 말을 활용하여 영작하시오.

15 두부는 콩으로 만들어진다. (tofu, make, soybeans)

→ ______________________________

16 나는 나중에 오라는 말을 들었다.
(tell, come back later)

→ ______________________________

17 이 행사는 온라인으로 시청될 수 있다.
(event, watch, online)

→ ______________________________

18 그의 할머니는 그의 삼촌에 의해 돌봐진다.
(grandmother, look after, uncle)

→ ______________________________

19 그녀는 사실을 말하도록 강요당했다.
(make, tell the truth)

→ ______________________________

20
A Look at that building! It's amazing.
B 그것은 유명한 건축가에 의해 설계되었어.
(design, a famous architect)

→ ______________________________

21
A What's the matter?
B It's raining. 우리의 현장 학습이 연기될지도 몰라.
(field trip, might, put off)

→ ______________________________

집중 훈련 4 조건 영작하기
우리말과 의미가 같도록 〈조건〉에 맞게 영작하시오.

22 네 언니는 새 직장에 만족하니?

조건 1 주어진 단어를 활용할 것
(satisfy, her new job)
2 8단어의 수동태 문장으로 쓸 것

→ ______________________________

23 그 사무실은 경찰에 의해 빈 채로 발견되었다.

조건 1 수동태로 쓸 것
2 〈보기〉의 단어를 활용할 것

보기　the office　the police　find　empty

→ ______________________________

24 성적표는 각 학생에게 보내졌다.

조건 1 현재완료 수동태를 사용할 것
2 9단어의 문장으로 쓸 것
3 다음 중 필요한 단어를 골라 활용할 것
(a report card, send, each, by, for, to)

→ ______________________________

25 모든 손님은 정시에 도착할 것으로 예상된다.

조건 1 수동태로 쓸 것
2 주어진 단어를 활용할 것
(all guests, expect, arrive, on time)
3 모두 8단어로 쓸 것

→ ______________________________

서술형 1   (6점, 각 3점)

우리말과 의미가 같도록 주어진 말을 활용하여 문장을 완성하시오.

(1) 그의 정원은 꽃들로 가득 차 있다.

→ His garden ________________________ .
(fill, flowers)

(2) 전화기는 수업 중에 꺼져 있어야 한다.

→ Phones ________________________ .
(should, turn off, in class)

서술형 2   (4점)

우리말과 의미가 같도록 〈조건〉에 맞게 문장을 완성하시오.

> 화재는 어떤 피해도 입히기 전에 소방관들에 의해 진화되었다.

> 조건 1 수동태를 사용하시오.
>   2 주어진 말을 활용하시오. (put out)

→ The fire __________ __________ __________
__________ the firefighters before it caused
any damage.

서술형 3   (3점)

그림을 보고, 주어진 말을 바르게 배열하여 문장을 완성하시오.

> seen, the road, a cat, was, crossing

→ ________________________________

서술형 4   (4점, 각 2점)

다음 문장에서 어법상 **틀린** 부분을 찾아 바르게 고쳐 쓰시오.

(1) 새 병원이 공원 근처에 지어지고 있다.

A new hospital is be built near the park.

____________ → ____________

(2) 그 창문들은 나에 의해 이미 청소되었다.

The windows have already been cleaning
by me.

____________ → ____________

서술형 5   (9점, 각 3점)

다음 문장들의 의미가 같도록 주어진 말로 시작하는 문장을 완성하시오.

(1) Lisa told us a funny story.

→ We ________________________ .

→ A funny story ________________________ .

(2) He may sing the song at the concert.

→ The song ________________________
at the concert.

(3) My mother made me bring the blanket.

→ I ________________________ .

서술형 6   (4점)

그림을 보고, 〈조건〉에 맞게 문장을 완성하시오.

> 조건 1 현재진행시제를 사용하시오.
>   2 주어진 말을 활용하시오. (collect)

→ The donations ________________________
the volunteers.

관계사 1

1 관계대명사의 역할과 종류

2 관계대명사 that

3 관계대명사 what

관계대명사의 역할과 종류

A 관계대명사는 두 문장을 연결하는 접속사와 대명사의 역할을 하며, 앞에 나온 명사인 선행사를 수식하는 절을 이끈다.

I have *a friend*. + **She** speaks both English and German.

↓

I have *a friend* **who** speaks both English and German.   나는 **영어와 독일어 둘 다 말하는** 친구가 있다.
선행사 ─── 관계대명사절

B 선행사의 종류와 관계사절에서 관계대명사의 역할에 따라 구분하여 쓴다.

선행사＼격	주격	목적격	소유격
사람	who, that	who(m), that	whose
사물/동물	which, that		

주격 I found a website **which** contains useful information.
⟶ 주격 관계대명사절의 동사는 선행사의 인칭과 수에 일치시킨다.

목적격 The girl **who(m)** I met at the math contest was very smart.
⟶ 목적격 관계대명사는 생략할 수 있다.

소유격 I have a friend **whose** mother is a police officer.
⟶ 소유격 관계대명사 뒤에는 항상 명사가 온다.

cf. 관계대명사 that은 선행사의 종류에 관계없이 주격 또는 목적격 관계대명사로 쓸 수 있다.
Peter is *the tall man* **that**〔**who**〕 sits next to Harry.
I watched *the documentary* **that**〔**which**〕 my father made.

---

1 **알맞은 관계대명사 쓰기**

e.g. 요리를 잘하는 남자   → a man _who〔that〕_ cooks well

1 그가 원했던 선물   → the gift __________ he wanted

2 머리가 긴 소녀   → the girl __________ hair is long

3 그녀가 좋아하는 가수   → the singer __________ she likes

4 제때 도착한 소포   → the package __________ arrived on time

5 표지가 파란색인 책   → the book __________ cover is blue

6 은행에서 일하는 여자   → a woman __________ works at a bank

7 우리가 찾고 있는 가방   → the bag __________ we are looking for

2 관계대명사 사용하여 **문장 연결하기**

1 I love stories. They have happy endings.

→ I love stories _________ _________ _________ _________.

2 We entered a room. Its door was open.

→ We entered a room _________ _________ _________ _________.

3 The boy is John. He is right behind you.

→ The boy _________ _________ _________ _________ _________ is John.

4 Tom gave me the letter. He had just written it.

→ Tom gave me the letter _________ _________ _________ _________ _________.

5 The man was kind. I met him yesterday.

→ The man _________ _________ _________ _________ was kind.

3 관계대명사절 **형태 익히기**

1 Paul은 정직하지 않은 사람들을 싫어한다. (people, be)

→ Paul hates _________ _________ _________ not honest.

2 저것이 공항에 가는 버스이다. (the bus, go)

→ That is _________ _________ _________ _________ to the airport.

3 나는 별명이 백설 공주인 여자아이를 안다. (a girl, nickname)

→ I know _________ _________ _________ _________ is Snow White.

4 저 아이들이 그녀가 돌보고 있는 아이들이다. (the kids)

→ Those are _________ _________ _________ _________ taking care of.

5 Kate가 추천했던 영화는 매우 재미있었다. (recommend, be)

→ The movie _________ _________ _________ _________ very interesting.

6 나는 작가가 알려지지 않은 책을 읽고 있다. (a book, author)

→ I'm reading _________ _________ _________ _________ is unknown.

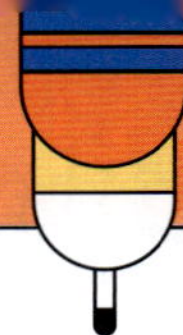

영작 기본 훈련

STEP 1 관계대명사 사용하여 의미 **확장하기**

e.g.
- **a** Ian은 우리 옆집에 살았다.
  Ian lived next door to us.
- **b** Ian은 **우리 옆집에 살던** 소년이다.
  Ian is the boy ___who(that) lived next door to us___.

1
- **a** 나는 지갑을 잃어버렸다.
  I lost my wallet.
- **b** **내가 잃어버린** 지갑은 빨간색이다.
  The wallet ___________________________ is red.

2
- **a** 내 친구의 취미는 독서이다.
  My friend's hobby is reading.
- **b** 나는 **취미가 독서인** 친구가 있다.
  I have a friend ___________________________.

3
- **a** 그 집은 100년 되었다.
  The house is 100 years old.
- **b** **100년 된** 집이 있다.
  There is a house ___________________________.

4
- **a** 그는 한 소녀를 도와주었다.
  He helped a girl.
- **b** Anne은 **그가 도와준** 소녀이다.
  Anne is the girl ___________________________.

5
- **a** 그 자전거는 벽에 기대어 있다.
  The bike is leaning against the wall.
- **b** **벽에 기대어 있는** 자전거는 내 것이다.
  The bike ___________________________ is mine.

6
- **a** Jane은 파티에서 한 소년을 만났다.
  Jane met a boy at the party.
- **b** 저 애가 **Jane이 파티에서 만난** 그 소년이다.
  That is the boy ___________________________.

7
- **a** 한 가수가 이 노래를 썼다.
  A singer wrote this song.
- **b** 나는 **이 노래를 쓴** 가수를 만나고 싶다.
  I want to meet the singer ___________________________.

8
- **a** 몇몇 과일의 가격은 매우 저렴했다.
  The price of some fruit was very low.
- **b** 우리는 **가격이 매우 저렴한** 과일을 좀 샀다.
  We bought some fruit ___________________________.

STEP **2** 영작 **완성하기**

1 네가 내게 한 질문들은 무례했다. (ask me)

→ The questions ___________ ___________ ___________ ___________ were rude.

2 그는 큰소리로 시간을 말해 주는 시계를 가지고 있다. (say the time)

→ He has a clock ___________ ___________ ___________ ___________ aloud.

3 Eric은 꿈이 유명한 가수가 되는 것인 소년이다. (dream)

→ Eric is a boy ___________ ___________ ___________ to become a famous singer.

4 나는 4개 국어를 말하는 사람을 안다. (speak, four languages)

→ I know a person ___________ ___________ ___________ ___________.

5 부산은 많은 관광객들이 방문하는 곳이다. (a place, many tourists)

→ Busan is ___________ ___________ ___________ ___________ ___________ visit.

STEP **3** 배열 **영작하기**

1 Brian은 우리 학교에서 내가 가장 좋아하는 소년이다.   like, the boy, is, whom, most, I, Brian

→ ____ in my school.

2 아이들은 그림들로 가득 찬 책을 좋아한다.   are full of, books, pictures, that, like, children

→ ____

3 우리가 함께 보았던 콘서트는 멋졌다.   the concert, was, together, we, wonderful, watched, that

→ ____

4 나는 부모님이 영화배우인 친구가 한 명 있다.   whose, are, parents, I, movie stars, have, a friend

→ ____

5 벤치에 앉아 있는 여성은 우리 엄마이다.   the woman, is sitting, is, who, my mom, on the bench

→ ____

관계대명사 that은 선행사의 종류에 관계없이 주격 또는 목적격 관계대명사로 쓸 수 있다.
또한, 다음과 같은 경우에는 주로 관계대명사 that을 쓴다.

선행사가 「사람+사물」일 때	The book is about *a man and a cat* **that** traveled together.
선행사가 -thing, -body일 때	I learned *everything* **that** I know from books.
선행사에 최상급이 있을 때	This is *the best restaurant* **that** I've ever visited.
선행사에 the only, the very, the same, all, every, 서수 등이 있을 때	Mina was *the first person* **that** we called. He has *the same backpack* **that** you have.

1 관계대명사 that절의 의미 익히기

e.g. They did all <u>that was possible</u>. → 그들은 ＿＿＿＿＿ 가능한 모든 것을 ＿＿＿＿＿ 했다.

1 <u>The pasta that I ate</u> was delicious. → ＿＿＿＿＿＿＿＿＿＿＿ 맛있었다.

2 I need <u>somebody that I can trust</u>. → 나는 ＿＿＿＿＿＿＿＿＿＿＿ 필요하다.

3 That is <u>the very phone that I want to buy</u>. → 저것이 ＿＿＿＿＿＿＿＿＿＿＿이다.

4 He was <u>the first person that I met in this town</u>. → 그가 ＿＿＿＿＿＿＿＿＿＿＿이었다.

2 관계대명사 that 형태 적용하기

1 이것이 내가 좋아하는 유일한 선물이다. (only, gift)

→ This is ＿＿＿＿＿ ＿＿＿＿＿ ＿＿＿＿＿ ＿＿＿＿＿ I like.

2 우리가 한 첫 번째 일은 청소였다. (thing)

→ ＿＿＿＿＿ ＿＿＿＿＿ ＿＿＿＿＿ ＿＿＿＿＿ we did was clean up.

3 나는 너를 놀라게 할 무언가를 가지고 있다. (something)

→ I have ＿＿＿＿＿ ＿＿＿＿＿ will surprise you.

4 그것은 나에게 일어난 최고의 일이었다. (best, thing)

→ It was ＿＿＿＿＿ ＿＿＿＿＿ ＿＿＿＿＿ ＿＿＿＿＿ ever happened to me.

5 그 가수는 그의 팬들이 그에게 보내는 모든 편지를 읽는다. (every, letter)

→ The singer reads ＿＿＿＿＿ ＿＿＿＿＿ ＿＿＿＿＿ his fans send him.

3 관계대명사 what

A 관계대명사 what은 '~하는 것'이라는 의미로 선행사를 포함하며, 문장에서 주어, 목적어, 보어 역할을 하는 명사절을 이끈다.

주어	**What** I like about Steve **is** his creativity.
목적어	Don't tell anybody **what** I told you.
보어	This is **what** the poet wrote last year.

what이 이끄는 관계대명사절이
주어로 쓰이면 단수 취급한다.

B 관계대명사 that *vs.* 관계대명사 what: that 앞에는 관계사절의 수식을 받는 선행사가 와야 하는 반면에, what은 이미 선행사를 포함하므로 앞에 별도의 선행사가 오지 않는다.

that (선행사 수식)	I have *the book* **that** you wanted to read.	네가 읽고 싶어 했던 책
what (선행사 포함)	I have **what** you wanted to read. (= *the thing* that)	네가 읽고 싶어 했던 것

1 관계대명사 that과 what의 쓰임 익히기

1   내 흥미를 끄는 것 → __________ interests me

  내 흥미를 끄는 영화 → the movie __________ interests me

2   그가 아는 것 → __________ he knows

  그가 아는 사실 → the fact __________ he knows

3   우리가 너에게 말해 주고 싶은 이야기 → the story __________ we want to tell you

  우리가 너에게 말해 주고 싶은 것 → __________ we want to tell you

2 관계대명사 what 형태 적용하기

1 그 상점은 내가 필요로 하는 것을 판다. (need)

  → The store sells __________ __________ __________.

2 이것이 교장 선생님께서 말씀하신 것이다. (the principal, say)

  → This is __________ __________ __________ __________.

3 Tony에게 일어난 일은 수수께끼이다. (happen to)

  → __________ __________ __________ __________ is a mystery.

영작 기본 훈련

STEP 1 관계대명사절 의미 **비교하기** (that 또는 what을 사용할 것)

1
ⓐ 나는 **네가 말하는 것**에 동의한다.
I agree with __________ __________ say.

ⓑ 나는 **네가 말하는** 모든 것에 동의한다.
I agree with everything __________ __________ __________.

2
ⓐ 그것은 **그가 물었던** 똑같은 질문이다.
That is the same question __________ __________ asked.

ⓑ 그것은 **그가 물었던 것**이다.
That is __________ __________ __________.

3
ⓐ 이것이 **그들이 제공하는 것**이다.
This is __________ __________ provide.

ⓑ 이것이 **그들이 제공하는** 서비스이다.
This is the service __________ __________ __________.

4
ⓐ **네가 들은** 소문은 사실이 아니다.
The rumor __________ __________ heard is not true.

ⓑ **네가 들은 것**은 사실이 아니다.
__________ __________ __________ is not true.

5
ⓐ 이것이 크리스마스에 **내가 받은 것**이다.
This is __________ __________ got for Christmas.

ⓑ 이것이 크리스마스에 **내가 받은** 선물이다.
This is the gift __________ __________ __________ for Christmas.

6
ⓐ 나는 중국에서 **내가 먹은** 모든 음식을 즐겼다.
I enjoyed all the food __________ __________ ate in China.

ⓑ 나는 중국에서 **내가 먹은 것**을 즐겼다.
I enjoyed __________ __________ __________ in China.

7
ⓐ 나는 **그녀가 만든 것**을 샀다.
I bought __________ __________ made.

ⓑ 나는 **그녀가 만든** 유일한 꽃병을 샀다.
I bought the only vase __________ __________ __________.

8
ⓐ 나는 **내가 본 것**을 기억한다.
I remember __________ __________ watched.

ⓑ 나는 **내가 본** 첫 번째 영화를 기억한다.
I remember the first movie __________ __________ __________.

STEP **2** 영작 완성하기 (that 또는 what을 사용할 것)

1 이 책가방은 내가 어제 산 것이다. (buy)

→ This backpack is ___________ ___________ ___________ yesterday.

2 나는 오빠가 사용하는 것과 같은 책상을 쓴다. (same, desk)

→ I use ___________ ___________ ___________ ___________ my brother uses.

3 나를 두렵게 하는 것은 아무것도 없다. (nothing, scare)

→ There is ___________ ___________ ___________ me.

4 내가 읽고 있었던 것은 과학 잡지였다. (read)

→ ___________ ___________ ___________ ___________ was a science magazine.

5 그녀가 가져온 유일한 것은 그녀의 전화기였다. (only, bring)

→ ___________ ___________ ___________ ___________ ___________ ___________ was her phone.

STEP **3** 배열 영작하기

1 이것은 내가 먹어 본 최고의 햄버거이다.　I, have, the best, that, hamburger, ever eaten

→ This is ____.

2 Sam이 말한 것은 매우 이상했다.　said, strange, Sam, what, very, was

→ ____

3 이것은 Joe가 잃어버린 바로 그 우산이다.　that, this, Joe, the very, lost, umbrella, is

→ ____

4 나는 Amy가 찾고 있던 것을 발견했다.　I, looking, was, what, for, found, Amy

→ ____

5 우리가 모르는 무언가가 있다.　don't, we, know, is, something, there, that

→ ____

집중 훈련 1 틀린 부분 고치기
어법상 틀린 부분을 찾아 바르게 고치시오.

집중 훈련 2 영작 완성하기 (관계대명사를 사용할 것)
주어진 말을 활용하여 문장을 완성하시오.

01
This is not that I want for my birthday.
이것은 내 생일에 내가 원하는 것이 아니다.

______ → ______

02
I know the girl who live next door.
나는 옆집에 사는 그 여자애를 안다.

______ → ______

03
She met a writer who novel won a prize.
그녀는 소설이 상을 받은 작가를 만났다.

______ → ______

04
I did all which I could do for him.
나는 그를 위해 내가 할 수 있는 모든 것을 했다.

______ → ______

05
Jack is an old friend which I like very much.
Jack은 내가 매우 좋아하는 오랜 친구이다.

______ → ______

06
That is the very boy what stole my bike.
저 아이가 내 자전거를 훔쳤던 바로 그 소년이다.

______ → ______

07
These are not the glasses what I left on the bus. 이것은 내가 버스에 두고 내렸던 안경이 아니다.

______ → ______

08 내가 쓰고 있는 모자는 내 언니의 것이다. (wear)

→ The cap ________________
   is my sister's.

09 James는 꿈이 수의사인 친절한 소년이다.
(friendly, dream)

→ James is ________________
   is to become a vet.

10 네가 손에 가지고 있는 것을 내게 보여 줘. (have)

→ Show me ________________
   in your hand.

11 나는 서랍이 두 개 있는 책상을 샀다. (a desk, have)

→ I bought ________________
   two drawers.

12 축제에서 노래했던 그 소녀는 누구니? (the girl, sing)

→ Who is ________________
   at the festival?

13 Alex는 내가 지금까지 만나 본 사람 중 가장 똑똑한 사람
이다. (ever, meet)

→ Alex is the smartest person ________________
   ________________.

14 너는 네가 알고 싶은 어떤 것이든 내게 물어도 된다.
(want, know)

→ You can ask me anything ________________
   ________________.

집중 훈련 **3** 통문장 영작하기
주어진 말을 활용하여 영작하시오.

집중 훈련 **4** 조건 영작하기
우리말과 의미가 같도록 〈조건〉에 맞게 영작하시오.

15 나는 이 감독이 만든 모든 영화들을 좋아한다.
(all the movies, director)

→ ____________________

16 그는 어제 내 사무실을 방문했던 그 남자이다.
(visit, office)

→ ____________________

17 내가 말한 것을 잊지 마. (forget, say)

→ ____________________

18 이것은 모래가 흰 아름다운 해변이다.
(a beautiful beach, sand)

→ ____________________

19 이것은 내가 남동생에게 사 준 것과 같은 장난감이다.
(the same toy, buy, for my brother)

→ ____________________

20
A Who do you respect most?
B My parents. 그들은 나를 위해 그들이 할 수 있는 모든 것을 하셔. (do, everything)

→ ____________________

21
A Did you take a swimming lesson?
B Yes, I did. 오늘 배운 것은 배영이었어.
(learn, the backstroke)

→ ____________________

22 나는 그 답을 찾아낸 유일한 학생이었다.

조건 **1** 주어진 말을 활용할 것
(the only, find the answer)
2 9단어의 문장으로 쓸 것

→ ____________________

23 그가 내게 말한 것은 충격적이었다.

조건 **1** that, which, what 중 알맞은 말을 쓸 것
2 tell과 shocking을 활용할 것
3 6단어의 문장으로 쓸 것

→ ____________________

24 그녀는 그가 남긴 메모를 보았다.

조건 **1** 괄호 안에 주어진 말을 활용할 것
(leave, the note)
2 관계대명사를 반드시 포함할 것
3 모두 7단어로 쓸 것

→ ____________________

25 그들은 지붕이 빨간색인 집에 산다.

조건 **1** 관계대명사를 사용할 것
2 roof와 in a house를 사용할 것
3 red로 끝나는 9단어의 문장으로 쓸 것

→ ____________________

서술형 1　　(4점)

우리말과 의미가 같도록 〈조건〉에 맞게 문장을 완성하시오.

> 당신이 필요한 어떤 것이든 나에게 부탁하세요.

> 조건　1　관계대명사를 사용하시오.
> 　　　2　주어진 말을 사용하시오. (anything, need)

→ Please ask me for ___________ ___________

　___________ ___________.

서술형 2　　(4점, 각 2점)

다음 문장에서 어법상 **틀린** 부분을 바르게 고쳐 문장을 다시 쓰시오.

> (1) That you drew surprised us.
> (2) I like singers which voice is powerful.

(1) ____

(2) ____

서술형 3　　(8점, 각 2점)

(A)와 (B)에 주어진 말을 <u>한 번씩</u> 사용하여 문장을 완성하시오.

(A)	(B)
who	· Kate gave me
that	· exists on Earth
what	· the whole world admires
whose	· rules are very difficult

(1) I like ____________________________.

(2) Kim is a skater ____________________________.

(3) This is a game ____________________________.

(4) The blue whale is the biggest animal ________

　____________.

서술형 4　NEW　　(6점, 각 3점)

그림을 보고, 주어진 말을 활용하여 문장을 완성하시오.
(관계대명사를 사용할 것)

(1)

→ I have a dog ___________ ___________

　___________. (name, Jerry)

(2)

→ He is ___________ ___________
　___________ ___________ the marathon last
year. (same, runner, win)

서술형 5　NEW　　(8점, 각 4점)

표를 보고, 다음 글의 밑줄 친 우리말과 의미가 같도록 관계대명사를 사용하여 문장을 완성하시오.

the Louvre	It has over 38,000 works of art.
the *Mona Lisa*	I want to see it most.

> 　I want to visit the Louvre someday. (1)<u>그곳은 38,000점 이상의 예술 작품을 가진 유명한 박물관이다.</u> There are a lot of great paintings there. (2)<u>그중에서 내가 가장 보고 싶은 것은 '모나리자'이다.</u>

(1) It is a famous museum ____________________

　________________________________.

(2) Among them, ____________________________
　is the *Mona Lisa*.

관계사 2

1 관계대명사의 생략

2 관계대명사의 계속적 용법

3 관계부사 ① | when, where

4 관계부사 ② | why, how

1 관계대명사의 생략

목적격 관계대명사와 「주격 관계대명사+be동사」는 생략할 수 있다.

목적격 관계대명사의 생략	The movie (**that**) you recommended was very exciting.
「주격 관계대명사+be동사」의 생략	The man (**who is**) waving to me is my father. I like the pictures (**which were**) taken by this photographer.

주의 관계대명사가 전치사의 목적어인 경우, 「전치사+관계대명사」 형태일 때는 관계대명사를 생략할 수 없다.

I know the boy **to whom** Sarah is talking.
　　　　　　　　　　⌐----------➔ 전치사 뒤에는 목적격 관계대명사로 who나 that을 쓸 수 없다.

I know the boy (**who(m)**)(**that**)) Sarah is talking **to**.　(전치사가 관계사절의 끝에 올 때는 관계대명사 생략 가능)

1 목적격 관계대명사 생략 형태 익히기

e.g.

그가 듣고 있던 노래　　➔ the song _that(which)_ he was listening to

➔ the song ___to___ ___which___ he was listening

➔ the song ___he___ ___was___ ___listening___ ___to___

1　우리가 고른 꽃들　　➔ the flowers ___________ we chose

➔ the flowers ___________ ___________

2　네가 보고 있는 소년　➔ the boy ___________ you are looking at

➔ the boy ___________ ___________ you are looking

➔ the boy ___________ ___________ ___________ ___________

2 「주격 관계대명사+be동사」 생략 형태 익히기

1　The man who is waiting in front of the house is Kevin.

➔ ___________ ___________ ___________ in front of the house is Kevin.

2　I didn't get the email that was sent to customers.

➔ I didn't get the email ___________ ___________ ___________.

3　She has a watch which was made in China.

➔ She has ___________ ___________ ___________ in China.

4　Have you seen the people who are sitting next to you?

➔ Have you seen ___________ ___________ ___________ next to you?

 2 관계대명사의 계속적 용법

선행사에 추가적인 설명을 더할 때 쓰며, 관계대명사 앞에 콤마(,)를 쓴다. 계속적 용법의 관계대명사는 생략할 수 없다.

선행사가 사람일 때	I like *Tom Cruise*, **who** starred in the movie *Mission Impossible*. (← I like *Tom Cruise*, **and he** starred in the movie *Mission Impossible*.)
선행사가 사물일 때	My favorite book is *The Little Prince*, **which** I've read ten times so far. (← My favorite book is *The Little Prince*, **and** I've read **it** ten times so far.)
선행사가 앞 문장 전체일 때	*He quit smoking*, **which** surprised everyone. (← *He quit smoking*, **and it** surprised everyone.)

선행사가 앞 문장 전체일 때 관계대명사는 반드시 which를 쓴다.

주의 관계대명사 that은 계속적 용법으로 쓸 수 없다.
The carpet, that was damaged by fire, was thrown away. (×)
The carpet, **which** was damaged by fire, was thrown away. (○)

---

1 계속적 용법의 관계대명사로 문장 연결하기

1 They visited the British Museum. It was built in 1753.

→ They visited the British Museum, ____.

2 This is Ben. He plays the guitar in our band.

→ This is Ben, ____.

3 She was late. It disappointed me.

→ She was late, ____.

2 계속적 용법의 관계대명사 형태 적용하기

1 내 여동생은 채식주의자인데, 절대 고기를 먹지 않는다.

→ My sister, __________ is a vegetarian, never eats meat.

2 Eric이 그 경기에서 졌는데, 그것은 믿기 어렵다.

→ Eric lost the game, __________ is hard to believe.

3 이들은 내 친구들인데, 그들을 네게 소개해 주고 싶다.

→ These are my friends, __________ I want to introduce to you.

4 내 휴대 전화는 어제 고장 났는데, 곧 수리될 것이다.

→ My cell phone, __________ broke yesterday, will be fixed soon.

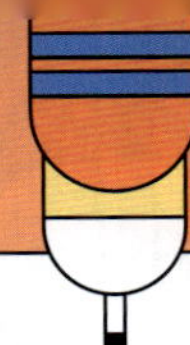

영작 기본 훈련

STEP 1 관계대명사 사용하여 의미 **확장하기** (가능한 경우 관계대명사를 생략할 것)

1
- ⓐ 나는 Lisa와 이야기했다.

  I talked with Lisa.

- ⓑ Lisa가 **나와 이야기한** 그 친구이다.

  Lisa is the friend __________ __________ I talked.

2
- ⓐ 그는 그림을 그렸다.

  He painted a picture.

- ⓑ 그는 **그가 그린 그림**을 내게 보여 주었다.

  He showed me the picture __________ __________.

3
- ⓐ 그것이 나를 놀라게 했다.

  It surprised me.

- ⓑ 그는 그 시험에 합격했는데, **그것이 나를 놀라게 했다**.

  He passed the test, __________ __________ __________.

4
- ⓐ 우리 가족은 그 집에 산다.

  My family lives in the house.

- ⓑ 이것이 **우리 가족이 살고 있는** 집이다.

  This is the house __________ __________ __________ __________ lives.

5
- ⓐ 그 영화는 극장에서 상영 중이다.

  The movie is playing at the theater.

- ⓑ **극장에서 상영 중인 그 영화**는 내가 가장 좋아하는 것이다.

  __________ __________ __________ __________ __________ is my favorite.

6
- ⓐ Jim은 용감한 군인이다.

  Jim is a brave soldier.

- ⓑ 나는 Jim을 만났는데, **그는 용감한 군인이다**.

  I met Jim, __________ __________ __________ __________.

7
- ⓐ 그 개는 Tim에게 훈련 받았다.

  The dog was trained by Tim.

- ⓑ 그녀는 **Tim에게 훈련 받은 개**를 키운다.

  She has __________ __________ __________ __________.

8
- ⓐ 우리는 이 공원을 매우 좋아한다.

  We love this park.

- ⓑ 이 공원은 **우리가 매우 좋아하는데** 우리 집에서 멀다.

  This park, __________ __________ __________, is far from our house.

STEP **2** 배열 영작하기 (필요시 콤마(,)를 추가할 것)

1 나는 Ian에게 전화를 했는데, 그는 내 누나의 친구이다.   called, I, who, a friend, Ian, is

→ ____ of my sister.

2 이것이 네가 찾고 있는 책이니?   looking, for, are, is, the book, you, this

→ ____

3 2층에 살고 있는 여자는 의사이다.   a doctor, living, is, the second floor, the woman, on

→ ____

4 그녀는 그 미술관에 갔는데, 그곳은 문을 닫았다.   was, which, she, went, the gallery, closed, to

→ ____

5 내가 어제 만난 아이들은 지금 아프다.   met, yesterday, are, I, the kids, sick, now

→ ____

STEP **3** 부분 영작하기 (필요시 콤마(,)를 추가할 것)

1 네가 방문하고 싶어 했던 박물관에 가자. (want, visit)

→ Let's go to the museum ____.

2 사람들은 Kate를 좋아하는데, 그녀는 친절하고 쾌활하다. (kind and cheerful)

→ People like ____.

3 이 분이 우리가 존경하는 선생님이다. (look up to)

→ This is the teacher ____.

4 Joe가 아직 집에 안 돌아왔는데, 그것이 나를 걱정시킨다. (worry me)

→ Joe hasn't come home yet, ____.

5 웃긴 모자를 쓰고 있는 그 소녀는 내 룸메이트이다. (wearing, the funny hat)

→ ____ is my roommate.

A 관계부사는 「접속사＋부사」의 역할을 하며, 관계부사가 이끄는 절은 시간, 장소, 이유, 방법을 나타내는 선행사를 꾸며 준다. 관계부사는 「전치사＋관계대명사」로 바꿔 쓸 수 있다.

> 2024 was *the year*. ＋ France hosted the Olympic Games **then**(= **in** that year).
> → 2024 was *the year* **when** France hosted the Olympic Games.
>   선행사   관계부사
> → 2024 was *the year* **in which** France hosted the Olympic Games.
>   선행사   전치사＋관계대명사

B 선행사가 시간을 나타내는 명사일 때는 관계부사 when을, 장소를 나타내는 명사일 때는 관계부사 where를 쓴다.

	선행사	관계부사	전치사＋관계대명사
시간	the time, the day, the year 등	when	at/on/in＋which
장소	the place, the house, the city 등	where	at/on/in/to＋which

I still remember *the day* **when** we got our dog.
Now is *the time* **when** we have to make a decision.

This is *the city* **where** he grew up.
She lives in *a place* **where** the winters are very cold.

---

1 알맞은 관계부사 쓰기

1 내가 이곳으로 이사 온 해 → the year ___________ I moved here

2 David가 여행한 곳 → the place ___________ David traveled

3 우리가 수업을 듣는 교실 → the classroom ___________ we have classes

4 비가 많이 내리는 계절 → the season ___________ it rains a lot

2 관계부사 사용하여 문장 완성하기

1 다음 주 월요일은 학교가 시작하는 날이다.

→ Next Monday is ___________ ___________ ___________ school starts.

2 2월은 매년 우리가 스키 타러 가는 달이다.

→ February is ___________ ___________ ___________ we go skiing every year.

3 우리가 휴가를 보낸 도시는 아름다웠다.

→ ___________ ___________ ___________ we spent our holidays was beautiful.

 4 관계부사 2 | why, how

선행사가 이유를 나타내는 명사일 때는 관계부사 why를, 방법을 나타내는 명사일 때는 관계부사 how를 쓴다.

	선행사	관계부사	전치사＋관계대명사
이유	the reason	why	for＋which
방법	the way	how	in＋which

I don't know *the reason* **why** he is angry with me.
Please tell me *the reason* **why** she left so early.

This is *the way* I prepared for the audition.
= This is **how** I prepared for the audition.

주의 방법을 나타내는 선행사 the way와 관계부사 how는 함께 쓸 수 없고, 둘 중 하나만 써야 한다.
I'll explain to you <u>the way how</u> I solved the problem. (×)

1 알맞은 관계부사 쓰기

1 내가 늦게까지 깨어 있던 이유 → the reason __________ I stayed up late

2 네가 영어를 공부하는 방법 → __________ you study English

3 그가 아침 식사를 거른 이유 → the reason __________ he skipped breakfast

4 그들이 그 문제를 푼 방법 → __________ they solved the problem

2 관계부사 사용하여 문장 완성하기

1 Clark는 나에게 그가 시험에 합격한 방법을 말해 주었다.

→ Clark told me __________ he passed the test.

→ Clark told me __________ __________ he passed the test.

2 그들이 싸운 이유는 확실치 않다.

→ __________ __________ __________ they had a fight is not clear.

3 Kelly는 그 기계가 작동하는 방식을 모른다.

→ Kelly doesn't know __________ the machine works.

→ Kelly doesn't know __________ __________ the machine works.

4 네가 숙제를 할 수 없었던 어떤 이유가 있니?

→ Is there any __________ __________ you couldn't do your homework?

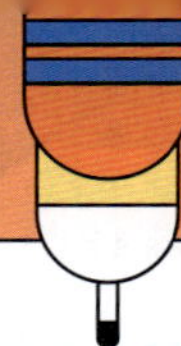

영작 기본 훈련

STEP 1 관계부사 사용하여 의미 **확장하기**

1
- **ⓐ** 나는 그 날을 기억한다.
- **ⓑ** 나는 **우리가 처음 만난 날**을 기억한다.
- **ⓒ** **우리가 처음 만난 날**은 추웠다.

I remember the day.

I remember the day _________ we first met.

_________ _________ _________ we first met was cold.

2
- **ⓐ** 나는 그 마을을 방문했다.
- **ⓑ** 나는 **내가 자란 마을**을 방문했다.
- **ⓒ** **내가 자란 마을**은 작다.

I visited the village.

I visited the village _________ I grew up.

_________ _________ _________ I grew up is small.

3
- **ⓐ** 이것이 그 이유이다.
- **ⓑ** 이것이 **내가 결석한 이유**이다.
- **ⓒ** **내가 결석한 이유**는 비밀이다.

This is the reason.

This is the reason _________ I was absent.

_________ _________ _________ I was absent is a secret.

4
- **ⓐ** 나는 그 방법을 모른다.
- **ⓑ** 나는 **그가 성공한 방법**을 모른다.
- **ⓒ** 그는 내게 **그가 성공한 방법**을 알려 줬다.

I don't know the way.

I don't know _________ _________ he succeeded.

He told me _________ he succeeded.

5
- **ⓐ** 너는 그 날짜를 기억하니?
- **ⓑ** 너는 **우리가 뮤지컬을 본 날짜**를 기억하니?
- **ⓒ** **우리가 뮤지컬을 본 날짜**는 5월 10일이었다.

Do you remember the date?

Do you remember the date _________ we saw the musical?

_________ _________ _________ we saw the musical was May 10.

6
- **ⓐ** 그녀는 한 장소를 알고 있다.
- **ⓑ** 그녀는 **우리가 수영할 수 있는 장소**를 알고 있다.
- **ⓒ** **우리가 수영할 수 있는 장소**는 여기서 멀다.

She knows a place.

She knows a place _________ we can swim.

The place _________ _________ _________ _________ is far from here.

STEP 2 배열 영작하기

1 Tom이 학교에 지각한 이유는 나를 놀라게 했다. late for, the reason, was, Tom, why, school

→ ____ surprised me.

2 이것이 내가 시험을 준비했던 방식이다. how, this, prepared, I, the test, is, for

→ ____

3 목요일은 내가 피아노 수업이 있는 날이다. a piano lesson, the day, have, when, Thursday, I, is

→ ____

4 블로그는 우리가 생각을 공유할 수 있는 공간이다. spaces, ideas, we, are, where, share, blogs, can

→ ____

5 나는 그가 그렇게 많은 돈을 번 방법을 모르겠다. I, he, so much money, made, don't, the way, know

→ ____

STEP 3 부분 영작하기 (관계부사를 사용할 것)

1 그녀는 혼자 있을 수 있는 시간을 즐긴다. (be alone)

→ She enjoys time ____.

2 그들은 네가 피곤한 이유를 이해하지 못한다. (the reason, be tired)

→ They don't understand ____.

3 여름은 나무들이 더 푸르러지는 계절이다. (the season, become greener)

→ Summer is ____.

4 이곳이 그가 그의 친구들과 야구를 했던 공원이다. (the park, play baseball)

→ This is ____.

5 우리는 네가 이 맛있는 피자를 만든 방법을 알고 싶다. (know, make, delicious)

→ We want to ____.

집중 훈련 1 틀린 부분 고치기
어법상 틀린 부분을 찾아 바르게 고치시오.

집중 훈련 2 영작 완성하기
주어진 말을 활용하여 문장을 완성하시오.

01
Julie, that is my best friend, was elected school president.
Julie는 나의 가장 친한 친구인데, 학급 회장으로 뽑혔다.

___________ → ___________

02
This is the office at that I work.
이곳이 내가 일하는 사무실이다.

___________ → ___________

03
She told me the way how this dish is made.
그녀는 나에게 이 음식이 만들어지는 방법을 알려 줬다.

___________ → ___________

04
The friend to who I'm writing lives in L.A.
내가 편지를 쓰고 있는 친구는 L.A.에 산다.

___________ → ___________

05
There were some reasons how I left early.
내가 일찍 떠난 몇 가지 이유가 있었다.

___________ → ___________

06
I visited Paris, that is famous for fashion.
나는 파리를 방문했는데, 그곳은 패션으로 유명하다.

___________ → ___________

07
The milk that delivered today was fresh.
오늘 배달된 우유는 신선했다.

___________ → ___________

08 우리가 가장 존경하는 선생님이 지난주에 은퇴하셨다.
(respect most)

→ ___________________________ retired last week.

09 나는 네가 보고 있는 사진들이 마음에 든다. (look at)

→ I like the photos ___________________.

10 Brian은 뉴질랜드에 사는데, 두 명의 사촌이 있다.
(live in, New Zealand)

→ Brian, ___________________,
has two cousins.

11 Amy는 거짓말을 했는데, 그것은 그녀의 부모님을 화나게 만들었다. (make, parents, upset)

→ Amy told a lie, ___________________.

12 내 여동생은 무대 위에서 춤추고 있는 소녀이다.
(dance, on the stage)

→ My sister is the girl ___________________
___________.

13 우리가 졸업했던 날은 매우 추웠다.
(when, the day, graduate)

→ ___________________________ was very cold.

14 우리는 우리가 공부할 수 있는 조용한 곳을 찾고 있다.
(where, study)

→ We are looking for a quiet place ___________
___________.

집중 훈련 3 통문장 영작하기
주어진 말을 활용하여 영작하시오.

15 저것이 John에 의해 수리된 그 차이다. (repair, by)

→ _______________________________________

16 우리가 머물렀던 그 방은 매우 작았다.
(where, stay, very small)

→ _______________________________________

17 그는 그 마라톤에서 우승했는데, 그것은 놀라웠다.
(win the marathon, amazing)

→ _______________________________________

18 Sally는 어제 그녀가 산 잡지를 읽고 있다.
(read, the magazine)

→ _______________________________________

19 나는 오래된 반지를 발견했는데, 그것은 비싸 보였다.
(find, ring, look expensive)

→ _______________________________________

20
A 너는 그가 오지 않은 이유를 알고 있니?
(the reason, come)
B No, I don't. He said nothing to me.

→ _______________________________________

21
A Have you ever been to Italy?
B Yes. 나는 내가 그곳에 갔던 그때를 결코 잊을 수 없을 거야. (will, never, the time, go)

→ _______________________________________

집중 훈련 4 조건 영작하기
우리말과 의미가 같도록 〈조건〉에 맞게 영작하시오.

22 런던은 네가 유명한 박물관들을 방문할 수 있는 도시이다.

조건 **1** 주어진 말을 사용할 것
(London, a city, visit, famous)
2 관계부사를 사용할 것
3 10단어의 문장으로 쓸 것

→ _______________________________________

23 커다란 선글라스를 쓰고 있는 그 남자가 코치이다.

조건 **1** 주어진 말을 활용할 것
(wear, big sunglasses, a coach)
2 생략할 수 있는 표현은 생략할 것
3 8단어의 문장으로 쓸 것

→ _______________________________________

24 Kate는 그녀가 가장 좋아하는 가수를 만났는데, 그것은 정말 놀라운 일이었다.

조건 **1** who, which, that 중 알맞은 것을 쓸 것
2 주어진 말을 사용할 것
(favorite, a big surprise)
3 모두 10단어로 쓸 것

→ _______________________________________

25 이것이 내가 별을 그리는 방법이다.

조건 **1** draw stars를 사용할 것
2 총 7단어의 문장으로 쓸 것

→ _______________________________________

서술형 실전 TEST

서술형 1　(9점, 각 3점)

〈보기〉에서 알맞은 말을 골라 문장을 완성하시오.

> 보기
> • I told you about
> • parked at the gate
> • which is next Saturday

(1) This is the popular TV show ＿＿＿＿＿＿＿.

(2) I'll have a picnic on my birthday, ＿＿＿＿＿＿
＿＿＿＿＿＿＿＿＿.

(3) The bike ＿＿＿＿＿＿＿＿＿＿＿ is mine.

서술형 2 NEW　(3점)

그림을 보고, 〈조건〉에 맞게 문장을 완성하시오.

> 조건　1　관계대명사를 사용하시오.
> 　　　2　주어진 말을 활용하시오. (make, happy)

→　I found money in my jacket, ＿＿＿＿＿＿
＿＿＿＿＿ ＿＿＿＿＿ ＿＿＿＿＿.

서술형 3　(4점)

우리말과 의미가 같도록 〈조건〉에 맞게 문장을 완성하시오.

> 나의 도시에는 사람들이 그들의 개를 산책시킬 수 있는 공원이 있다.

> 조건　1　관계부사를 사용하시오.
> 　　　2　주어진 말을 활용하시오. (walk one's dogs)

→　My city has a park ＿＿＿＿＿＿＿＿
＿＿＿＿＿＿＿＿＿＿＿.

서술형 4　(4점)

우리말과 의미가 같도록 주어진 말을 활용하여 문장을 완성하시오.

> 2015년은 나의 가족이 부산으로 이사한 해였다.

2015 was the year ＿＿＿＿＿＿＿＿＿.
　　　　　　　　　　　(move to Busan)

서술형 5　(4점)

그림을 보고, 주어진 말을 바르게 배열하여 완전한 문장으로 쓰시오.

> caused, a car accident, there, a traffic jam, by, is

→　＿＿＿＿＿＿＿＿＿＿＿＿＿＿＿

서술형 6 NEW　(6점, 각 3점)

다음 글에서 밑줄 친 우리말을 〈조건〉에 맞게 영작하시오.

> 조건　1　관계대명사 또는 관계부사를 사용하시오.
> 　　　2　주어진 말을 활용하시오.
> 　　　　(everybody, like, make friends, easily)

> 　(1)Jenny는 모두가 좋아하는 여자아이다. She says "hello" to others first and is nice to everyone. Also, she is always smiling. (2)그것이 그녀가 쉽게 친구를 사귀는 방법이다.

(1) Jenny is a girl ＿＿＿＿＿＿＿＿＿.

(2) That's ＿＿＿＿＿＿＿＿＿＿＿.

접속사

1 시간·이유를 나타내는 접속사

2 조건·양보를 나타내는 접속사

3 상관접속사

4 기타 접속사

5 의문사가 있는 간접의문문

6 의문사가 없는 간접의문문

A 시간을 나타내는 접속사

when	~할 때	Let's have dinner **when** everyone arrives.
as	~하면서, ~할 때	I met my old friend **as** I was shopping.
since	~한 이래로	We have been best friends **since** we met in 2020.
while	~하는 동안	Don't drink too much water **while** you're eating.

> **TIP** 시간을 나타내는 부사절에서는 현재시제를 사용하여 미래의 일을 나타낸다.
> He will call you **when** he *comes* home.

B 이유를 나타내는 접속사

because (as/since)	~하기 때문에	Lucy was sad, **as** her cat was sick. I don't eat peanuts, **since** I'm allergic to them.

cf. because of는 전치사구이므로 뒤에는 절이 아닌 명사(구)를 쓴다.
He missed school **because of** *a cold*.
= He missed school **because** *he caught a cold*.

---

1 알맞은 접속사 쓰기

1 She will attend fashion shows
- ___________ she is in Paris. 파리에 있는 동안
- ___________ she is interested in fashion. 패션에 관심 있기 때문에

2 I went to the beach every day
- ___________ I was young. 어렸을 때
- ___________ I loved surfing. 서핑을 아주 좋아했기 때문에

3 He has been making videos
- ___________ he left his job. 일을 그만둔 이후로
- ___________ he travels. 여행을 하면서

2 문맥에 맞는 접속사 쓰기 (<보기>의 접속사를 한 번씩만 쓸 것)

1 ___________ I heard the doorbell, I was in the kitchen.

2 We haven't seen Tim ___________ we met him at the party last year.

3 Lisa cleared the table ___________ her mom was washing the dishes.

4 Jake avoids talking with strangers, ___________ he is very shy.

보기
while
since
as
when

 2 조건·양보를 나타내는 접속사

A 조건을 나타내는 접속사

| if | (만약) ~하면 | **If** it keeps raining, the event will be canceled. |
| unless | (만약) ~하지 않으면 | I can't trust you **unless** you keep your promises. |

TIP 조건을 나타내는 부사절에서는 현재시제를 사용하여 미래의 일을 나타낸다.

If the weather *is* nice tomorrow, we will go hiking.

B 양보를 나타내는 접속사

| although(though/ even though) | 비록 ~이지만, ~에도 불구하고 | **Although** I had a big lunch, I still feel hungry.
The bag **is** popular **even though** it is very expensive. |

cf. '~에도 불구하고'라는 의미의 despite 또는 in spite of는 전치사(구)이므로 뒤에는 절이 아닌 명사(구)를 쓴다.

Despite *my mistake*, the show was successful.
= **Although** *I made a mistake*, the show was successful.

---

1 접속사 의미 익히기

e.g.
Although I felt tired, I helped my mother.

→ ______나는 비록 피곤했지만______ 엄마를 도와드렸다.

1 If it snows, we will take a taxi to the station.

→ __________________________ 우리는 역까지 택시를 탈 것이다.

2 We found a table even though the restaurant was crowded.

→ __________________________ 우리는 테이블을 찾았다.

3 I'll call the police unless you leave right now.

→ __________________________ 나는 경찰을 부를 것이다.

2 문맥에 맞는 접속사 쓰기 (<보기>의 접속사를 한 번씩만 쓸 것)

1 You will fail the test __________ you study harder.

2 __________ anyone knows the answer, please raise your hand.

3 The fans didn't leave the stadium __________ the game was over.

보기
though
if
unless

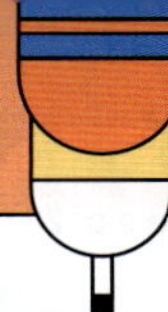

STEP 1 접속사 사용하여 문장 연결하기

1
ⓐ 나는 쇼핑몰에 갔다. 나는 즐거운 시간을 보냈다.
I went to the shopping mall. I had a great time.

ⓑ **나는 쇼핑몰에 갔을 때** 즐거운 시간을 보냈다.
I had a great time ______________________________.

2
ⓐ 날씨가 추웠다. 나는 외투를 입었다.
It was cold. I put on a coat.

ⓑ **날씨가 추웠기 때문에** 나는 외투를 입었다.
I put on a coat ______________________________.

3
ⓐ 나는 돈이 거의 없다. 나는 행복하다.
I have little money. I'm happy.

ⓑ **비록 나는 돈이 거의 없지만** 행복하다.
______________________________, I'm happy.

4
ⓐ 네가 벨을 누른다. 그 버스는 멈출 것이다.
You ring the bell. The bus will stop.

ⓑ **네가 벨을 누르면** 그 버스는 멈출 것이다.
______________________________, the bus will stop.

5
ⓐ 그는 8살이었다. 그는 그때부터 그녀를 알고 지냈다.
He was 8 years old. He has known her since then.

ⓑ **그는 8살 때 이래로** 그녀를 알고 지냈다.
He has known her ______________________________.

6
ⓐ 나는 자전거를 타고 있었다. 나는 Sam을 만났다.
I was riding my bike. I met Sam.

ⓑ **나는 자전거를 타고 있는 동안에** Sam을 만났다.
______________________________, I met Sam.

7
ⓐ 나는 앉았다. 전화벨이 울렸다.
I sat down. The phone rang.

ⓑ **내가 앉았을 때** 전화벨이 울렸다.
The phone rang ______________________________.

8
ⓐ 당신은 표를 가지고 있지 않다. 당신은 극장에 입장할 수 없다.
You don't have a ticket. You can't enter the theater.

ⓑ **당신은 표를 가지고 있지 않으면** 극장에 입장할 수 없다.
You can't enter the theater ______________________________.

STEP **2** 영작 **완성하기** (<보기>의 접속사를 한 번씩만 사용할 것)

| 보기 | if | as | though | because | unless |

1 길이 얼었기 때문에 그들은 천천히 걸었다. (the road, icy)

→ They walked slowly ________________________________.

2 그녀가 내일 제시간에 도착한다면 회의에 참석할 것이다. (arrive on time)

→ ________________________________, she will attend the meeting.

3 비록 그것은 그의 실수였지만, 그는 내게 사과하지 않았다. (his mistake)

→ ________________________________, he didn't apologize to me.

4 그는 기차에서 내리면서 나에게 미소 지었다. (get off the train)

→ ________________________________, he smiled at me.

5 너는 일찍 잠자리에 들지 않으면 내일 피곤할 것이다. (go to bed early)

→ You'll be tired tomorrow ________________________________.

STEP **3** 배열 **영작하기**

1 내가 그 방에 들어갔을 때 사람들이 나를 쳐다보았다. I, people, entered, looked at, the room, when, me

→ ____

2 네가 다른 계획이 있는 것이 아니라면 같이 외식을 하자. you, let's, have, together, other plans, eat out, unless

→ ____

3 방이 어두웠기 때문에 나는 불을 켰다. dark, turned on, the room, was, because, I, the light

→ ____

4 만약 날씨가 좋으면 우리는 그 공원에 갈 것이다. the weather, we, is, if, go to, will, good, the park

→ ____

5 비록 교통이 혼잡했지만 우리는 일찍 도착했다. was, early, heavy, arrived, the traffic, even though, we

→ ____

3 상관접속사

상관접속사는 두 개 이상의 단어가 짝을 이루어 쓰이는 접속사로, 문법적으로 대등한 단어/구/절을 연결한다.

both A and B	A와 B 둘 다	**Both** you **and** I are responsible for the accident.
not A but B	A가 아니라 B	Our new class president is **not** Mia **but** Joan.
not only A but (also) B = B as well as A	A뿐만 아니라 B도	Tony Stark is **not only** a millionaire **but also** a hero. = Tony Stark is a hero **as well as** a millionaire.
either A or B	A나 B 둘 중 하나	**Either** James **or** I am going to win the race.
neither A nor B	A도 B도 아닌	**Neither** Ron **nor** I know the answer to that question.

주의 상관접속사가 주어로 쓰일 경우 「both A and B」는 복수 취급하고, 나머지는 B에 수를 일치시킨다.
Both you **and** Jake *run* very fast.
Not only you **but also** Jake *runs* very fast.

1 상관접속사 형태 익히기

1 결과가 아니라 과정 → ___________ the result ___________ the process

2 아이스크림과 케이크 둘 다 → ___________ ice cream ___________ cake

3 교사들뿐만 아니라 학생들도 → students ___________ ___________ ___________ teachers

4 천재도 바보도 아닌 → ___________ a genius ___________ a fool

2 상관접속사 형태 적용하기

1 너는 집에 있거나 나와 함께 외출할 수 있다. (stay home)

→ You can ___________ ___________ ___________ ___________ go out with me.

2 Steve는 수학과 역사 둘 다에서 좋은 성적을 받았다. (math, history)

→ Steve got a good grade in ___________ ___________ ___________ ___________.

3 그 수업은 재미있지도 유익하지도 않았다. (interesting, helpful)

→ The class was ___________ ___________ ___________ ___________.

4 우리는 집에서가 아니라 도서관에서 공부했다. (at home)

→ We studied ___________ ___________ ___________ ___________ at the library.

5 그들은 서울뿐만 아니라 다른 도시들도 방문했다. (Seoul)

→ They visited ___________ ___________ ___________ ___________ ___________ other cities.

4 기타 접속사

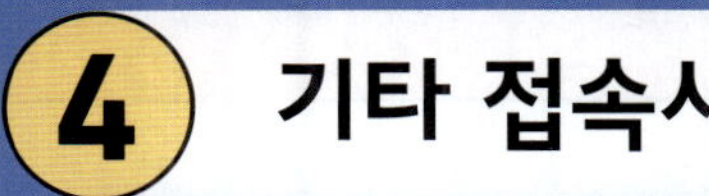

A 명사절을 이끄는 접속사 whether/if

| whether/if | ~인지 (아닌지) | **Whether** you believe it (or not) is not important. 〈주어〉
= **It** is not important **whether** you believe it (or not).
Please let me know **if**〔**whether**〕 you can join us. 〈목적어〉 |

TIP whether가 이끄는 명사절은 주어, 목적어, 보어 역할을 할 수 있지만, if가 이끄는 명사절은 목적어로만 쓰인다.
The question is **whether** she will agree with us. (○) 〈보어〉
The question is if she will agree with us. (×)

B 명령문+and/or

| 명령문, and ... | ~해라. 그러면
…할 것이다. | **Turn** right, **and** you'll find the gas station.
(← If you turn right, you'll find the gas station.) |
| 명령문, or ... | ~해라. 그러지 않으면
…할 것이다. | **Do** your best, **or** you'll regret it.
(← If you don't do your best, you'll regret it.)
(← Unless you do your best, you'll regret it.) |

1 whether / if 형태 익히기

1 이번 주말에 눈이 올지는 확실하지 않다.

→ ____________ it will snow this weekend is not certain.

2 우리는 그 계획이 가능한지 알아야 한다.

→ We need to know ____________ the plan is possible.

3 그 문제점들 중 하나는 우리에게 충분한 시간이 있는지 아닌지이다.

→ One of the issues is ____________ we have enough time ____________ ____________.

2 「명령문+and/or」 의미 익히기

1 Hurry up, or you will miss the train.

→ 서둘러라. ____

2 Open the window, and fresh air will come in.

→ 창문을 열어라. ____

3 Say sorry to him, or he won't forgive you.

→ 그에게 미안하다고 말해라. ____

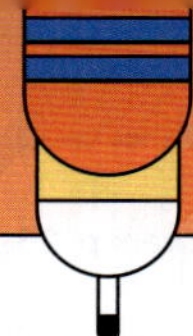

STEP 1 접속사 사용하여 문장 완성하기

1 The store sells accessories as well as clothing.

→ The store sells ________ ________ ________ ________ ________ ________.

2 We are going to visit Italy. Or we are going to visit Germany.

→ We are going to visit ________ ________ ________ ________.

3 His birthday is not today. It is next Thursday.

→ His birthday is ________ ________ ________ ________ ________.

4 I don't want tea. I don't want juice, either.

→ I want ________ ________ ________ ________.

5 Jessica got an A on the test. I got an A on the test, too.

→ ________ ________ ________ ________ got an A on the test.

6 If you finish your homework, you can go out.

→ ________ ________ ________, ________ you can go out.

7 If you don't get some rest, you'll be very tired.

→ ________ ________ ________, ________ you'll be very tired.

8 Will it rain? Will it not rain? I don't know.

→ I don't know ________ ________ ________ ________ ________.

STEP **2** 영작 **완성하기** (접속사를 사용할 것)

1 나는 돈도 시간도 없다. (money, time)

→ I have ___________ ___________ ___________ ___________.

2 너는 택시나 지하철로 공항에 갈 수 있다. (by taxi)

→ You can go to the airport ___________ ___________ ___________ ___________ by subway.

3 그가 외국인인지는 중요하지 않다. (a foreigner)

→ It is not important ___________ ___________ ___________ ___________.

4 Tom뿐만 아니라 Ken도 K-pop에 관심이 있다. (be)

→ ___________ ___________ Tom ___________ ___________ Ken ___________ interested in K-pop.

5 나는 내 대답이 맞는지 아닌지 궁금하다. (my answer, right)

→ I wonder ___________ ___________ ___________ ___________ ___________ or not.

STEP **3** 배열 **영작하기**

1 Peter와 나는 둘 다 학교 버스를 기다리고 있다. I, both, waiting, and, are, for, Peter, the school bus

→ ____

2 그가 진실을 말하고 있는지 나는 모른다. don't know, he, whether, the truth, is, I, telling

→ ____

3 그녀는 아침이 아니라 밤에 샤워한다. but, in the morning, not, she, showers, at night

→ ____

4 우리는 박물관이나 고궁 중 한 곳을 방문할 것이다. or, visit, the museum, we, either, the palace, will

→ ____

5 Kate도 나도 내일에 대해 아무런 계획이 없다. any plans, have, neither, I, for tomorrow, nor, Kate

→ ____

의문사가 있는 간접의문문

간접의문문은 의문문이 어떤 문장의 일부로 쓰여, 질문의 내용을 간접적으로 묻는 것을 말한다. 의문사가 있는 간접의문문은 「의문사+주어+동사」의 형태로 쓴다.

be동사가 있는 경우	Can you tell me? + Where is Tom? → Can you tell me **where Tom is**? 주어 동사	
일반동사가 있는 경우	I'm not sure. + When does the store open? → I'm not sure **when the store opens**. 주어 동사	의문문의 do/does/did를 삭제하고, 간접의문문의 동사에 시제와 수를 적용한다.
의문사가 주어인 경우	Please tell me. + What happened? → Please tell me **what happened**. 의문사(주어) 동사	의문사가 간접의문문의 주어인 경우 「의문사+동사」 순서로 쓴다.

TIP 생각이나 추측을 나타내는 think, believe, guess, imagine 등이 주절의 동사인 의문문은 간접의문문의 의문사를 문장 맨 앞에 쓴다.

Do you *think*? + Where did you lose your phone?
→ **Where** do you *think* **you lost** your phone?

---

1 의문문을 간접의문문으로 **바꿔 쓰기**

1 "Where is the subway station?" → I don't know __________________.

2 "How did you make this cake?" → Please tell me __________________.

3 "How old is she?" → Do you know __________________?

4 "Who stole my wallet?" → I wonder __________________.

5 "When did she call?" → Do you remember __________________?

2 간접의문문 사용하여 **한 문장으로 쓰기**

1 Do you think? + When will you finish your work?

→ __________________

2 Do you think? + What did the cat eat last night?

→ __________________

3 Do you believe? + Who will be the next president?

→ __________________

 6 의문사가 없는 간접의문문

의문사가 없는 간접의문문은 '~인지 (아닌지)'라는 뜻의 명사절을 이끄는 접속사 if〔whether〕를 사용하여
「if〔whether〕+주어+동사」의 형태로 쓴다.

I'm not sure. + Does she have a dog?
→ I'm not sure **if〔whether〕 she has** a dog.
　　　　　　　　　　　주어　동사

Do you know? + Did he pass the exam?
→ Do you know **if〔whether〕 he passed** the exam?
　　　　　　　　　　주어　　동사

1 의문문을 간접의문문으로 바꿔 쓰기

1 "Is he from Spain?"

→ Do you know ______________________________?

2 "Does she know my name?"

→ I'm wondering ______________________________.

3 "Can I have a seat here?"

→ I'm not sure ______________________________.

4 "Has he been to Korea?"

→ She wants to know ______________________________.

2 간접의문문 사용하여 한 문장으로 쓰기

1 I wonder. + Can you come to my birthday party?

→ I wonder ______________________________.

2 I want to know. + Is Jane in the library?

→ I want to know ______________________________.

3 Can you tell me? + Did you send me these flowers?

→ Can you tell me ______________________________?

4 We are not sure. + Is she angry at us?

→ We are not sure ______________________________.

영작 기본 훈련

STEP 1 의문문과 간접의문문 **비교하기**

1
ⓐ 누가 내 우산을 가져갔니?

Who took my umbrella?

ⓑ 너는 **누가 내 우산을 가져갔는지** 알고 있니?

Do you know ___________________?

2
ⓐ 그는 자동차를 가지고 있니?

Does he have a car?

ⓑ 나는 **그가 자동차를 가지고 있는지** 궁금하다.

I wonder ___________________.

3
ⓐ 그녀는 언제 호주로 떠나니?

When does she leave for Australia?

ⓑ 나는 **그녀가 언제 호주로 떠날지** 잘 모르겠다.

I'm not sure ___________________.

4
ⓐ 그녀가 그에게 뭐라고 말했니?

What did she say to him?

ⓑ 너는 **그녀가 그에게 뭐라고 말했다고** 생각하니?

_________ do you think ___________________?

5
ⓐ 이 시계는 비싸니?

Is this watch expensive?

ⓑ 그는 **이 시계가 비싼지** 알지 못한다.

He doesn't know ___________________.

6
ⓐ 그들은 어디에서 그 축제를 열까?

Where will they hold the festival?

ⓑ 너는 **그들이 어디에서 그 축제를 열 거라고** 생각하니?

_________ do you think ___________________?

7
ⓐ 그녀는 어떻게 그 문제를 풀었니?

How did she solve the problem?

ⓑ 나는 **그녀가 어떻게 그 문제를 풀었는지** 알고 싶다.

I want to know ___________________.

8
ⓐ 그 쇼는 몇 시에 시작하니?

What time does the show start?

ⓑ 너는 **그 쇼가 몇 시에 시작하는지** 내게 말해 주겠니?

Can you tell me ___________________?

STEP 2 영작 완성하기 (의문사 또는 접속사를 사용할 것)

1 나는 어젯밤에 무슨 일이 일어났는지 궁금하다. (wonder, happen)

→ I ___________ ___________ ___________ last night.

2 나는 우리가 그를 파티에 초대해야 할지 잘 모르겠다. (should, invite)

→ I'm not sure ___________ ___________ ___________ ___________ ___________ to the party.

3 너는 누가 이 편지를 썼다고 생각하니? (believe)

→ ___________ ___________ ___________ ___________ wrote this letter?

4 그녀는 그가 언제 캐나다로 이사 갔는지 나에게 물었다. (move to Canada)

→ She asked me ___________ ___________ ___________ ___________ ___________.

5 나는 이 공책이 네 것인지 알고 싶다. (notebook, yours)

→ I want to know ___________ ___________ ___________ ___________.

STEP 3 배열 영작하기

1 이 접시가 얼마인지 제게 말씀해 주시겠어요? me, this plate, is, how much, tell

→ Could you ___________________________________?

2 그들이 전에 만난 적이 있는지 너는 아니? know, have met, whether, you, do, they

→ ___________________________________ before?

3 너는 그녀가 지금 어디에 가고 있다고 생각하니? you, where, is, think, she, do, going

→ ___________________________________ now?

4 나는 이 단어가 무엇을 의미하는지 모른다. this word I, know, what, don't, means

→ ___________________________________

5 나는 그들이 나를 채용할지 잘 모르겠다. I'm, if, me, not, hire, they, sure, will

→ ___________________________________

집중 훈련 1 틀린 부분 고치기
어법이나 의미가 <u>틀린</u> 부분을 찾아 바르게 고치시오.

집중 훈련 2 영작 완성하기
주어진 말을 활용하여 문장을 완성하시오.

01
I want to know that she likes cats or not.
나는 그녀가 고양이를 좋아하는지 아닌지 알고 싶다.

______________ → ______________

02
We played outside if it was cold.
추웠음에도 불구하고 우리는 밖에서 놀았다.

______________ → ______________

03
Not only the driver but also his kids was wearing a seat belt.
운전자뿐만 아니라 그의 아이들도 안전벨트를 매고 있었다.

______________ → ______________

04
I don't know what are they talking about.
나는 그들이 무엇에 대해 이야기하고 있는지 모르겠다.

______________ → ______________

05
Both Nancy and Josh lives in Japan.
Nancy와 Josh 둘 다 일본에 산다.

______________ → ______________

06
Go now, and you will miss the bus.
지금 가라. 그러지 않으면 너는 버스를 놓칠 것이다.

______________ → ______________

07
Do you think what your brother wants for his birthday?
너는 네 남동생이 생일에 무엇을 원한다고 생각하니?

______________ → ______________

08 그녀는 항상 쾌활하기 때문에 모든 사람들이 그녀를 좋아한다. (always, cheerful)

→ Everyone likes her ______________

______________.

09 너는 걸어가거나 버스를 탈 수 있다.
(take a bus, either)

→ You can ______________.

10 그가 결혼했는지 아닌지는 확실하지 않다.
(is married, not)

→ ______________ is not clear.

11 내가 브라질에 사는 동안 Susan과 나는 친구가 되었다.
(live, Brazil)

→ Susan and I became friends ______________

______________.

12 나는 그가 왜 울고 있는지 잘 모르겠다. (cry)

→ I'm not sure ______________.

13 그것이 네 가방이 아니라면 너는 그것을 만져서는 안 된다.
(your bag)

→ ______________, you shouldn't touch it.

14 나는 영어뿐만 아니라 프랑스어도 말할 수 있다.
(English, French, as)

→ I can speak ______________.

집중 훈련 3 통문장 영작하기
주어진 말을 활용하여 영작하시오.

집중 훈련 4 조건 영작하기
우리말과 의미가 같도록 〈조건〉에 맞게 영작하시오.

15 너는 저 남자가 누구인지 아니? (know, that man)

→ ______________________________

16 그 영화는 감동적일 뿐만 아니라 웃기기도 하다.
(also, touching, funny)

→ ______________________________

17 아침을 먹어라. 그러지 않으면 너는 기운이 없을 것이다.
(have breakfast, have no energy)

→ ______________________________

18 나는 그녀가 채식주의자인지 궁금하다.
(wonder, a vegetarian)

→ ______________________________

19 Tom도 Jane도 놀라지 않았다. (surprised, nor)

→ ______________________________

20
A Are you going on a picnic tomorrow?
B Yes. But 비가 오면 나는 집에 있을 거야.
(stay home, it, rain)

→ ______________________________

21
A 네가 어디 사는지 내게 말해 주겠니?
(can, tell me, live)
B Sure. I live in that house over there.

→ ______________________________

22 비록 나는 졸렸지만 숙제를 끝냈다.

조건 1 주어진 말을 활용할 것
(sleepy, finish my homework)
2 접속사로 시작할 것
3 9단어의 문장으로 쓸 것

→ ______________________________

23 네가 외투를 입지 않으면 너는 감기에 걸릴지도 모른다.

조건 1 괄호 안에 주어진 말을 사용할 것
(may, catch a cold, a coat)
2 not을 쓰지 말 것
3 10단어의 문장으로 쓸 것

→ ______________________________

24 왼쪽으로 돌아라. 그러면 너는 은행을 찾을 것이다.

조건 1 명령문을 포함할 것
2 모두 8단어로 쓸 것
3 〈보기〉의 표현을 사용할 것

보기   turn left   find the bank

→ ______________________________

25 너는 그녀가 언제 돌아올 것이라고 생각하니?

조건 1 think, come back을 사용할 것
2 총 8단어로 쓸 것

→ ______________________________

서술형 **1** (3점)

우리말과 의미가 같도록 문장을 완성하시오.

> 그가 나를 도울 수 있을지는 확실하지 않다.

→ It is not clear ___________ ___________

___________ ___________ ___________ .

서술형 **2** (3점)

우리말과 의미가 같도록 〈조건〉에 맞게 문장을 완성하시오.

> 비록 그들이 무척 빠르게 말했지만, 나는 거의 모든 것을
> 알아들었다.

조건　1　접속사를 사용하시오.
　　　2　주어진 말을 활용하시오.
　　　　(speak, very fast)

___________________________________ , I understood nearly everything.

서술형 **3** (6점, 각 3점)

우리말과 의미가 같도록 어법상 틀린 부분을 바르게 고쳐 문장
을 다시 쓰시오.

> (1) She will try *dalgona* when she will visit
> 　　Korea.
> 　　(그녀는 한국을 방문할 때 달고나를 먹어볼 것이다.)
> (2) We can't start the game unless everyone
> 　　isn't here.
> 　　(모두가 여기에 있지 않으면 우리는 게임을 시작할 수
> 　　없다.)

(1) _______________________________________

(2) _______________________________________

서술형 **4** (6점, 각 2점)

다음 문장을 지시대로 바꿔 쓰시오.

(1) They didn't serve beef. They served fish.
　　(상관접속사를 사용할 것)
　　→ They served _____________________________ .

(2) If you visit the website, you can learn more
　　about our projects. (명령문을 사용할 것)
　　→ _____________________________ you
　　can learn more about our projects.

(3) "When did he arrive?" (간접의문문을 사용할 것)
　　→ Do you know _____________________________ ?

서술형 **5** (6점, 각 2점)

(A)와 (B)에 주어진 말을 한 번씩 사용하여 문장을 완성하시오.

(A)	(B)
when	· it rains
unless	· I have a sore throat
because	· I saw my report card

(1) I will go camping _____________________________ .

(2) I can't sing today _____________________________ .

(3) I was surprised _____________________________ .

서술형 **6** NEW (6점, 각 3점)

그림을 보고, 주어진 말을 사용하여 문장을 완성하시오.
(상관접속사를 사용할 것)

(1) (2)

(1) Junho wants to play _____________________
_____________________ . (baseball, soccer)

(2) Susan is interested in plants _______________
_____________________ . (animals)

가정법

1 가정법 과거

2 가정법 과거 *vs.* 직설법 현재

3 가정법 과거완료

4 가정법 과거완료 *vs.* 직설법 과거

5 I wish 가정법

6 as if 가정법

1 가정법 과거

A 가정법 과거는 현재 사실과 반대되거나 실현 가능성이 거의 없는 일이나 소망을 가정할 때 쓴다.

| If+주어+ 동사의 과거형 / were ~, | 주어+ would / could / might +동사원형 … | 만약 ~한다면, …할 텐데. / 만약 ~한다면, …할 수 있을 텐데. / 만약 ~한다면, …할지도 모를 텐데. |

→ if절의 동사가 be동사인 경우 주어에 관계없이 were를 쓴다.

If she **had** time, she **would take** a break.
If I **were not** full, I **could eat** more.
If he **didn't have** an injury, he **might play** better.

B 가정법이 실현 가능성이 거의 없는 일을 나타내는 것과 달리 조건문은 현재나 미래에 일어날 수 있는 일을 나타낸다.

| 가정법 | If I **had** some money, I **would buy** a new backpack. |

내가 돈을 좀 가지고 있다면, 새로운 배낭을 하나 살 텐데. (돈이 있을 가능성이 거의 없음)

| 조건문 | If I **have** some money next week, I **will buy** a new backpack. |

내가 다음 주에 돈을 좀 가지고 있다면, 새로운 배낭을 하나 살 거야. (돈이 있을 가능성이 있음)

1 가정법 과거 형태 익히기

1 네가 시간이 좀 더 있다면, (have) 　너는 나를 찾아올 수 있을 텐데. (visit)

→ If you ___________ more time, you ___________ ___________ me.

2 그가 용감하다면, (be) 　그는 그것을 시도할 텐데. (try)

→ If he ___________ brave, he ___________ ___________ it.

3 그녀가 패스트푸드를 먹지 않는다면, (eat) 　그녀는 더 건강해질 텐데. (get)

→ If she ___________ ___________ fast food, she ___________ ___________ healthier.

4 그가 지금 화나 있지 않다면, (be) 　나는 그에게 이야기해 볼 수 있을 텐데. (talk)

→ If he ___________ angry now, I ___________ ___________ to him.

5 네가 방을 매일 청소한다면, (clean) 　네 방은 그렇게 지저분하지 않을 텐데. (be)

→ If you ___________ your room every day, it ___________ ___________ messy like that.

2 가정법 과거 *vs.* 직설법 현재

가정법 과거는 직설법 현재 문장으로 바꿔 쓸 수 있다.

가정법   **If I were** a scientist, **I could discover** the secrets of the universe.

내가 과학자라면, 우주의 비밀을 발견할 수 있을 텐데.

직설법   **As I am not** a scientist, **I can't discover** the secrets of the universe.

나는 과학자가 아니기 때문에, 우주의 비밀을 발견할 수 없다.

TIP 가정법 과거는 형태가 과거이지만 현재에 대한 내용을 나타내므로 직설법에서는 현재시제를 써야 한다. 또한 반대 사실을 가정하므로 가정법이 긍정이면 직설법은 부정으로, 가정법이 부정이면 직설법은 긍정으로 바꿔 쓴다.

If I **had** a TV in my room, I **could watch** my favorite shows anytime.
(← I *don't have* a TV in my room, so I *can't watch* my favorite shows anytime.)

1 가정법 과거 문장으로 바꿔 쓰기

1   As it isn't sunny, I won't walk to school.

→ _________________________________, I would walk to school.

2   You play games all day, so your parents are angry at you.

→ _________________________________, your parents wouldn't be angry at you.

3   As school doesn't finish early, I won't go to the movies.

→ If school finished early, _________________________________.

4   As they don't know the truth, they may not forgive him.

→ If they knew the truth, _________________________________.

2 가정법 과거 형태 적용하기

1   네가 천천히 말한다면, 우리는 네 말을 더 잘 이해할 수 있을 텐데. (speak, understand)

→ If you __________ slowly, we __________ __________ you better.

2   그가 매운 음식을 좋아한다면, 그는 김치 먹는 것을 즐길 텐데. (like, enjoy)

→ If he __________ spicy food, he __________ __________ eating kimchi.

3   그녀가 병원에 있지 않다면, 그녀는 이번 마라톤을 달릴 수 있을 텐데. (be, run)

→ If she __________ in the hospital, she __________ __________ this marathon.

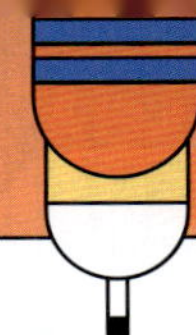

STEP 1 조건문과 가정법 과거 문장 비교하기

1

ⓐ 내가 바쁘지 않으면, 너를 데리러 갈 것이다.

If I'm not busy, I will pick you up.

ⓑ 내가 바쁘지 **않다면**, 너를 데리러 **갈 텐데**.

If I __________ busy, I ______________ you up.

2

ⓐ 눈이 오면, 우리는 눈사람을 만들 것이다.

If it snows, we will build a snowman.

ⓑ **눈이 온다면**, 우리는 눈사람을 **만들 텐데**.

If it __________, we ______________ a snowman.

3

ⓐ 피곤하지 않으면, 그녀는 밖에서 놀 수 있다.

If she isn't tired, she can play outside.

ⓑ 피곤하지 **않다면**, 그녀는 밖에서 **놀 수 있을 텐데**.

If she __________ tired, she ____________ outside.

4

ⓐ 그 앱이 무료이면, 나는 그것을 쓸지도 모른다.

If the app is free, I may use it.

ⓑ 그 앱이 무료**라면**, 나는 그것을 **쓸지도 모르는데**.

If the app __________ free, I ______________ it.

5

ⓐ 내가 복권에 당첨되면, 저 자동차를 살 수 있다.

If I win the lottery, I can buy that car.

ⓑ 내가 복권에 **당첨된다면**, 저 자동차를 **살 수 있을 텐데**.

If I __________ the lottery, I ____________ that car.

6

ⓐ 집에 차가 있으면, 우리는 커피를 마시지 않을 것이다.

If we have tea at home, we won't drink coffee.

ⓑ 집에 차가 **있다면**, 우리는 커피를 **마시지 않을 텐데**.

If we __________ tea at home, we ______________ coffee.

7

ⓐ 비가 내리지 않으면, 우리는 지금 산책을 할 수 있다.

If it isn't raining, we can take a walk now.

ⓑ **비가 내리지 않는다면**, 우리는 산책을 **할 수 있을 텐데**.

If it ______________, we ______________ a walk.

8

ⓐ 네가 열이 없으면, 수영하러 갈 수 있다.

If you don't have a fever, you can go swimming.

ⓑ 네가 열이 **없다면**, 수영하러 **갈 수 있을 텐데**.

If you ______________ a fever, you ______________ swimming.

STEP **2** 영작 **완성하기**

1 네가 그들을 안다면, 너는 절대 그렇게 말하지 않을 텐데. (know)

→ ___________ ____________ ____________ ___________, you would never say that.

2 내가 너라면, 수업 시간에 전화기를 사용하지 않을 텐데. (use my phone)

→ If I were you, I ___________ ___________ ___________ ___________ in class.

3 그가 좋은 드럼 연주자라면, 우리 밴드에 들어올 수 있을 텐데. (be, a good drummer)

→ If he ___________ ____________ ____________ ___________, he could join our band.

4 내가 충분한 돈을 가지고 있다면, 전 세계를 여행할지도 모를 텐데. (travel around the world)

→ If I had enough money, I ___________ ___________ ___________ ___________ ___________.

5 숙제가 많지 않다면, 나는 친구들과 외출할 수 있을 텐데. (have, go)

→ If I ___________ ___________ a lot of homework, I ___________ ___________ out with my friends.

STEP **3** 부분 **영작하기**

1 그녀가 내 비밀을 지킨다면, 나는 그녀를 신뢰할 텐데. (keep my secrets)

→ ________________________________, I would trust her.

2 내가 시력이 나쁘지 않다면, 나는 안경을 쓰지 않을 텐데. (wear glasses)

→ If I didn't have poor eyesight, ________________________________.

3 그가 더 열심히 공부한다면, 수학 시험을 통과할지도 모를 텐데. (study harder, pass)

→ If he ________________________________, ________________________________ the math test.

4 네가 프랑스어를 말한다면, 너는 Lucas와 이야기할 수 있을 텐데. (speak French, talk)

→ If ________________________________, ________________________________ with Lucas.

5 내가 가수라면, 내 노래들을 작곡할 텐데. (be, write)

→ ________________________________, ________________________________ my own songs.

3 가정법 과거완료

A 가정법 과거완료는 과거 사실과 반대되는 일을 가정할 때 쓴다.

If + 주어 + **had** + **p.p.** ~,	주어 + **would** / **could** / **might** + **have** + **p.p.** ...	만약 ~했다면, …했을 텐데. 만약 ~했다면, …할 수 있었을 텐데. 만약 ~했다면, …했을지도 모를 텐데.

If I **had known** your phone number, I **would have called** you.
If he **hadn't made** a mistake, he **could have won** a gold medal.
If we **had gone** to the market, we **might have bought** some fresh fruit.

B 가정법 과거는 현재 사실에 대한 가정을, 가정법 과거완료는 과거 사실에 대한 가정을 나타내므로, 가정법을 쓸 때 시제에 유의해야 한다.

가정법 과거   If you **were** free today, we **could watch** a movie together.
네가 오늘 한가하다면, 우리는 같이 영화를 볼 수 있을 텐데. (오늘 한가하지 않음)

가정법 과거완료   If you **had been** free yesterday, we **could have watched** a movie together.
네가 어제 한가했다면, 우리는 같이 영화를 볼 수 있었을 텐데. (어제 한가하지 않았음)

1 가정법 과거완료 형태 익히기

1 그녀가 그 사고를 봤다면, (see)

→ If she ＿＿＿＿ ＿＿＿＿ the accident,

그녀는 충격 받았을 텐데. (be)

she ＿＿＿＿ ＿＿＿＿ ＿＿＿＿ shocked.

2 네가 더 일찍 왔다면, (come)

→ If you ＿＿＿＿ ＿＿＿＿ earlier,

너는 더 좋은 자리를 찾았을지도 모를 텐데. (find)

you ＿＿＿＿ ＿＿＿＿ a better seat.

3 그들이 집에 가지 않았다면, (go)

→ If they ＿＿＿＿ ＿＿＿＿ home,

그들은 그 공연을 볼 수 있었을 텐데. (watch)

they ＿＿＿＿ ＿＿＿＿ ＿＿＿＿ the show.

4 그가 외투를 입었다면, (wear)

→ If he ＿＿＿＿ ＿＿＿＿ a coat,

그는 감기에 걸리지 않았을 텐데. (catch)

he ＿＿＿＿ ＿＿＿＿ ＿＿＿＿ a cold.

5 내게 돈이 좀 있었다면, (have)

→ If I ＿＿＿＿ ＿＿＿＿ some money,

나는 그 운동화를 샀을지도 모르는데. (buy)

I ＿＿＿＿ ＿＿＿＿ ＿＿＿＿ the sneakers.

 4 가정법 과거완료 *vs.* 직설법 과거

가정법 과거완료는 직설법 과거 문장으로 바꿔 쓸 수 있다.

| 가정법 | If I **had been** Sherlock Holmes, I **could have solved** the riddle. |

내가 셜록 홈즈였다면, 그 수수께끼를 풀 수 있었을 텐데.

| 직설법 | As I **wasn't** Sherlock Holmes, I **couldn't solve** the riddle. |

내가 셜록 홈즈가 아니었기 때문에, 그 수수께끼를 풀 수 없었다.

TIP 가정법 과거완료는 형태가 과거완료이지만 과거에 대한 내용을 나타내므로 직설법에서는 과거시제를 써야 한다.

If I **had taken** the medicine, I **would have gotten** better.
(← I *didn't take* the medicine, so I *didn't get* better.)

1 가정법 과거완료 문장으로 바꿔 쓰기

1 As she wasn't home, I didn't visit her.

→ ________________________________, I would have visited her.

2 Because you didn't see the sign, you parked your car there.

→ If you had seen the sign, ________________________________.

3 As I didn't have breakfast, I was hungry all morning.

→ ________________________________, I wouldn't have been hungry all morning.

4 As we didn't vote for Mark, he didn't become our class president.

→ If we had voted for Mark, ________________________________.

2 가정법 과거완료 형태 적용하기

1 어제 날이 흐리지 않았다면, 우리는 해변에 갔을 텐데. (be, go)

→ If it _________ _________ cloudy yesterday, we _________ _________ _________ to the beach.

2 내가 그 가수를 알아봤다면, 그녀의 사인을 받을 수 있었을 텐데. (recognize, get)

→ If I _________ _________ the singer, I _________ _________ _________ her autograph.

3 그가 등산을 했다면, 아름다운 풍경을 봤을 텐데. (go, see)

→ If he _________ _________ hiking, he _________ _________ _________ the beautiful scenery.

4 네가 제시간에 도착했다면, 우리와 함께 저녁을 먹을 수 있었을 텐데. (arrive, eat)

→ If you _________ _________ on time, you _________ _________ _________ dinner with us.

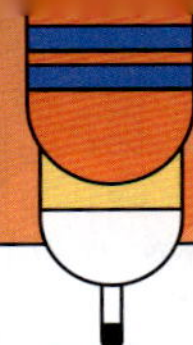

영작 기본 훈련

STEP 1 가정법 과거와 가정법 과거완료 **비교하기**

1 be / keep

ⓐ 내가 **너라면**, 약속을 **지킬 텐데**.
→ If I ________________ you, I ________________ my promise.

ⓑ 내가 **너였다면**, 약속을 **지켰을 텐데**.
→ If I ________________ you, I ________________ my promise.

2 be / go

ⓐ 날씨가 **좋다면**, 우리는 소풍을 **갈 텐데**.
→ If the weather ________________ nice, we ________________ on a picnic.

ⓑ 날씨가 **좋았다면**, 우리는 소풍을 **갔을 텐데**.
→ If the weather ________________ nice, I ________________ on a picnic.

3 be / meet

ⓐ 그가 여기에 **있다면**, 새로운 사람들을 **만날지도 모를 텐데**.
→ If he ________________ here, he ________________ new people.

ⓑ 그가 여기에 **있었다면**, 새로운 사람들을 **만났을지도 모를 텐데**.
→ If he ________________ here, he ________________ new people.

4 have / see

ⓐ 나에게 표가 **있다면**, 그 영화를 **볼 수 있을 텐데**.
→ If I ________________ a ticket, I ________________ the movie.

ⓑ 나에게 표가 **있었다면**, 그 영화를 **볼 수 있었을 텐데**.
→ If I ________________ a ticket, I ________________ the movie.

5 remember / send

ⓐ 그가 그녀의 전화번호를 **기억한다면**, 그녀에게 문자 메시지를 **보낼 텐데**.
→ If he ________________ her phone number, he ________________ her a text.

ⓑ 그가 그녀의 전화번호를 **기억했다면**, 그녀에게 문자 메시지를 **보냈을 텐데**.
→ If he ________________ her phone number, he ________________ her a text.

6 know / introduce

ⓐ 그녀가 그를 잘 **안다면**, 그에게 너를 **소개해 줄 텐데**.
→ If she ________________ him well, she ________________ you to him.

ⓑ 그녀가 그를 잘 **알았다면**, 그에게 너를 **소개해 줬을 텐데**.
→ If she ________________ him well, she ________________ you to him.

STEP **2** 배열 **영작하기**

1 네가 우리에게 사실을 말했다면, 우리는 너를 믿었을 텐데. would, you, have, we, believed

→ If you had told us the truth, _______________________________________.

2 그녀가 휴대 전화를 잃어버리지 않았다면, 내게 전화할 수 있었을 텐데. she, if, her cell phone, not, lost, had

→ _______________________________________, she could have called me.

3 그가 수업에 집중했다면, 시험에 합격할 수 있었을 텐데. focused, he, have, had, in class, he, if, passed, could

→ _______________________________________ the test.

4 네가 좀 더 일찍 출발했다면, 너는 교통 체증을 피할 수 있었을지도 모르는데.

earlier, the traffic, have, had, you, avoided, left, might

→ If you _______________________________________.

5 도로가 얼어붙지 않았다면, 그 사고가 일어나지 않았을 텐데.

happened, would, not, been, had, the accident, icy, not, have

→ If the road _______________________________________.

STEP **3** 부분 **영작하기**

1 네가 그 파티에 왔다면, 마술 공연을 봤을 텐데. (come to the party)

→ _______________________________, you would have seen the magic show.

2 내가 용돈을 모았다면, 그 앨범을 살 수 있었을 텐데. (buy the album)

→ If I had saved my allowance, _______________________________________.

3 너희들이 서로 싸우지 않았다면, 혼나지 않았을 텐데. (fight with each other)

→ _______________________________, you wouldn't have been scolded.

4 내가 한 골을 넣었다면, 우리 팀이 결승전에서 이겼을 텐데. (win the final game)

→ If I had scored a goal, _______________________________________.

5 내가 버스를 잘못 타지 않았다면, 늦지 않았을 텐데. (take the wrong bus, be late)

→ If I _______________________________________.

A 「I wish+가정법 과거」는 현재 이룰 수 없거나 실현 가능성이 거의 없는 일을 소망할 때 쓴다.

I wish	주어 +	동사의 과거형 were	(현재) ~한다면 좋을 텐데.

I wish I were a singer.　내가 가수라면 좋을 텐데.
(← I'm sorry that I am not a singer.)

I wish I knew his phone number.　내가 그의 전화번호를 안다면 좋을 텐데.
(← I'm sorry that I don't know his phone number.)

B 「I wish+가정법 과거완료」는 과거에 이루지 못한 일에 대한 아쉬움을 나타낼 때 쓴다.

I wish	주어 + **had** + **p.p.**	(과거에) ~했다면 좋을 텐데.

I wish I had joined the book club.　내가 그 독서 동아리에 가입했다면 좋을 텐데.
(← I'm sorry that I didn't join the book club.)

1　「I wish+가정법 과거」 형태 익히기

1　오늘이 내 생일이라면 좋을 텐데. (be)

→ I wish today ____________ my birthday.

2　그렇게 자주 비가 내리지 않는다면 좋을 텐데. (rain)

→ I wish it ____________ ____________ so often.

3　나에게 개가 있다면 좋을 텐데. (have)

→ I wish I ____________ a dog.

2　「I wish+가정법 과거완료」 형태 익히기

1　그가 그렇게 빨리 떠나지 않았다면 좋을 텐데. (leave)

→ I wish he ____________ ____________ so soon.

2　우리가 너의 문제에 대해 알았다면 좋을 텐데. (know)

→ I wish we ____________ ____________ about your problems.

3　우리가 여행 중에 사진을 더 많이 찍었다면 좋을 텐데. (take)

→ I wish we ____________ ____________ more photos during the trip.

6 as if 가정법

A 「as if+가정법 과거」는 주절의 시제와 같은 시점의 사실에 반대되는 일을 가정할 때 쓴다.

주어 + 동사 +	**as if** + 주어 +	**동사의 과거형** **were**	마치 ~하는 것처럼

He acts **as if** it **were** my fault.　그는 마치 그것이 내 잘못인 것처럼 행동한다.
(← In fact, it isn't my fault.)

She talks **as if** she **lived** in this neighborhood.　그녀는 마치 이 동네에 사는 것처럼 말한다.
(← In fact, she doesn't live in this neighborhood.)

B 「as if+가정법 과거완료」는 주절의 시제보다 앞선 시점의 사실에 반대되는 일을 가정할 때 쓴다.

주어 + 동사+	**as if** + 주어 + **had** + **p.p.**	마치 ~했던 것처럼

She talks **as if** she **had gotten** a perfect score.　그녀는 마치 만점을 받았던 것처럼 말한다.
(← In fact, she didn't get a perfect score.)

1 「as if+가정법 과거」 형태 익히기

1 Sarah는 마치 Nick을 좋아하는 것처럼 행동한다. (like)

→ Sarah behaves as if she ___________ Nick.

2 그는 마치 아무것도 모르는 것처럼 말한다. (know)

→ He talks as if he ___________ ___________ anything.

3 그녀는 마치 우리의 상사인 것처럼 행동한다. (be)

→ She acts as if she ___________ our boss.

2 「as if+가정법 과거완료」 형태 익히기

1 Amy는 마치 그 영화를 봤던 것처럼 말한다. (see)

→ Amy talks as if she ___________ ___________ the movie.

2 그는 마치 자신이 그 소설을 썼던 것처럼 말했다. (write)

→ He talked as if he ___________ ___________ the novel.

3 그들은 마치 그 소식을 듣지 못했던 것처럼 행동한다. (hear)

→ They act as if they ___________ ___________ the news.

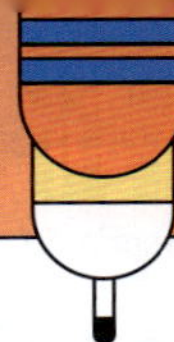

영작 기본 훈련

STEP 1 가정법 문장 의미 **비교하기**

1

ⓐ 그는 **마치** 내 남자 친구**인 것처럼** 행동한다.

He acts as if he ___________ my boyfriend.

ⓑ 그는 **마치** 내 남자 친구**였던 것처럼** 행동한다.

He acts as if he ___________ my boyfriend.

2

ⓐ 나에게 컴퓨터가 **있다면** 좋을 텐데.

___________ I ___________ a computer.

ⓑ 나에게 컴퓨터가 **있었다면** 좋을 텐데.

___________ I ___________ a computer.

3

ⓐ 그녀는 **마치** 책을 많이 **읽는 것처럼** 말한다.

She talks ___________ she ___________ a lot of books.

ⓑ 그녀는 **마치** 책을 많이 **읽었던 것처럼** 말한다.

She talks ___________ she ___________ a lot of books.

4

ⓐ 그가 더 열심히 **공부한다면** 좋을 텐데.

___________ he ___________ harder.

ⓑ 그가 더 열심히 **공부했다면** 좋을 텐데.

___________ he ___________ harder.

5

ⓐ 네가 나에게 결말을 **말하지 않으면** 좋을 텐데.

___________ you ___________ me the ending.

ⓑ 네가 나에게 결말을 **말하지 않았다면** 좋을 텐데.

___________ you ___________ me the ending.

6

ⓐ 네가 아프지 **않으면** 좋을 텐데.

___________ you ___________ sick.

ⓑ 네가 아프지 **않았다면** 좋을 텐데.

___________ you ___________ sick.

7

ⓐ 그녀는 **마치** 가고 **싶지 않은 것처럼** 말했다.

She talked ___________ she ___________ to go.

ⓑ 그녀는 **마치** 가고 **싶지 않았던 것처럼** 말했다.

She talked ___________ she ___________ to go.

8

ⓐ 그들은 **마치** 친한 친구가 **아닌 것처럼** 행동한다.

They act ___________ they ___________ close friends.

ⓑ 그들은 **마치** 친한 친구가 **아니었던 것처럼** 행동한다.

They act ___________ they ___________ close friends.

STEP **2** 문장 **전환하기**

1 I'm sorry that the exams weren't easy.

→ I wish ____ .

2 I'm sorry that I am not a superhero like Iron Man.

→ I wish ____ .

3 I'm sorry that my mom turned off my alarm clock.

→ I wish ____ .

4 They talk like they met the actor at the concert, but they didn't.

→ They talk ____ .

5 He knows her, but he acts like he doesn't know her.

→ He acts ____ .

STEP **3** 배열 **영작하기**

1 우리가 미래에 화성에서 살 수 있다면 좋을 텐데.   live, on Mars, I, we, could, wish

→ ____ in the future.

2 그 남자는 마치 전날 잠을 잘 못 잤던 것처럼 보였다.   if, looked, had, not, as, the man, he, slept well

→ ____ the day before.

3 내가 점심 식사로 다른 요리를 주문했다면 좋을 텐데.   wish, ordered, I, had, a different dish, I

→ ____ for lunch.

4 나의 아빠는 마치 내가 어린아이인 것처럼 대하신다.   a child, me, as, treats, were, my dad, if, I

→ ____

5 내가 그 연극의 주인공이었다면 좋을 텐데.   I, the main character, been, I, had, wish, of the play

→ ____

집중 훈련 **1** 틀린 부분 고치기
어법상 틀린 부분을 찾아 바르게 고치시오.

집중 훈련 **2** 영작 완성하기
주어진 말을 활용하여 문장을 완성하시오.

01 If this bag is a little bigger, I would buy it.
이 가방이 조금 더 크다면, 나는 그것을 살 텐데.

___________ → ___________

02 If we had an umbrella, we won't get wet.
우리에게 우산이 있다면, 젖지 않을 텐데.

___________ → ___________

03 Mike talks as if he is always right.
Mike는 마치 자신이 항상 옳은 것처럼 말한다.

___________ → ___________

04 I wish he hasn't talked about the problem.
그가 그 문제에 대해 말하지 않았다면 좋을 텐데.

___________ → ___________

05 If it didn't rain, I could have ridden my bike.
비가 오지 않았다면, 자전거를 탈 수 있었을 텐데.

___________ → ___________

06 I wish I can see my future.
내가 내 미래를 볼 수 있다면 좋을 텐데.

___________ → ___________

07 If yesterday had been Sunday, I might go shopping.
어제가 일요일이었다면 나는 쇼핑하러 갔을지도 모를 텐데.

___________ → ___________

08 내가 바쁘지 않다면, 너와 더 많은 시간을 보낼 텐데.
(busy)

→ _________________, I would spend more time with you.

09 내가 키가 더 크다면 좋을 텐데. (taller)

→ I wish _________________.

10 내가 아파트에 살지 않는다면, 정원을 가질 수 있을 텐데.
(a garden)

→ If I didn't live in an apartment, ___________
___________.

11 Steve는 마치 자신이 모든 것을 알고 있는 것처럼 말한다. (everything)

→ Steve talks _________________.

12 네가 그의 충고를 받아들이지 않았더라면 좋을 텐데.
(take)

→ _________________ his advice.

13 그 남자는 마치 그 사건을 보았던 것처럼 말한다.
(see, the accident)

→ The man talks _________________
___________.

14 네가 왔다면, 우리는 보드게임을 했을 텐데.
(come, play)

→ If you _________________
board games.

집중 훈련 3 통문장 영작하기
주어진 말을 활용하여 영작하시오.

집중 훈련 4 조건 영작하기
우리말과 의미가 같도록 〈조건〉에 맞게 영작하시오.

---

15 그가 자동차를 가지고 있다면, 언제든 운전할 수 있을 텐데.
(drive, anytime)

→ _______________________________________

16 나에게 여동생이 있다면 좋을 텐데. (a sister)

→ _______________________________________

17 눈이 왔다면, 우리는 스키 타러 갔을 텐데.
(snow, go skiing)

→ _______________________________________

18 사람들은 마치 아무 일도 일어나지 않았던 것처럼 행동했다. (act, nothing, happen)

→ _______________________________________

19 내가 내 카메라를 가져왔다면 좋을 텐데. (bring)

→ _______________________________________

20
A I often have a headache nowadays.
B 내가 너라면, 나는 진찰을 받으러 갈 텐데.
       (go see a doctor)

→ _______________________________________

21
A Everyone is here now, so let's start the meeting.
B 너는 마치 네가 우리의 팀 리더인 것처럼 말하는 구나. (talk, our team leader)

→ _______________________________________

---

22 내가 부유하다면, 요트를 살지도 모르는데.

> 조건 **1** 가정법 문장으로 쓸 것
>   **2** rich, may, a yacht를 활용할 것
>   **3** 9단어의 문장으로 쓸 것

→ _______________________________________

23 우리가 달걀을 좀 가지고 있었다면, 오믈렛을 만들 수 있었을 텐데.

> 조건 **1** 주어진 말을 활용할 것
>   (have some eggs, make an omelet)
>   **2** 가정법 문장으로 쓸 것

→ _______________________________________

24 그는 마치 그곳에 있지 않았던 것처럼 말한다.

> 조건 **1** 괄호 안에 주어진 말을 활용할 것
>   (talk, be, there)
>   **2** 모두 8단어로 쓸 것

→ _______________________________________

25 우리가 하와이에 더 오래 머물렀다면 좋을 텐데.

> 조건 **1** 주어진 말을 활용할 것
>   (stay longer, in Hawaii)
>   **2** I wish를 사용할 것

→ _______________________________________

서술형 실전 TEST

서술형 1 　(6점, 각 3점)

우리말과 의미가 같도록 어법상 <u>틀린</u> 부분을 바르게 고쳐 문장을 다시 쓰시오.

> (1) You talk as if you made the food yourself.
> 　　(너는 마치 직접 음식을 만들었던 것처럼 말한다.)
> (2) I wish I am at the concert.
> 　　(내가 그 콘서트에 있다면 좋을 텐데.)

(1) ____

(2) ____

서술형 2 　(8점, 각 4점)

다음 두 문장의 의미가 같도록 빈칸에 알맞은 말을 쓰시오.

(1) I'm sorry I can't speak English fluently.

　→ I wish ___________________________.

(2) I didn't hear the weather report, so I didn't bring my umbrella.

　→ If I ___________________________,
　　___________________________.

서술형 3 NEW 　(5점)

다음 대화의 밑줄 친 우리말을 〈조건〉에 맞게 영작하시오.

> 조건　1　가정법을 사용하시오.
> 　　　2　대화 속 표현을 활용하시오.

> A Did you watch the soccer game last night?
> B No, I didn't. I fell asleep.
> 　　<u>내가 잠들지 않았다면, 그것을 봤을 텐데.</u>

→ If I _________ _________ _________,
　I _________ _________ _________ it.

서술형 4 　(6점, 각 3점)

그림을 보고, 주어진 말을 활용하여 영작하시오.

(1)

→ I wish ___________________________.
　(this jacket, smaller)

(2)

→ She talks as if ___________________________.
　(visit New York)

서술형 5 NEW 　(5점)

다음 글을 읽고, 주어진 말을 활용하여 Lily에게 하는 조언을 가정법 문장으로 완성하시오.

> 　Lily wants to participate in the school talent show. The problem is that she is shy and nervous about performing in front of others. But she has a beautiful voice as well as a passion for singing.
>
> In this situation, what would you say to her?

You: Lily, if I _________ you, I _________
　_________. (be, believe in myself)
　Sign up for the show!

일치 및 특수구문

1 수 일치

2 시제 일치

3 강조 구문

4 부정 구문

A 주어가 다음과 같은 경우에는 단수 취급한다.

each, every, -thing, -one, -body	*Every person* **has** a different personality.
the number of+복수명사 (~의 수)	*The number of students* **is** 30.
복수 형태의 학문 이름, 국가 이름, 시간, 거리, 금액, 무게 등	*Mathematics* **is** my favorite subject. *Fifty dollars* **is** enough to buy a nice bag.
동명사구, to부정사구, 명사절	*Having good friends* **is** important.

cf. 복수 형태의 학문 이름: economics(경제학), mathematics(수학), physics(물리학), politics(정치학) 등
   복수 형태의 국가 이름: the Netherlands(네덜란드), the Philippines(필리핀), the United States(미국) 등

B 주어가 다음과 같은 경우에는 복수 취급한다.

(both) A and B, all+복수명사	*Both his father and mother* **work**.
a number of+복수명사 (많은 ~)	*A number of apples* **are** in the basket.
the+형용사 (~한 사람들)	*The elderly*(= Elderly people) **have** wisdom.

1 수 일치 형태 익히기

1　know　모든 선수는 규칙을 알고 있다.　→ Every player __________ the rules.
　　　　　　모든 선수들은 규칙을 알고 있다.　→ All players __________ the rules.

2　be　많은 차들이 주차장에 있다.　→ A number of cars __________ in the parking lot.
　　　　　주차장에 있는 차의 수는 50대이다.　→ The number of cars in the parking lot __________ 50.

3　have　두 책 모두 긴 제목을 가지고 있다.　→ Both books __________ long titles.
　　　　　각각의 책은 긴 제목을 가지고 있다.　→ Each book __________ a long title.

2 수 일치 형태 적용하기

1　그 책을 읽는 데 두 시간이면 충분하다. (be)

　→ Two hours __________ enough to read the book.

2　부자들은 종종 호화로운 저택에 산다. (live)

　→ The rich often __________ in luxurious mansions.

3　낯선 사람들과 이야기하는 것은 나를 긴장하게 만든다. (make)

　→ Talking with strangers __________ me nervous.

2 시제 일치

A 주절의 시제가 현재일 때 종속절에는 현재, 과거, 미래시제가 모두 올 수 있고, 주절의 시제가 과거일 때 종속절에는 과거나 과거완료시제가 올 수 있다.

주절의 시제	종속절의 시제	
현재	현재 과거 미래	I **know** that you **are** honest. I **remember** that she **called** me yesterday. He **says** that he **will arrive** next Monday.
과거	과거 과거완료	I **thought** that there **were** no problems. She **said** that she **had been** to Paris before.

B 다음과 같은 경우에는 주절의 시제에 관계없이 종속절에 항상 현재시제 또는 과거시제를 쓴다.

항상 현재시제를 쓰는 경우	She **said** that she **goes** swimming once a week. I **learned** that light **travels** faster than sound. My teacher **told** me that knowledge **is** power.	<현재의 습관> <과학적 사실> <속담·격언>
항상 과거시제를 쓰는 경우	The book **says** that the Korean War **broke out** in 1950.	<역사적 사실>

1 과거시제 문장으로 바꿔 쓰기

1 They say that they will clean the room.

→ They said that they ______________ ______________ the room.

2 He thinks that he needs more time to finish his work.

→ He thought that he ______________ more time to finish his work.

3 I know that we have met before.

→ I knew that we ______________ ______________ before.

2 시제 일치 형태 적용하기

1 나는 그 소문이 사실이 아니라고 믿었다. (be)

→ I believed that the rumor ______________ not true.

2 나의 엄마는 일찍 일어나는 새가 벌레를 잡는다고 말씀하셨다. (catch)

→ My mom said that the early bird ______________ the worm.

3 우리는 세종대왕이 1443년에 한글을 창제했다는 것을 배웠다. (create)

→ We learned that King Sejong ______________ Hangul in 1443.

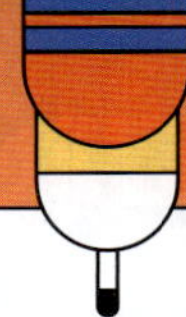

영작 기본 훈련

STEP 1 수와 시제 일치 **비교하기**

1 die
- ⓐ 모든 사람들은 죽는다.
  All people __________.
- ⓑ 모든 사람은 죽는다.
  Everyone __________.

2 be
- ⓐ 싱가포르는 일 년 내내 덥다.
  Singapore __________ hot all year round.
- ⓑ 필리핀은 일 년 내내 덥다.
  The Philippines __________ hot all year round.

3 need
- ⓐ 각 학생은 그 시험을 치러야 한다.
  Each student __________ to take the exam.
- ⓑ 모든 학생들은 그 시험을 치러야 한다.
  All students __________ to take the exam.

4 enjoy
- ⓐ 프랑스 사람들은 요리하는 것을 즐긴다.
  The French __________ cooking.
- ⓑ 프랑스 사람들은 요리하는 것을 즐긴다.
  French people __________ cooking.

5 be
- ⓐ 나는 그가 **용감하다고 생각한다**.
  I think he __________ brave.
- ⓑ 나는 그가 **용감하다고 생각했다**.
  I thought he __________ brave.

6 quit
- ⓐ 나는 Jim이 일을 **그만둘 거라고 생각한다**.
  I believe that Jim __________ __________ his job.
- ⓑ 나는 Jim이 일을 **그만둘 거라고 생각했다**.
  I believed that Jim __________ __________ his job.

7 be
- ⓐ 기름이 물보다 더 **가볍다**.
  Oil __________ lighter than water.
- ⓑ 나는 기름이 물보다 더 **가볍다고 배웠다**.
  I learned that oil __________ lighter than water.

8 land
- ⓐ 아폴로 11호는 1969년에 달에 **착륙했다**.
  Apollo 11 __________ on the Moon in 1969.
- ⓑ 우리는 아폴로 11호가 1969년에 달에 **착륙했다는 것을 배웠다**.
  We learned that Apollo 11 __________ on the Moon in 1969.

STEP **2** 영작 **완성하기**

1 경제학은 많은 학생들에게 어렵다. (economics, difficult)

→ _____________ _____________ _____________ for many students.

2 그는 소풍이 취소될 거라고 말했다. (the picnic, cancel)

→ He said that _____________ _____________ _____________ _____________.

3 나는 흰긴수염고래가 포유류라는 것을 배웠다. (blue whales, mammals)

→ I learned that _____________ _____________ _____________ _____________.

4 많은 사람들이 도시로 이동할 것이다. (a number of)

→ _____________ _____________ _____________ _____________ _____________ going to move to the city.

5 수업을 빠지는 것은 좋지 않은 생각이다. (skip, classes)

→ _____________ _____________ _____________ a bad idea.

STEP **3** 배열 **영작하기**

1 모든 건물들이 화재로 손상되었다.　damaged, the buildings, all, were

→ ____ in the fire.

2 선생님은 콜럼버스가 1492년에 아메리카에 도착했다고 말씀하셨다.

Columbus, America, reached, in 1492, that

→ The teacher said ____.

3 사람들은 내가 운이 좋다고 생각했다.　that, I, people, was, thought, lucky

→ ____

4 판다들의 수가 줄어들고 있다.　decreasing, is, the number, pandas, of

→ ____

5 젊은이들은 어르신들을 공경해야 한다.　the young, the elderly, need, respect, to

→ ____

3 강조 구문

A **동사 강조**: 「do/does/did + 동사원형」의 형태로 동사를 강조하여 '정말 ~하다/했다'라는 의미를 나타낸다.

Amy **does** *like* to read detective novels. Amy는 탐정 소설 읽는 것을 **정말 좋아한다**.
(← Amy *likes* to read detective novels.)

I **did** *send* a text message to John. 나는 John에게 문자 메시지를 **정말 보냈다**.
(← I *sent* a text message to John.)

B 「**It is/was ~ that** ...」 **강조**: It is/was와 that 사이에 강조하려는 말을 넣어 '…한 것은 바로 ~이다/이었다'라는 의미를 나타낸다.

Mia saw Sam yesterday. Mia는 어제 Sam을 보았다.
　주어　　　목적어　　　부사
→ **It was** *Mia* **that** saw Sam yesterday. 〈주어 강조〉 어제 Sam을 본 사람은 **바로 Mia였다**.
→ **It was** *Sam* **that** Mia saw yesterday. 〈목적어 강조〉 Mia가 어제 본 사람은 **바로 Sam이었다**.
→ **It was** *yesterday* **that** Mia saw Sam. 〈부사 강조〉 Mia가 Sam을 본 것은 **바로 어제였다**.

1 동사 강조하는 문장 쓰기

1 I <u>know</u> that you said it.

→ I ＿＿＿＿＿ ＿＿＿＿＿ that you said it.

2 They <u>enjoyed</u> the party.

→ They ＿＿＿＿＿ ＿＿＿＿＿ the party.

3 Brian <u>likes</u> to read comic books.

→ Brian ＿＿＿＿＿ ＿＿＿＿＿ to read comic books.

2 밑줄 친 부분 강조하는 문장 쓰기

1 I met Tom <u>at the library</u>.

→ It was ＿＿＿＿＿ ＿＿＿＿＿ ＿＿＿＿＿ that I met Tom.

2 Jack is riding <u>my bike</u> now.

→ It ＿＿＿＿＿ ＿＿＿＿＿ ＿＿＿＿＿ ＿＿＿＿＿ Jack is riding now.

3 <u>Dad</u> fixed the toilet last night.

→ ＿＿＿＿＿ ＿＿＿＿＿ ＿＿＿＿＿ ＿＿＿＿＿ ＿＿＿＿＿ the toilet last night.

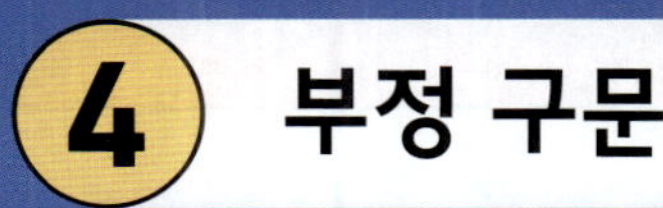

A   **전체 부정**: '아무도〔아무것도〕~ 않다'의 의미로, none, neither, never 등으로 나타낸다.

None of the students are〔is〕in the classroom.   학생들 중 어느 누구도 교실에 있지 않다.
Neither of them will come.   그들 둘 다 오지 않을 것이다.

cf. 「none of+복수(대)명사」는 단수 · 복수 모두 가능한데 보통 복수 취급하고, 「neither of+복수(대)명사」는 주로 단수 취급한다.

B   **부분 부정**: '모두〔항상〕~인 것은 아니다'의 의미로 「not+all, every, always」 등으로 나타낸다.

Not all my cousins are tall.   내 사촌들 모두가 키가 큰 것은 아니다. (키가 작은 사촌도 있음)
He **doesn't always** come late.   그가 항상 늦게 오는 것은 아니다. (일찍 오는 경우도 있음)

1   부정 구문 의미 익히기

1   The weather forecast is <u>not always right</u>.

→ 일기 예보가 ______________________________________.

2   <u>None of us heard</u> about last night's accident.

→ 어젯밤의 사고에 대해 ______________________________.

3   <u>Neither of them will join</u> the cooking club.

→ ______________________ 요리 동아리에 ______________________.

4   <u>Not everyone is happy</u>.

→ ______________________________________.

2   부정 구문 형태 적용하기

1   이 앨범에 있는 모든 곡이 인기 있는 것은 아니다. (every, song)

→ ____________ ____________ ____________ on this album is popular.

2   그 상자들 중 어느 것도 비어 있지 않다. (none, the boxes)

→ ____________ ____________ ____________ ____________ are empty.

3   내가 항상 걸어서 학교에 가는 것은 아니다. (always, walk)

→ I ____________ ____________ ____________ to school.

4   모든 옷이 깨끗한 것은 아니었다. (all, the clothes)

→ ____________ ____________ ____________ ____________ were clean.

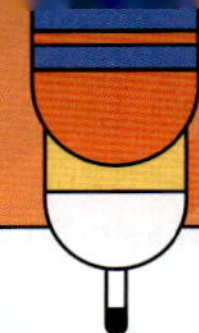

영작 기본 훈련

STEP 1 강조와 부정 구문 의미 **확장하기**

1
ⓐ Tom이 개를 산책시킨다.
Tom walks the dog.

ⓑ 개를 산책시키는 사람은 **바로 Tom이다**.
__________ __________ __________ that walks the dog.

2
ⓐ 나는 Amy에게 전화했다.
I called Amy.

ⓑ 내가 전화한 사람은 **바로 Amy였다**.
__________ __________ __________ __________ I called.

3
ⓐ 그 드레스는 네게 잘 어울린다.
The dress looks good on you.

ⓑ 그 드레스는 네게 **정말 잘 어울린다**.
The dress __________ __________ __________ on you.

4
ⓐ 나는 이 경기에서 최선을 다했다.
I did my best in this game.

ⓑ 나는 이 경기에서 **정말 최선을 다했다**.
I __________ __________ __________ __________ in this game.

5
ⓐ 모든 직원이 열심히 일한다.
Every worker works hard.

ⓑ **모든 직원이** 열심히 일하는 **것은 아니다**.
__________ __________ __________ works hard.

6
ⓐ 내 친구들은 키가 크다.
My friends are tall.

ⓑ **내 친구들 중 누구도** 키가 크지 **않다**.
__________ __________ __________ __________ are tall.

7
ⓐ 모든 컴퓨터 게임은 해롭다.
All computer games are harmful.

ⓑ **모든 컴퓨터 게임이** 해로운 **것은 아니다**.
__________ __________ __________ __________ are harmful.

8
ⓐ 이 두 책 모두 베스트셀러이다.
Both of these books are bestsellers.

ⓑ **이 두 책 중 어느 것도** 베스트셀러가 **아니다**.
__________ __________ __________ __________ is a bestseller.

STEP 2 영작 완성하기

1 Jones 씨는 아이들을 정말 좋아한다. (like, kids)

→ Ms. Jones __________ __________ __________.

2 그 축구 경기가 시작하는 시각은 바로 정오이다. (at noon)

→ __________ __________ __________ __________ __________ the soccer game starts.

3 여름에 항상 더운 것은 아니다. (it, hot, always)

→ __________ __________ __________ __________ __________ in summer.

4 나는 그 시험에서 문제들 중 아무것도 풀 수 없었다. (the problems)

→ I could solve __________ __________ __________ __________ on the exam.

5 밤새 시끄럽게 한 것은 바로 내 이웃이었다. (my neighbor, make noise)

→ __________ __________ __________ __________ __________ __________ all night.

STEP 3 배열 영작하기

1 모든 K-pop 노래가 일본에서 인기 있는 것은 아니다. K-pop song, popular, every, is, not

→ ____ in Japan.

2 그 마라톤에서 우승한 사람은 바로 Linda였다. the marathon, Linda, won, that, was, it

→ ____

3 그녀의 두 아이 중 누구도 캠핑을 즐기지 않는다. camping, her kids, neither, enjoys, of

→ ____

4 그들은 마감일 전에 그 프로젝트를 정말 끝냈다. the due date, did, the project, finish, before, they

→ ____

5 내가 우산을 잃어버린 것은 바로 공원에서였다. was, I, lost, that, in the park, it, my umbrella

→ ____

집중 훈련 1 틀린 부분 고치기

어법상 틀린 부분을 찾아 바르게 고치시오.

집중 훈련 2 영작 완성하기

주어진 말을 활용하여 문장을 완성하시오.

01 The news did shocked me.
그 소식은 나에게 정말 충격을 주었다.

__________ → __________

02 Two kilometers are a long distance.
2킬로미터는 먼 거리이다.

__________ → __________

03 He said that it will rain the next week.
그는 그 다음 주에 비가 올 거라고 말했다.

__________ → __________

04 Not all students didn't go on the field trip.
모든 학생들이 현장 학습을 간 것은 아니었다.

__________ → __________

05 Decorating my room with photos were fun.
내 방을 사진들로 꾸미는 것은 재미있었다.

__________ → __________

06 The number of houses in this town are not known.
이 마을의 주택 수는 알려져 있지 않다.

__________ → __________

07 People in the past did not know that the Earth was round.
옛날 사람들은 지구가 둥글다는 것을 몰랐다.

__________ → __________

08 내가 런던을 방문한 것은 바로 지난여름이었다.
(last summer)

→ __________________ I visited London.

09 그녀는 그녀의 엄마와 정말 닮았다. (look like, do)

→ __________________ her mother.

10 10달러는 그 책을 사기에 충분하지 않다.
(ten dollars, enough)

→ __________________ to buy the book.

11 그 학생들 중 아무도 그 질문에 답하지 않았다. (none)

→ __________________ answered the question.

12 젊은 사람들은 새로운 것들을 빠르게 배운다.
(the young, learn, thing)

→ __________________ quickly.

13 우리는 주문한 모든 음식을 먹은 것은 아니었다.
(all the food)

→ __________________ that we ordered.

14 그는 미국이 북아메리카에 있다고 말했다.
(the United States)

→ He said that __________________ in North America.

주어진 말을 활용하여 영작하시오.

15 내가 서점에서 만난 사람은 Jane이었다.
(it, at the bookstore)

→ ______________________________

16 모든 사람은 각기 다른 의견을 가지고 있다.
(everybody, different opinions)

→ ______________________________

17 Helen이 모든 종류의 음악을 좋아하는 것은 아니다.
(every kind of music)

→ ______________________________

18 많은 사람들이 그 광장에서 춤을 추고 있다.
(number, dance, in the square)

→ ______________________________

19 나는 그녀가 늦게 도착할지도 모른다고 생각했다.
(may, arrive late)

→ ______________________________

20
A I enjoyed both of the movies. What about you?
B <u>나는 그것들 둘 다 마음에 들지 않았어.</u>
(like, neither)

→ ______________________________

21
A Not many people came to Jane's party.
B I know. <u>그렇지만 우리는 정말 재밌었잖아.</u>
(but, have fun, do)

→ ______________________________

우리말과 의미가 같도록 〈조건〉에 맞게 영작하시오.

22 우리는 물이 섭씨 100도에서 끓는다는 것을 배웠다.

> 조건 1 주어진 문장을 사용할 것
>   Water boils at 100℃.
>   2 that을 포함할 것
>   3 7단어의 문장으로 쓸 것

→ ______________________________

23 각 학급에는 20명의 학생들이 있다.

> 조건 1 주어진 말을 모두 활용할 것
>   (each, class, have)
>   2 현재시제로 쓸 것
>   3 숫자는 영어로 쓸 것

→ ______________________________

24 그들 중 아무도 진실을 말하지 않았다.

> 조건 1 괄호 안에 주어진 말을 활용할 것
>   (none, tell, the truth)
>   2 모두 6단어로 쓸 것

→ ______________________________

25 우리가 수영 강습을 받은 것은 바로 지난 일요일이었다.

> 조건 1 take, the swimming lesson, last
>   Sunday를 활용할 것
>   2 총 10단어의 문장으로 쓸 것

→ ______________________________

서술형 **1**   (6점, 각 2점)

다음 문장의 밑줄 친 (1)~(3)을 강조하는 문장을 완성하시오.

> David bought a nice jacket at this store.
>   (1)   (2)   (3)

(1) It was ________________________________ .

(2) It was ________________________________ .

(3) It was ________________________________ .

서술형 **2**   (4점, 각 2점)

다음 두 문장을 한 문장으로 완성하시오.

(1) I practice the piano every day. I told Amy.

→ I told Amy that ________________________
________________________ .

(2) Tom will win the race. My coach said so.

→ My coach said that ______________________
________________________ .

서술형 **3** NEW   (8점, 각 4점)

우리말과 의미가 같도록 〈보기〉에서 알맞은 말을 골라 문장을 완성하시오.

보기	should talk	none	my
	the students	room	don't
	every week	clean	of

(1) 학생들 중 아무도 시험 중에 말을 해서는 안 된다.

→ ________________________________
during the exam.

(2) 나는 매주 내 방을 청소하는 것은 아니다.

→ I ______________________________ .

서술형 **4**   (3점)

다음 그림을 설명하는 문장을 완성하시오. (his dog를 강조할 것)

→ __________ __________ __________
__________ __________ saved him.

서술형 **5**   (3점)

우리말과 의미가 같도록 〈조건〉에 맞게 영작하시오.

> 기술이 항상 도움이 되는 것은 아니다.

조건 1 부정어를 사용하시오.
      2 주어진 말을 사용하시오.
         (technology, always, helpful)

→ ________________________________

서술형 **6** NEW   (6점, 각 3점)

다음 글에서 문장 (1), (2)를 〈조건〉에 맞게 각각 다시 쓰시오.

> Our school held a special competition last week. It was a kind of singing contest, but there were no losers. (1) All the participants won a prize. (2) Everybody enjoyed the competition.

조건 1 (1)은 not을 사용하여 부분 부정문으로 쓰시오.
      2 (2)는 밑줄 친 부분을 강조하는 문장으로 쓰시오.

(1) ________________________________

(2) ________________________________

MEMO

MEMO

동아출판 영어 교재 가이드

영역	브랜드	초1~2	초3~4	초5~6	중1	중2	중3	고1	고2	고3
문법	[초·중등] 개념서 **그래머 클리어 스타터** **중학 영문법 클리어**		Grammar CLEAR Starter 1	Grammar CLEAR Starter 2	중학 영문법 클리어 1	중학 영문법 클리어 2	중학 영문법 클리어 3			
	[중등] 문법 문제서 **그래머 클라우드 3000제**				그래머 클라우드 3000제 1	그래머 클라우드 3000제 2	그래머 클라우드 3000제 3			
	[중등] 실전 문제서 **빠르게 통하는 영문법** **핵심 1200제**				빠르게 통하는 영문법 1200 1	빠르게 통하는 영문법 1200 2	빠르게 통하는 영문법 1200 3			
	[중등] 서술형 영문법 **서술형에 더 강해지는** **중학 영문법** [고등] 시험 영문법 **시험에 더 강해지는** **고등 영문법**				서술형에 더 강해지는 중학 영문법 1	서술형에 더 강해지는 중학 영문법 2	서술형에 더 강해지는 중학 영문법 3	시험에 더 강해지는 고등영문법		
	 [고등] 개념서 **Supreme 고등 영문법**							Supreme 고등영문법		
어법	[고등] 기본서 **Supreme 수능 어법** 기본 실전							Supreme 수능 어법 (기본)	Supreme 수능 어법 (실전)	
쓰기	 [중등] 영작 집중 훈련서 **중학 문법+쓰기 클리어**				중학 문법+쓰기 클리어 1	중학 문법+쓰기 클리어 2	중학 문법+쓰기 클리어 3			
기출	[중등] 기출예상문제집 **특급기출 (중간, 기말)** 윤정미, 이병민				특급기출 중학 영어 1-1	특급기출 중학 영어 2-2	특급기출 중학 영어 3-2			

Grammar & Writing

중학 문법+쓰기

클리어.

Level **3**

Answers

동아출판

중학 문법+쓰기

클리어.

Level 3

Answers

chapter 1 to부정사와 동명사

1 to부정사의 역할 1   p. 8

1 1 To see   2 to finish   3 to find
2 1 for, to miss   2 for, to learn   3 of, to visit

2 to부정사의 역할 2   p. 9

1 1 to drink   2 to sell   3 to write with
   4 to live in
2 1 이해하기에   2 그 사진을 올리다니   3 늦지 않기 위해

영작 기본 훈련   pp. 10~11

STEP 1

A

1 ⓐ to blame   ⓑ for you to blame
2 ⓐ to say   ⓑ of him to say
3 ⓐ to cross   ⓑ for us to cross

B

1 happy to finish
2 went to Spain to learn
3 some bread to make
4 must be kind to help
5 grew up to be

STEP 2

1 decided to hold   2 of you to ask
3 woke up to find   4 a topic to write about
5 shocked to hear

STEP 3

1 use my smartphone to take selfies
2 promised not to be late for school
3 We were excited to go to the concert.
4 This app is easy to use.
5 She was the first person to finish the race.

3 to부정사 구문 1   p. 12

1 1 too, to have   2 too, for me to catch
   3 too, for him to wear
2 1 too, to finish   2 too, for him to upload
   3 too, to ride   4 too, for her to lift

4 to부정사 구문 2   p. 13

1 1 enough to carry   2 enough, to read
   3 enough to surprise
2 1 seems to know   2 seem to work
   3 seemed to enjoy

영작 기본 훈련   pp. 14~15

STEP 1

1 ⓐ too small to hold   ⓑ small enough to fit
2 ⓐ too old to try   ⓑ old enough to go
3 ⓐ warm enough, to play
   ⓑ too warm, to wear
4 ⓐ too big for me to wear
   ⓑ big enough for you to wear
5 ⓐ low enough for dogs to jump
   ⓑ too low for me to hide

STEP 2

1 simple enough to help
2 too exhausted to walk
3 large enough to hold
4 seems to get along well
5 too loud for us to hear

STEP 3

1 I am too busy to hang out with my friends.
2 Joan seems to be worried about the test.
3 These letters are too small for me to read.
4 This wooden knife is safe enough for children to use.
5 They seem to have fun at school.

5 to부정사와 동명사 p. 16

1 1 eating 2 opening 3 driving 4 to meet
2 1 drinking 2 to send 3 feeding

6 동명사 관용 표현 p. 17

1 1 arriving 2 meeting 3 jogging
   4 laughing 5 eating
2 1 worth taking 2 mind changing
   3 no knowing 4 felt like crying

영작 기본 훈련 pp. 18~19

STEP 1

1 remember visiting   2 is used to working
3 like playing   4 is no fishing
5 avoid going   6 plan to buy
7 forgot to send
8 looks forward to traveling

STEP 2

1 you mind waiting
2 On hearing the news
3 worth considering carefully
4 expected to arrive
5 looking forward to visiting

STEP 3

1 decided to give up drinking coffee
2 We couldn't help laughing at his idea.
3 He forgot changing the date of his appointment.
4 There is no parking in this area.
5 I am used to staying up late at night.

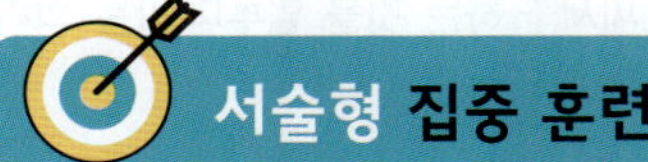

서술형 집중 훈련 pp. 20~21

집중 훈련 1

01 enough smart → smart enough
02 sit → sit on   03 to play → playing
04 seem to likes → seems to like
05 we → us
06 to answer → answering
07 cry → crying

집중 훈련 2

08 He finished painting his house
09 Would you mind taking
10 I cannot(can't) help smiling
11 I was not(wasn't) used to wearing glasses
12 I did not(didn't) feel like talking
13 too narrow for trucks to pass through
14 seemed to have a secret

집중 훈련 3

15 The museum is worth visiting twice.
16 He forgot to lock the door.
17 This board game is easy enough for kids to play.
18 I remember leaving my smartphone in the classroom.
19 I will do my best not to disappoint you.
20 I'm pleased to hear the good news.
21 It is nice of you to help people in need.

집중 훈련 4

22 It will be difficult for her to persuade him.
23 The gallery is too big for us to see all in one day.
24 People are used to sharing their ideas on social media.
25 She grew up to be(become) a great artist.

01 '…할 만큼 충분히 ~한'은 「형용사＋enough＋to부정사」로 나타내므로 형용사 smart 뒤에 enough를 쓴다.
02 'sit on a bench(벤치에 앉다)'이므로 to부정사 뒤에 전치사 on을 쓴다.

03 stop은 동명사를 목적어로 써서 '~하는 것을 멈추다'라는 의미를 나타낸다.

04 '~인 것 같다'는 「seem+to부정사」로 쓴다. 주어(The dog)가 3인칭 단수이므로 seems가 알맞고, to 뒤에는 동사원형을 쓴다.

05 to부정사의 의미상 주어는 「for+목적격」으로 쓴다.

06 avoid는 동명사를 목적어로 쓴다.

07 '~하지 않을 수 없다'는 「cannot〔can't〕help -ing」로 쓴다.

08 finish는 동명사를 목적어로 쓴다.

09 '~해 주시겠어요?'는 「Would you mind -ing …?」로 쓴다.

10 '~하지 않을 수 없다'는 「cannot〔can't〕help -ing」로 쓴다.

11 '~하는 데〔것에〕익숙하다'는 「be used to -ing」로 쓴다.

12 '~하고 싶다'는 「feel like -ing」로 쓴다.

13 '…하기에 너무 ~한'은 「too+형용사+to부정사」로 나타내고, to부정사의 의미상 주어는 to부정사 앞에 「for+목적격」으로 쓴다.

14 '~해 보이다, ~인 것 같다'는 「seem+to부정사」로 쓴다.

15 '~할 가치가 있다'는 「be worth -ing」로 쓴다.

16 '(미래에) ~할 것을 잊다'는 「forget+to부정사」로 쓴다.

17 '…할 만큼 충분히 ~한'은 「형용사+enough+to부정사」로 나타내고, to부정사의 의미상 주어는 to부정사 앞에 「for+목적격」으로 쓴다.

18 '(과거에) ~한 것을 기억하다'는 「remember+동명사」로 쓴다.

19 목적을 나타내는 부사적 용법의 to부정사를 쓴다. to부정사의 부정은 to부정사 앞에 not을 붙여 나타낸다.

20 감정의 원인을 나타내는 to부정사는 감정을 나타내는 형용사(pleased) 뒤에 쓴다.

21 사람의 성격, 태도를 나타내는 형용사(nice) 뒤에서 to부정사의 의미상 주어는 「of+목적격」으로 쓴다.

22 일반적인 형용사(difficult) 뒤에서 to부정사의 의미상 주어는 to부정사 앞에 「for+목적격」으로 쓴다.

23 '…하기에 너무 ~한'은 「too+형용사+to부정사」로 나타내고, to부정사의 의미상 주어는 to부정사 앞에 「for+목적격」으로 쓴다.

24 '~하는 데〔것에〕익숙하다'는 「be used to -ing」로 쓴다.

25 '(~해서) …되다'라는 결과의 의미를 나타내는 부사적 용법의 to부정사를 동사 뒤에 쓴다.

1 (1) Sam forgot **to buy** some milk on the way home.
(2) It was rude **of** you to ask that question.

2 three dogs to take care of

3 (1) well enough to become a singer
(2) seems to be excited on the stage

4 (1) afraid that we could not〔couldn't〕look down
(2) smart that he can read that difficult book

5 I'm looking forward to going on vacation.

6 (1) to watch a game (2) for us to buy tickets
(3) seeing

1 (1) '(미래에) ~할 것을 잊다'는 「forget+to부정사」를 써서 나타낸다.
(2) 사람의 성격, 태도를 나타내는 형용사(rude) 뒤에서 to부정사의 의미상 주어는 「of+목적격」으로 쓴다.

2 앞에 있는 명사를 꾸며 주는 형용사적 용법의 to부정사를 쓴다.

3 해석 K-pop 스타가 되는 것은 민재의 꿈이다. 그는 가수가 될 만큼 충분히 잘 노래 부른다. 그의 꿈을 실현시키기 위해 그는 오디션에 참가하기로 결심했다. 다음이 그의 차례이다. 그는 무대에서 신나 보인다.
(1) 부사+enough+to부정사: …할 만큼 충분히 ~하게
(2) seem+to부정사: ~해 보이다, ~인 것 같다

4 (1) too+형용사+to부정사: …하기에 너무 ~한 (→ so+형용사+that+주어+can't+동사원형: 너무 ~해서 …할 수 없는)
(2) 형용사+enough+to부정사: …할 만큼 충분히 ~한 (→ so+형용사+that+주어+can+동사원형: 매우 ~해서 …할 수 있는)

5 look forward to -ing: ~하기를 고대하다

6 해석 Diana에게,
　　우리는 지난 주말에 런던에 도착했어. 우리는 이곳에서 재미있게 지내고 있어. 어제 우리는 경기를 보러 축구 경기장에 갔어. 우리가 표를 사는 것은 쉽지 않았지만, 우리는 마침내 표를 샀어. 그 경기는 볼 가치가 있었어. 우리는 멋진 시간을 보냈어.
→ (1) 목적을 나타내는 부사적 용법의 to부정사를 쓴다.
(2) to부정사의 의미상 주어인 「for+목적격」과 진주어인 to부정사구를 쓴다.
(3) be worth -ing: ~할 가치가 있다

chapter ❷ 시제

① 현재완료의 의미와 용법   p. 24

1 1 have known   2 has tried   3 has, left
    4 have gone   5 has been

2 1 공부해 왔다   2 써 버렸다   3 막 도착했다
    4 먹어 본 적이 있니

② 현재완료의 형태와 현재완료진행   p. 25

1 1 has, started / hasn't started / Has, started
    2 has been / has not(never) been / Has, been
    3 have, paid / have not paid / Have, paid

2 1 has been playing   2 have been cooking
    3 has been snowing

영작 기본 훈련   pp. 26~27

STEP 1

1 ⓐ finished   ⓑ have, finished
2 ⓐ didn't clear   ⓑ hasn't cleared
3 ⓐ Did, meet   ⓑ Have, met
4 ⓐ didn't come   ⓑ hasn't come
5 ⓐ was watching   ⓑ have been watching
6 ⓐ worked   ⓑ has worked
7 ⓐ were playing   ⓑ have been playing
8 ⓐ Did, see   ⓑ Have, seen

STEP 2

1 has lived in the countryside for two years
2 has left her umbrella at home
3 The wind has been very strong since last night.
4 They have been waiting for her for an hour.

STEP 3

1 I have just received a text message
2 has not called me since Monday
3 We have been listening to the same song
4 has never been absent from school before
5 They have known each other since childhood.

③ 과거완료의 의미와 형태   pp. 28~29

1 1 had worked   2 had prepared
    3 had not(never) traveled   4 had taken

2 1 had seen   2 had passed   3 had bought
    4 had, started   5 had, studied

3 1 had not(never) been   2 had not(never) rained
    3 Had they seen   4 Had she been
    5 had not(never) taken

영작 기본 훈련   pp. 30~31

STEP 1

1 ⓐ began   ⓑ had, begun
2 ⓐ lived   ⓑ had lived
3 ⓐ met   ⓑ had met
4 ⓐ visited   ⓑ had visited
5 ⓐ didn't hear   ⓑ hadn't heard
6 ⓐ left   ⓑ had, left
7 ⓐ knew   ⓑ had known
8 ⓐ didn't say   ⓑ hadn't said

STEP 2

1 had hurt her leg
2 had already scored
3 had gotten the wrong change
4 had not eaten
5 Had he lived by himself

STEP 3

1 it had already stopped raining
2 They had lived in Toronto for 10 years before they moved
3 I had bought for his birthday
4 Our class had practiced the song over and over
5 didn't realize that I hadn't turned off the light

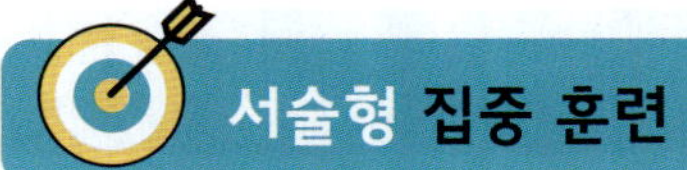

서술형 집중 훈련 pp. 32~33

집중 훈련 1

01 have gone → went
02 had → has had
03 gone → been
04 have you met → did you meet
05 use → have used(have been using)
06 Did you ever eat → Have you ever eaten
07 hasn't studied → hadn't studied

집중 훈련 2

08 They have not(haven't) decided where to go
09 We have been waiting for
10 had owned the car for five years
11 Have you ever been late for school
12 The baby has been sleeping
13 Nobody had told me about the event
14 has stolen his bike

집중 훈련 3

15 They have grown up together since childhood.
16 He had worked for 20 years when he retired. / When he retired, he had worked for 20 years.
17 I have never seen a giant panda.
18 She has been taking this course for three months.
19 I couldn't enter the building because I had lost my ID. / Because I had lost my ID, I couldn't enter the building.
20 She has just gone out.
21 Emma has moved to another city.

집중 훈련 4

22 Steve has not(hasn't) spoken to me since last week.
23 Lucy had been a photographer before she became a writer. / Before Lucy became a writer, she had been a photographer.
24 Have you been to the Grand Canyon?
25 Sue has been playing the piano for two hours.

01 과거를 나타내는 말(last week)이 있으므로 과거시제로 쓴다.

02 세 살 때부터 지금까지 계속 키우고 있는 것이므로 현재완료로 쓴다.

03 '~에 가 본 적이 없다'라는 의미로 경험을 나타낼 때는 「have+not(never)+been to」로 쓴다. (have gone to: ~에 가 버렸다)

04 when은 과거의 특정 시점을 묻는 말이므로 현재완료가 아니라 과거시제로 쓴다.

05 과거(last month)부터 현재까지 계속되고 있는 일을 나타내므로 현재완료 또는 현재완료진행으로 쓴다.

06 과거부터 현재까지의 경험에 대해 묻고 있으므로 현재완료로 쓴다.

07 과거(traveled)의 특정 시점 이전의 경험을 나타내므로 과거완료로 써야 하며, 과거완료의 부정은 「had not(hadn't)+p.p.」 형태로 쓴다.

08 yet과 함께 쓰여 아직 완료되지 않은 일을 나타내는 현재완료의 부정은 「have not(haven't)+p.p.」 형태로 쓴다.

09 과거에 시작되어 현재까지 진행 중인 일을 나타내므로 「have been+-ing」 형태의 현재완료진행으로 쓴다.

10 과거(sold)의 특정 시점까지 그 이전부터 지속된 일을 나타내므로 「had+p.p.」 형태의 과거완료로 쓴다.

11 과거부터 현재까지의 경험에 대해 묻고 있으므로 현재완료로 쓴다. 현재완료 의문문은 「Have+주어+(ever+)p.p. ~?」 형태로 쓴다.

12 과거에 시작되어 현재까지 진행 중인 일을 나타내고, 주어(The baby)가 3인칭 단수이므로 「has been+-ing」 형태의 현재완료진행으로 쓴다.

13 과거(saw)의 특정 시점까지 지속된 일을 나타내므로 '말해 주지 않았었다'는 과거완료로 써야 하며, nobody가 부정의 의미이므로 동사에 부정어를 쓰지 않는다.

14 과거에 일어난 일의 결과가 현재까지 영향을 미치는 상태를 나타내므로 현재완료로 쓴다.

15 과거부터 현재까지 계속되고 있는 일을 나타내므로 since와 함께 현재완료로 쓴다.

16 과거(retired)의 특정 시점까지 지속된 일을 나타내므로 '20년 동안 일해왔었다'는 for와 함께 과거완료로 쓴다.

17 과거부터 현재까지의 경험을 나타내므로 현재완료로 쓴다. 현재완료의 부정은 「have+not(never)+p.p.」 형태로 쓴다.

18 과거에 시작되어 현재까지 진행 중인 일을 나타내고, 주어(She)가 3인칭 단수이므로 「has been+-ing」 형태의 현재완료진행으로 쓴다.

19 '신분증을 잃어버린 것'이 '건물에 들어갈 수 없었던 것'보다 더 앞선 과거(대과거)의 일이므로 과거완료형으로 쓴다.

20 이제 막 완료된 일을 나타내므로 현재완료로 쓴다.

21 과거에 일어난 일의 결과가 현재까지 영향을 미치는 상태를 나타내므로 현재완료로 쓴다.

22 과거부터 현재까지 계속되고 있는 일을 나타내므로 현재완료로 쓴다. 현재완료의 부정은 「have/has+not〔never〕+p.p.」 형태로 쓴다.

23 과거(became)의 특정 시점 이전의 상태를 나타내므로 '사진작가였었다'는 과거완료로 쓴다.

24 과거부터 현재까지의 경험에 대해 묻고 있으므로 현재완료로 쓴다. 현재완료 의문문은 「Have+주어+p.p. ~?」 형태로 쓴다.

25 과거에 시작되어 현재까지 진행 중인 일을 나타내고, 주어(Sue)가 3인칭 단수이므로 「has been+-ing」 형태의 현재완료진행으로 쓴다.

CHAPTER 2 서술형 실전 TEST
p. 34

1 (1) He **has visited** 10 countries so far.
(2) She **hadn't** eaten kimchi before she visited Korea.

2 (1) has gone to Canada
(2) has been staying at my house since last weekend

3 (1) my mother had already prepared dinner
(2) has been running for 35 minutes

4 was exhausted, hadn't slept well

5 (1) I have just arrived in Busan.
(2) I have never been here before.

6 (1) amazed → has amazed
(2) has been found → was found

1 (1) so far(지금까지)가 있으므로 과거부터 현재까지의 경험을 나타내는 현재완료로 쓴다.
(2) 과거(visited)의 특정 시점 이전의 경험을 나타내므로 과거완료로 쓴다.

2 (1) 과거에 일어난 일의 결과가 현재까지 영향을 미치는 상태를 나타내므로 현재완료로 쓴다.
(2) 과거부터 현재까지 계속 진행되고 있는 일은 현재완료진행으로 쓴다.

3 (1) 과거(got)의 특정 시점 이전에 완료된 일을 나타내므로 과거완료로 쓴다.
(2) 과거에 시작되어 현재까지 계속 진행 중인 일을 나타내므로 현재완료진행으로 쓴다.

4 '지쳤다'는 과거의 특정 시점(last night)의 일이므로 과거시제로 쓰고, '잠을 잘 자지 못했었다'는 그때까지 지속된 일을 나타내

므로 과거완료로 쓴다. 과거완료의 부정은 「had not〔hadn't〕+p.p.」 형태로 쓴다.

5 <u>해석</u> 안녕, 민호야. 나는 부산에 막 도착했어. 나는 전에 이곳에 와 본 적이 없어. 나는 여기에 일주일간 머물며 많은 장소들을 방문할 예정이야. 나는 너무 신이 나!
→ (1) 완료를 나타내는 현재완료로 쓴다.
(2) 경험을 나타내는 현재완료로 쓴다.

6 <u>해석</u> 드래곤 성의 신비
여러분은 드래곤 성에 대해 들어본 적이 있나요? 그것은 신비로운 성입니다. 그 성은 수백 년 동안 사람들을 놀라게 해왔습니다. 지난주, 그 성에 관한 오래된 문서가 발견되었습니다. 연구자들은 이 문서가 그 성의 비밀들을 밝혀내기를 바라고 있습니다.
→ (1) 과거부터 현재까지 수백 년 동안 계속되고 있는 일을 나타내므로 현재완료로 쓴다.
(2) 과거를 나타내는 말(last week)이 있으므로 과거시제로 쓴다.

chapter 3 조동사

1 can, may
p. 36

1 1 can〔may〕 2 may〔might〕 3 cannot〔can't〕
2 1 can〔may〕 borrow
2 may〔might〕 not attend
3 will be able to explain

2 must, have to
p. 37

1 1 must be 2 had to cancel
3 must register
2 1 must not run 2 doesn't have to bring
3 don't have to pay

영작 기본 훈련
pp. 38~39

STEP 1

1 ⓐ may〔might〕 call ⓑ must call
2 ⓐ must be ⓑ cannot〔can't〕 be
3 ⓐ must not rush ⓑ don't have to rush
4 ⓐ may〔might〕 know ⓑ must know

5 ⓐ is able to play   ⓑ has to play

6 ⓐ can(may) park   ⓑ must(may) not park

7 ⓐ had to reply   ⓑ will have to reply

8 ⓐ can find   ⓑ was able to find

STEP 2

1 might go to Paris   2 can stand on

3 have to finish this project

4 must be nervous   5 can't be yours

STEP 3

1 may get an A on the math test

2 must be excited to meet her new classmates

3 don't have to make a reservation for dinner

4 can't be angry with you because of that

5 Could you drive Dan to school?

3 여러 가지 조동사   p. 40

1 1 had better drive   2 ought to leave
   3 would rather take   4 used to watch

2 1 말하는 것이 낫다
   2 들어야 한다(듣는 게 좋겠다)
   3 말해서는 안 된다

4 조동사+have+p.p.   p. 41

1 1 may(might) have fallen
   2 must have been
   3 cannot(can't) have left
   4 should have read
   5 should not have overslept

2 1 cannot(can't) have eaten
   2 should have booked
   3 may(might) have heard
   4 must have forgotten
   5 should not have quit

영작 기본 훈련   pp. 42~43

STEP 1

1 may(might) have moved

2 must have arrived

3 should have worn   4 used to be

5 cannot(can't) have spoken

6 would rather go

7 had better pack

8 should not have bought

STEP 2

1 cannot(can't) have broken

2 may(might) have seen

3 should have paid   4 had better get

5 used to be

STEP 3

1 He must have changed his phone number.

2 You ought not to shout at your friends.

3 You had better not go to the party.

4 She cannot have failed the exam.

5 The problem might have been too easy for Sam.

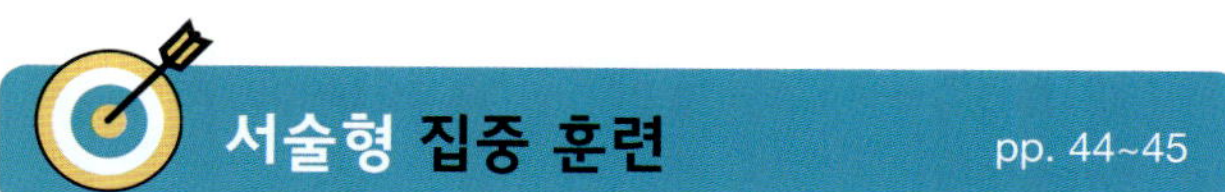 서술형 집중 훈련   pp. 44~45

집중 훈련 1

01 May → Can(Could)

02 have better → had better

03 should sleep → should have slept

04 ought to not → ought not to

05 have to → has to   06 use to → used to

07 must studied → had to study

집중 훈련 2

08 does not(doesn't) have to take this class

09 I will be able to help you

10 You had better not eat anything

11 They may(might) have left

12 We should have bought

13 must have lost his wallet

14 He cannot(can't) have forgotten

집중 훈련 3

15 You may(can) put your bag here.

16 He must be tired after the competition. / After
   the competition, he must be tired.

17 They used to〔would〕go to the library every Monday. / Every Monday, they used to〔would〕 go to the library.

18 I would rather watch TV tonight.

19 You ought to visit your grandparents.

20 You should have set the alarm last night.

21 He must have turned it off.

집중 훈련 **4**

22 She doesn't have to follow the recipe.

23 He will be able to speak Spanish fluently next year. / Next year, he will be able to speak Spanish fluently.

24 You cannot〔can't〕have seen Jane.

25 I should not have made that joke.

01 '~해 주시겠어요?'라는 요청의 의미는 Can〔Could〕you ~?로 나타낸다.

02 '~하는 것이 낫다'는 주어의 인칭과 수에 상관없이 had better 로 쓴다.

03 '(과거에) ~했어야 했다'는 「should have+p.p.」로 쓴다.

04 ought to의 부정은 ought not to로 쓴다.

05 주어가 3인칭 단수이고 현재시제이므로 has to로 쓴다.

06 '(과거에) ~이었다'라는 과거의 상태는 「used to+동사원형」으 로 나타낸다.

07 must의 과거형은 had to로 쓴다. had to 뒤에는 동사원형을 쓴다.

08 '~할 필요가 없다'는 don't/doesn't have to로 쓴다. 주어 (He)가 3인칭 단수이므로 doesn't를 쓴다.

09 '~할 수 있을 것이다'는 「will be able to+동사원형」으로 쓴다.

10 '~하지 않는 것이 낫다'는 「had better not+동사원형」으로 쓴 다.

11 '(과거에) ~했을지도 모른다'는 「may〔might〕have+p.p.」로 쓴다.

12 '(과거에) ~했어야 했다'는 「should have+p.p.」로 쓴다.

13 '(과거에) ~했던 게 틀림없다'는 「must have+p.p.」로 쓴다.

14 '(과거에) ~했을 리가 없다'는 「cannot〔can't〕have+p.p.」로 쓴다.

15 '~해도 된다'라는 허가의 의미는 may 또는 can을 써서 나타낸 다.

16 '~임이 틀림없다'라는 강한 추측의 의미는 must를 써서 나타낸 다.

17 '~하곤 했다'라는 과거의 습관은 used to 또는 would를 써서 나타낸다.

18 '(차라리) ~하겠다'는 「would rather+동사원형」으로 쓴다.

19 '~해야 한다'는 「ought to+동사원형」으로 쓴다.

20 '(과거에) ~했어야 했다'는 「should have+p.p.」로 쓴다.

21 '(과거에) ~했던 게 틀림없다'는 「must have+p.p.」로 쓴다.

22 '~할 필요가 없다'는 don't/doesn't have to로 쓴다. 주어 (She)가 3인칭 단수이므로 doesn't를 쓴다.

23 '~할 수 있을 것이다'는 「will be able to+동사원형」으로 쓴다.

24 '(과거에) ~했을 리가 없다'는 「cannot〔can't〕have+p.p.」로 쓴다.

25 '(과거에) ~하지 말았어야 했다'는 「should not have+p.p.」 로 쓴다.

서술형 실전 TEST

1 (1) used to (2) don't have to

2 (1) apologizes → apologize
　(2) must don't → must not

3 (1) must be (2) used to wear

4 (1) cannot〔can't〕have painted the picture
　(2) may〔might〕have taken the wrong bus

5 I would rather keep silent.

6 (1) should not〔shouldn't〕have fallen asleep
　(2) should have listened

1 (1) 과거의 습관을 나타내는 used to를 쓴다.
　(2) don't have to+동사원형: ~할 필요가 없다

2 (1) had better 뒤에는 동사원형을 쓴다.
　(2) must의 부정은 must 뒤에 not을 붙여 쓴다.

3 (1) 중국 국기를 들고 있으므로 강한 추측을 나타내는 must를 쓴다.
　(2) 어릴 때는 안경을 썼으나 지금은 그렇지 않으므로 과거의 상 태를 나타내는 used to를 쓴다.

4 (1) '나는 그녀가 그 그림을 그리지 않았다고 확신한다'라는 의미 는 '그녀가 그 그림을 그렸을 리가 없다'로 바꾸어 말할 수 있으 므로 「cannot〔can't〕have+p.p.」를 써서 나타낸다.
　(2) '어쩌면 그들은 잘못된 버스를 탔을지도 모른다'는 말은 과거 의 일에 대한 추측을 나타내므로 「may〔might〕have+p.p.」 를 써서 나타낸다.

5 would rather+동사원형: 차라리 ~하겠다

6 해석 지난 학기, 태우는 태도가 좋지 않았다. 그는 자주 수업 시간에 잠들었다. 또한, 그는 선생님 말씀을 듣지 않았다. 그것이 그가 기말시험에서 낮은 점수를 받은 이유이다.
　→ (1) should not have+p.p.: (과거에) ~하지 말았어야 했다
　(2) should have+p.p.: (과거에) ~했어야 했다

① 분사의 종류와 쓰임　p. 48

1　1 smiling / girl smiling　2 stolen / watch stolen
　　3 running / people running
2　1 playing　2 published　3 setting

② 감정을 나타내는 분사　p. 49

1　1 confused　2 disappointed　3 amazing
　　4 satisfying　5 embarrassing　6 interested
　　7 touching

영작 기본 훈련　pp.50~51

STEP ①

1　ⓐ satisfied　　ⓑ satisfying
2　ⓐ burning　　ⓑ burned(burnt)
3　ⓐ surprising　　ⓑ surprised
4　ⓐ touching　　ⓑ touched
5　ⓐ shocking　　ⓑ shocked
6　ⓐ building　　ⓑ built
7　ⓐ annoyed　　ⓑ annoying
8　ⓐ boring　　ⓑ bored

STEP ②

1　the bridge connecting the two islands
2　The fireworks festival was very disappointing.
3　The boy wearing a Batman costume is my cousin.
4　She looked annoyed by the loud noise.
5　We visited the museum designed by a famous
　　architect.

STEP ③

1　buy a used car
2　a child crying loudly
3　The mountain covered with snow
4　were confused by the new rules
5　a dog lying on the grass

③ 분사구문의 형태　p. 52

1　1 Growing older
　　2 Turning right at the corner
　　3 Entering the park
　　4 Not having enough money
2　1 Waving　2 Waiting　3 Living　4 Having

④ 분사구문의 의미　p. 53

1　1 조건 / 버스를 타면
　　2 이유 / 열심히 일했기 때문에
　　3 동시동작 / 팝콘을 먹으면서
2　1 Standing　2 Putting　3 Not feeling
　　4 Walking

영작 기본 훈련　pp. 54~55

STEP ①

1　Eating　　　　　　2　Walking
3　Seeing　　　　　　4　Giving up
5　Not knowing　　　6　Feeling
7　Reading　　　　　8　Listening

STEP ②

1　Being tired
2　Talking about their day
3　Not understanding his question
4　Launching a new product
5　Crossing the finish line

STEP ③

1　Walking on the beach
2　After arriving at the airport
3　Not wanting to go hiking
4　While waiting for the bus
5　Completing all the courses

1 1 It being 2 Today being
  3 The price being
2 1 (Being) Hit 2 (Being) Born
  3 (Being) Stuck 4 (Being) Used

6 「with+(대)명사+분사」 구문 p. 57

1 1 with, running 2 with, folded 3 with, turned
  4 with, blowing 5 with, locked
  6 with, delayed
2 1 with, covered 2 with, shouting
  3 with, closed 4 with, shining 5 with, bent

영작 기본 훈련 pp. 58~59

STEP 1

A

1 It being a national holiday
2 A storm coming
3 (Being) Lost in the forest
4 (Being) Satisfied with his report

B

1 with, crossed 2 with, ringing
3 with, pouring 4 with, raised

STEP 2

1 Surrounded by fans
2 Produced by local farmers
3 with your legs crossed
4 with her eyes closed
5 Tomorrow being Sunday

STEP 3

1 (Being) Written in simple English
2 (Being) Tired of the song
3 with her dog sleeping
4 with his seat belt fastened
5 It being noon

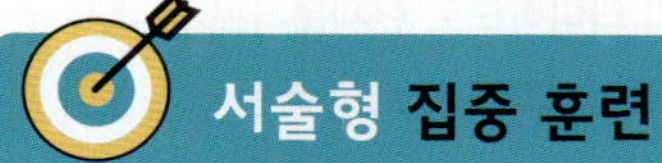

서술형 집중 훈련 pp. 60~61

집중 훈련 1

01 teaching → taught
02 shocked → shocking
03 Making → (Being) Made
04 Turned → Turning
05 publishing → published
06 Having not → Not having
07 closing → closed

집중 훈련 2

08 the ideas suggested by James
09 The store selling these shoes
10 Working hard
11 (Being) Broken into pieces
12 a few surprising facts
13 (Being) Painted yellow
14 with their hands raised high

집중 훈련 3

15 This is a photo taken by a famous photographer.
16 Hearing the doorbell, he ran to the door.
17 (Being) Covered by a thick fog, the building was invisible.
18 Visiting the website, you can get more information.
19 She can't eat anything containing milk.
20 The ending was very disappointing.
21 I was satisfied with the food and the service.

집중 훈련 4

22 Jane is tired of boring work.
23 The car driven by the thief hit another car.
24 Traveling in Paris, we visited the Eiffel Tower.
25 He looked at the players with his arms folded.

01 수업이 '가르쳐지는' 수동의 의미이므로 과거분사로 쓴다.
02 이야기의 결말이 감정을 불러일으키는 것이므로 현재분사로 쓴다.
03 노트북이 '만들어진' 수동 및 완료의 의미이므로 수동형 분사구문인 (Being) Made로 써야 하며, Being은 주로 생략한다.

04 네가 왼쪽으로 '도는' 능동의 의미이므로 현재분사로 쓴다.

05 소설이 '출간된' 수동 및 완료의 의미이므로 과거분사로 쓴다.

06 분사구문의 부정은 분사 앞에 not을 써서 나타낸다.

07 '~이 …한/된 채로'라는 의미를 나타내는 「with＋명사＋분사」 구문으로, 명사(the door)와 close와의 관계가 수동이므로 과거분사로 쓴다.

08 아이디어가 '제안된' 수동의 의미이므로 suggest를 과거분사로 쓴다. 구를 이루는 분사는 명사(the ideas)를 뒤에서 수식한다.

09 가게가 신발을 '파는' 능동의 의미이므로 sell을 현재분사로 쓴다. 구를 이루는 분사는 명사(The store)를 뒤에서 수식한다.

10 모두가 '일하는' 능동의 의미이므로 work를 현재분사로 써서 분사구문을 만든다.

11 거울이 '부서진' 수동 및 완료의 의미이므로 수동형 분사구문인 (Being) Broken으로 써야 하며, Being은 주로 생략한다.

12 분사가 수식하는 대상(facts)이 감정을 불러일으키는 것이므로 surprise를 현재분사로 쓴다.

13 신호등이 '칠해진' 수동 및 완료의 의미이므로 수동형 분사구문인 (Being) Painted로 써야 하며, Being은 주로 생략한다.

14 「with＋명사＋분사」 구문에서 명사(their hands)와 raise와의 관계가 수동이므로 과거분사로 쓴다.

15 사진이 '찍힌' 수동의 의미이므로 take를 과거분사로 쓴다. 구를 이루는 분사는 명사(a photo)를 뒤에서 수식한다.

16 그가 '듣는' 능동의 의미이므로 hear를 현재분사로 써서 분사구문을 만든다.

17 건물이 '가려진' 수동의 의미이므로 수동형 분사구문인 (Being) Covered로 써야 하며, Being은 주로 생략한다.

18 여러분이 '방문하는' 능동의 의미이므로 visit를 현재분사로 써서 분사구문을 만든다.

19 어떤 것이 우유를 '함유하고' 있는 능동의 의미이므로 contain을 현재분사로 쓴다. 구를 이루는 분사는 대명사(anything)를 뒤에서 수식한다.

20 주어가 감정을 불러 일으키는 것이므로 disappoint를 현재분사로 쓴다.

21 주어가 감정을 느끼는 것이므로 satisfy를 과거분사로 쓴다.

22 주어가 지친 감정을 느끼는 것이므로 과거분사 tired를 be동사 뒤에 쓰고, 분사가 수식하는 대상(work)이 지루한 감정을 불러일으키는 것이므로 현재분사 boring을 명사 앞에 쓴다.

23 자동차가 '운전되는' 수동의 의미이므로 drive를 과거분사로 쓴다. 구를 이루는 분사는 명사(The car)를 뒤에서 수식한다.

24 우리가 '여행하는' 능동의 의미이므로 travel을 현재분사로 써서 분사구문을 만든다.

25 「with＋명사＋분사」 구문에서 명사(his arms)와 fold와의 관계가 수동이므로 과거분사로 쓴다.

---

1 The flowers given to me by John

2 Seen from the Moon

3 with my eyes covered

4 (1) touched (2) amazing

5 Turning off the alarm

6 (1) Today, on the way to school, my purse was **stolen**.
(2) I was so **shocked**.
(3) **Hearing** the news, I was glad.

1 구를 이루는 분사는 명사를 뒤에서 수식한다.

2 부사절의 접속사와 주어를 생략하고 부사절의 동사 is를 분사 being으로 바꿔 쓴다. 수동형 분사구문에서 being은 주로 생략한다.

3 「with＋명사＋분사」 구문에서 명사(my eyes)와 cover와의 관계가 수동이므로 과거분사로 쓴다.

4 해석 Kate는 어제 그녀가 가장 좋아하는 작가의 책을 다 읽었다. 그녀는 그 결말에 감동받았다. 그녀는 이 놀라운 책을 친구들에게 추천할 것이다.
→ (1) 주어(She)가 감정을 느끼는 것이므로 과거분사로 쓴다.
(2) 분사가 수식하는 대상(book)이 감정을 불러일으키는 것이므로 현재분사로 쓴다.

5 주어(I)가 알람을 '끄는' 능동의 의미이므로 turn을 현재분사로 써서 분사구문을 만든다.

6 해석 오늘 학교 가는 길에, 내 지갑이 도난당했다. 나는 너무 충격 받았다. 방과 후에, 나는 경찰로부터 전화를 받았다. 경찰은 누군가 내 지갑을 발견했다고 말했다. 그 소식을 듣고, 나는 기뻤다. 하지만 내 지갑을 확인했을 때, 그 안에는 돈이 하나도 없었다.
→ (1) 지갑이 '도난당한' 수동의 의미이므로 과거분사 stolen으로 쓴다.
(2) 주어가 감정을 느끼는 것이므로 과거분사 shocked로 쓴다.
(3) 내가 소식을 '듣는' 능동의 의미이므로 현재분사 Hearing으로 쓴다.

chapter **5** 비교급

1 원급/비교급 비교　　p. 64

1 1 as fast as / faster than

2 as cold as / not as(so) cold as

3 as useful as / more useful than

4 easier than / much(even/still/far) easier than

2 1 as famous as　2 not as(so) comfortable as

3 more popular than

2 원급과 비교급을 이용한 표현　　p. 65

1 1 twice as wide as　2 as soon as, can

3 as quietly as possible

2 1 the better　2 more and more popular

3 three times thicker than

STEP 1

1 ⓐ as heavy as　　ⓑ heavier than

2 ⓐ deeper than　　ⓑ three times deeper

3 ⓐ as fast as　　ⓑ as fast as possible

4 ⓐ larger than　　ⓑ as(so) large as

5 ⓐ better than　　ⓑ much(even/still/far) better than

6 ⓐ as narrow as　　ⓑ twice as narrow

7 ⓐ hotter than　　ⓑ hotter and hotter

8 ⓐ happier than　　ⓑ the happier

STEP 2

1 as successful as　　2 more difficult than

3 not as(so) thin as　　4 as calm as possible

5 The more, the less

STEP 3

1 travels faster than sound

2 four times as big as this model

3 a lot more important than money

4 is getting more and more interesting

5 finish our homework as quickly as we can

3 최상급 비교　　p. 68

1 1 the happiest moment　2 the worst situation

3 the most popular song

2 1 the brightest　2 the most positive

3 the most responsible　4 the most helpful

4 원급과 비교급을 이용한 최상급 의미 표현　　p. 69

1 1 as large as / larger than

2 as wealthy as / wealthier than

3 colder than

2 1 more important than

2 No other, as exciting as

3 older than any other

STEP 1

1 ⓑ the fastest player

ⓒ one of the fastest players

2 ⓑ the most amazing show (that)

ⓒ more amazing than

3 ⓑ the tallest girl　　ⓒ taller than

4 ⓑ the most diligent person　　ⓒ as diligent as

5 ⓑ the most fantastic painting

ⓒ one of the most fantastic paintings

6 ⓑ the most touching　　ⓒ more touching than

STEP 2

1 the hottest of all seasons

2 more valuable than

3 better than any other

4 the most exciting film

5 No, as long as

STEP 3

1 bought the cheapest watch in the store

2 is one of the greatest inventions in history

3 the happiest moment I have ever experienced

4 No other sea in the world is saltier than

5 No other game is as difficult as this game.

집중 훈련 **1**

01 more and more warm → warmer and warmer

02 as three times → three times as

03 bigger → biggest   **04** girls → girl

05 very → much(even/still/far/a lot)

06 the angry → the angrier

07 can → we can 또는 possible

집중 훈련 **2**

08 not as(so) new as

09 the largest ocean in the world

10 went to bed later than usual

11 the lower the temperature becomes

12 It is the most unbelievable story (that)

13 No other activity was as boring as

14 No one in this office is busier

집중 훈련 **3**

15 The Sahara Desert is one of the hottest deserts on Earth.

16 Their performance became more and more enjoyable.

17 This subway line is twice as short as that one.

18 It is the most amazing discovery (that) they have ever made.

19 No (other) tower in this area is taller than this one(tower).

20 It was the most embarrassing moment in my life.

21 He is friendlier than any other person at my school.

집중 훈련 **4**

22 His story was not as(so) scary as yours.

23 No other bird in the world is larger than the ostrich.

24 This is the funniest article (that) I have(I've) ever read.

25 The longer she walked, the more relaxed she became.

01 '점점 더 ~한'은 「비교급+and+비교급」으로 쓴다. warm의 비교급은 -er을 붙여 warmer로 쓴다.

02 '…보다 -배 더 ~한'은 배수사를 앞에 써서 「배수사+as+원급+as」로 나타낸다.

03 '가장 ~한 …들 중 하나'는 「one of the+최상급+복수명사」로 쓰므로 최상급인 biggest를 쓴다.

04 비교급을 이용한 최상급 표현은 「비교급+than any other+단수명사」로 쓴다.

05 비교급 강조는 비교급 앞에 much, even, still, far, a lot 등을 쓴다.

06 '~할수록 더 …하다'는 「the+비교급 ~, the+비교급 …」으로 나타낸다.

07 '가능한 한 ~하게'는 「as+원급+as+주어+can」 또는 「as+원급+as possible」로 쓴다.

08 '…만큼 ~하지 않은'은 「not as(so)+원급+as」로 쓴다.

09 최상급 뒤에 장소나 범위가 올 때는 전치사 in을 쓴다.

10 비교급 비교는 「비교급+than」으로 쓴다.

11 '~할수록 더 …하다'는 「the+비교급 ~, the+비교급 …」으로 쓴다.

12 '지금껏 …한 것들 중에서 가장 ~한'은 「the+최상급+명사(+that)+주어+have ever+p.p.」로 쓴다.

13 원급을 이용한 최상급 표현을 써서 「No (other)+단수명사 ~ as+원급+as」로 쓴다.

14 비교급을 이용한 최상급 표현을 써서 「No one ~ 비교급+than」으로 쓴다. busy의 비교급은 y를 i로 바꾸고 -er을 붙여 쓴다.

15 '가장 ~한 …들 중 하나'는 「one of the+최상급+복수명사」로 쓴다.

16 '점점 더 ~한'은 「비교급+and+비교급」으로 나타내며, 비교급이 「more+원급」 형태인 경우에는 「more and more+원급」으로 쓴다.

17 배수사를 이용한 원급 비교 표현은 「배수사+as+원급+as」로 쓴다.

18 '지금껏 …한 것들 중에서 가장 ~한'은 「the+최상급+명사(+that)+주어+have ever+p.p.」로 쓴다.

19 비교급을 이용한 최상급 표현을 써서 「No (other)+단수명사 ~ 비교급+than」으로 쓴다.

20 '…에서 가장 ~한'은 「the+최상급 ~ in+장소/범위」로 쓴다.

21 비교급을 이용한 최상급 표현을 써서 「비교급+than any other+단수명사」로 쓴다. friendly의 비교급은 y를 i로 바꾸고 -er을 붙여 쓴다.

22 '…만큼 ~하지 않은'은 「not as(so)+원급+as」로 쓴다.

23 비교급을 이용한 최상급 표현을 써서 「No (other)+단수명사 ~ 비교급+than」으로 쓴다.

24 '지금껏 …한 것들 중에서 가장 ~한'은 「the+최상급+명사 (+that)+주어+have ever+p.p.」로 쓴다. funny의 최상급은 y를 i로 바꾸고 -est를 붙여 쓴다.

25 '~할수록 더 …하다'는 「the+비교급 ~, the+비교급 …」으로 나타내며, long과 relaxed의 비교급은 각각 longer와 more relaxed로 쓴다.

서술형 실전 TEST
p. 74

1 becoming more and more violent
2 (1) This screen is not as **wide** as that one.
(2) It is one of the bestselling **books** of all time.
3 as(so) exciting / than any other
4 (1) far more comfortable than
(2) the most delicious dessert of
5 (1) three times more expensive
(2) the lightest of (3) twice as heavy as

1 '점점 더 ~한'은 「비교급+and+비교급」으로 나타내며, 비교급이 「more+원급」 형태인 경우에는 「more and more+원급」으로 쓴다.

2 (1) '…만큼 ~하지 않은'은 「not as(so)+원급+as」이므로 원급 wide를 써야 한다.
(2) '가장 ~한 …들 중 하나'는 「one of the+최상급+복수명사」이므로 복수명사 books로 써야 한다.

3 the+최상급
→ No (other)+단수명사 ~ as(so)+원급+as
→ 비교급+than any other+단수명사

4 (1) 두 가지 대상의 차이를 비교하는 비교급 비교는 「비교급+than」으로 쓰며, 비교급을 강조하는 far는 비교급 앞에 쓴다.
(2) '… 중에서 가장 ~한'은 「the+최상급 ~ of+비교 대상」으로 나타낸다.

5 (1) than이 있으므로 「배수사+비교급+than」으로 나타내며, '세 배'는 three times로 쓴다.
(2) '… 중에서 가장 ~한'은 「the+최상급+of+비교 대상」으로 나타낸다.
(3) '…보다 −배 더 ~한'은 「배수사+as+원급+as」로 나타내며, '두 배'는 twice로 쓴다.

chapter ❻ 수동태

❶ 수동태의 형태
p. 76

1　**1** is delayed / is being delayed
　　2 were canceled / will be canceled
　　3 has, been accepted / won't be accepted
2　**1** must be made　**2** may be announced
　　3 can be led

❷ 4형식과 5형식 문장의 수동태
p. 77

1　**1** were taught Spanish　**2** were cooked for us
　　3 were shown those pictures
　　4 was painted green　**5** was made to choose

영작 기본 훈련
pp. 78~79

STEP 1

A
1 ⓐ was found　　ⓑ will be found
2 ⓐ are destroyed　　ⓑ are being destroyed
3 ⓐ are influenced　　ⓑ can(may) be influenced

B
1 ⓑ was told to her　　ⓒ was told the news
2 was advised to lose
3 was made to get off
4 was seen dancing

STEP 2

1 will be invited　　**2** has been read
3 was allowed to use　　**4** were asked to sign
5 was seen entering

STEP 3

1 A boy was heard calling for help
2 We were given no information
3 The film will be made by a Korean director.
4 I was made to change seats.
5 The thief was being chased by the police.

> **1** 1 was dealt with   2 may be cut off
>   3 was turned off
> **2** 1 is looked up to   2 be turned on
>   3 were turned down   4 was put off

4 by 이외의 전치사를 쓰는 수동태   p. 81

> **1** 1 known as   2 covered with
>   3 worried about   4 surprised at(by)
> **2** 1 was filled with   2 is crowded with
>   3 is known as   4 is made from

영작 기본 훈련   pp. 82~83

STEP 1

1 ⓐ looked after   ⓑ taken care of
2 ⓐ turned on   ⓑ turned off
3 ⓐ looked up to   ⓑ looked down on
4 ⓐ pleased with   ⓑ satisfied with
5 ⓐ filled with   ⓑ covered with
6 ⓐ known as   ⓑ known to
7 ⓐ made of   ⓑ made from
8 ⓐ broken into   ⓑ put off

STEP 2

1 was covered with   2 were satisfied with
3 were pleased with   4 were dealt with
5 was turned down by

STEP 3

1 The airport was crowded with travelers
2 Many consumers are worried about food safety.
3 I was surprised at the price of the festival tickets.
4 The homeless are looked after by the community.
5 These bags are made of recycled plastic bottles.

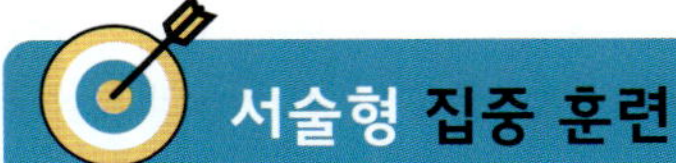

서술형 집중 훈련   pp. 84~85

집중 훈련 1

01 will given → will be given   02 to → for
03 cry → crying(to cry)   04 by → with
05 was taken care → was taken care of
06 is painting → is being painted
07 show → to show

집중 훈련 2

08 were made to stay
09 The desk was made for Jane
10 Her car is being fixed
11 He was awarded a flight ticket
12 is known as the symbol
13 These issues will be dealt with
14 was covered with posters

집중 훈련 3

15 Tofu is made from soybeans.
16 I was told to come back later.
17 This event can be watched online.
18 His grandmother is looked after by his uncle.
19 She was made to tell the truth.
20 It was designed by a famous architect.
21 Our field trip might be put off.

집중 훈련 4

22 Is your sister satisfied with her new job?
23 The office was found empty by the police.
24 A report card has been sent to each student.
25 All guests are expected to arrive on time.

01 미래시제 수동태는 「will be+p.p.」 형태로 쓴다.
02 직접목적어가 주어인 4형식 문장의 수동태에서 동사 cook은 간접목적어 앞에 전치사 for를 쓴다.
03 지각동사가 있는 5형식 문장의 수동태에서 목적격 보어는 현재분사(crying) 또는 to부정사(to cry)로 바꿔 쓴다.
04 '~로 가득 차다'는 be filled with로 쓴다.
05 take care of와 같은 구동사를 수동태로 쓸 때는 동사를 「be동사+p.p.」로 바꾸고 나머지는 동사 뒤에 그대로 쓴다.
06 진행시제 수동태는 「be동사+being+p.p.」 형태로 쓴다.

07 「ask+목적어+목적격 보어(to부정사)」 형태이므로 수동태 문장에서도 to부정사를 그대로 쓴다.

08 사역동사가 있는 5형식 문장의 목적격 보어(동사원형)는 수동태 문장에서 to부정사로 바꿔 쓴다.

09 직접목적어가 주어인 4형식 문장의 수동태에서 동사 make는 간접목적어 앞에 전치사 for를 쓴다.

10 진행시제 수동태는 「be동사+being+p.p.」 형태로 쓴다. 주어 (Her car)가 3인칭 단수이고 현재시제이므로, be동사는 is를 쓴다.

11 「award+간접목적어+직접목적어」 형태의 4형식 문장을 간접목적어가 주어인 수동태 문장으로 바꿔 쓴다.

12 '~로 알려져 있다'는 be known as로 쓴다.

13 '~을 다루다'라는 의미의 구동사 deal with의 수동태는 be dealt with로 쓴다.

14 '~로 덮여 있다'는 be covered with로 쓴다.

15 '~로 만들어지다'라는 의미는 be made of/from으로 나타내는데, 재료의 형태와 성질이 모두 변하는 경우에는 전치사 from을 쓴다.

16 「tell+목적어+목적격 보어(to부정사)」 형태이므로 수동태 문장에서도 to부정사를 그대로 쓴다.

17 조동사가 있는 문장의 수동태는 「조동사+be+p.p.」 형태로 쓴다.

18 '~을 돌보다'라는 의미의 구동사 look after의 수동태는 be looked after로 쓴다. 수동태 문장에서 행위자 앞에는 전치사 by를 쓴다.

19 사역동사가 있는 5형식 문장의 목적격 보어(동사원형)는 수동태 문장에서 to부정사로 바꿔 쓴다.

20 과거시제 수동태는 「was/were+p.p.」 형태로 쓰고, 수동태 문장에서 행위자 앞에는 전치사 by를 쓴다.

21 조동사가 있는 문장의 수동태는 「조동사+be+p.p.」 형태로 쓴다. '~을 연기하다'라는 의미의 구동사 put off의 수동태는 be put off로 쓴다.

22 '~에 만족하다'는 be satisfied with로 쓴다.

23 「find+목적어+목적격 보어(형용사)」 형태이므로 수동태 문장에서도 형용사를 그대로 쓴다.

24 현재완료 수동태는 「have/has+been+p.p.」 형태로 쓴다. 4형식 문장의 수동태에서 동사 send는 간접목적어 앞에 전치사 to를 쓴다. 행위자는 언급되지 않았으므로 생략한다.

25 「expect+목적어+목적격 보어(to부정사)」 형태이므로 수동태 문장에서도 to부정사를 그대로 쓴다.

1 (1) is filled with flowers
　(2) should be turned off in class
2 was put out by
3 A cat was seen crossing the road.
4 (1) be → being　(2) cleaning → cleaned
5 (1) were told a funny story by Lisa / was told to us by Lisa
　(2) may be sung by him
　(3) was made to bring the blanket by my mother
6 are being collected by

1 (1) be filled with: ~로 가득 차다
　(2) 조동사가 있는 문장의 수동태: 조동사+be+p.p.
2 '(불을) 끄다, 진화하다'라는 의미의 구동사 put out의 수동태는 be put out으로 쓴다. 주어(The fire)가 3인칭 단수이고 과거시제이므로 be동사는 was를 쓴다. 수동태 문장에서 행위자 앞에는 전치사 by를 쓴다.
3 5형식 문장에서 목적격 보어가 분사(crossing)이면 수동태 문장에서 그대로 쓴다.
4 (1) 진행시제의 수동태: be동사+being+p.p.
　(2) 현재완료시제의 수동태: have/has been+p.p.
5 (1) 「tell+간접목적어+직접목적어」 형태의 4형식 문장을 각각의 목적어를 주어로 하는 수동태 문장으로 바꿔 쓴다. 직접목적어가 주어인 경우에는 간접목적어 앞에 전치사 to를 쓴다.
　(2) 조동사가 있는 문장의 수동태: 조동사+be+p.p.
　(3) 사역동사가 있는 5형식 문장의 목적격 보어(동사원형)는 수동태 문장에서 to부정사로 바꿔 쓴다.
6 진행시제 수동태: be동사+being+p.p.

chapter 7 관계사 1

1 관계대명사의 역할과 종류 — pp. 88~89

1 1 that(which) 2 whose 3 who(m)(that)
 4 that(which) 5 whose 6 who(that)
 7 that(which)

2 1 that(which) have happy endings
 2 whose door was open
 3 who(that) is right behind you
 4 that(which) he had just written
 5 who(m)(that) I met yesterday

3 1 people who(that) are
 2 the bus that(which) goes
 3 a girl whose nickname
 4 the kids who(m)(that) she is
 5 that(which) Kate recommended was
 6 a book whose author

영작 기본 훈련 — pp. 90~91

STEP 1

1 that(which) I lost
2 whose hobby is reading
3 that(which) is 100 years old
4 who(m)(that) he helped
5 that(which) is leaning against the wall
6 who(m)(that) Jane met at the party
7 who(that) wrote this song
8 whose price was very low

STEP 2

1 that(which) you asked me
2 that(which) says the time
3 whose dream is
4 who(that) speaks four languages
5 a place that(which) many tourists

STEP 3

1 Brian is the boy whom I like most
2 Children like books that are full of pictures.
3 The concert that we watched together was wonderful.

4 I have a friend whose parents are movie stars.
5 The woman who is sitting on the bench is my mom.

2 관계대명사 that — p. 92

1 1 내가 먹은 파스타는
 2 내가 믿을 수 있는 누군가가
 3 내가 사고 싶은 바로 그 전화기
 4 내가 이 마을에서 만난 첫 번째 사람

2 1 the only gift that 2 The first thing that
 3 something that 4 the best thing that
 5 every letter that

3 관계대명사 what — p. 93

1 1 what / that 2 what / that 3 that / what
2 1 what I need 2 what the principal said
 3 What happened to Tony

영작 기본 훈련 — pp. 94~95

STEP 1

1 ⓐ what you   ⓑ that you say
2 ⓐ that he   ⓑ what he asked
3 ⓐ what they   ⓑ that they provide
4 ⓐ that you   ⓑ What you heard
5 ⓐ what I   ⓑ that I got
6 ⓐ that I   ⓑ what I ate
7 ⓐ what she   ⓑ that she made
8 ⓐ what I   ⓑ that I watched

STEP 2

1 what I bought 2 the same desk that
3 nothing that scares 4 What I was reading
5 The only thing that she brought

STEP 3

1 the best hamburger that I have ever eaten
2 What Sam said was very strange.
3 This is the very umbrella that Joe lost.
4 I found what Amy was looking for.
5 There is something that we don't know.

집중 훈련 1

01 that → what   **02** live → lives
03 who → whose
04 which → that (또는 which 삭제)
05 which → who(m)(that) (또는 which 삭제)
06 what → that
07 what → that(which) (또는 what 삭제)

집중 훈련 2

08 that(which) I am wearing
09 a friendly boy whose dream
10 what you have
11 a desk that(which) has
12 the girl who(that) sang
13 that I have ever met
14 that you want to know

집중 훈련 3

15 I like all the movies (that) this director made.
16 He is the man who(that) visited my office yesterday.
17 Don't(Do not) forget what I said.
18 This is a beautiful beach whose sand is white.
19 This is the same toy (that) I bought for my brother.
20 They do everything (that) they can do for me.
21 What I learned today was the backstroke.

집중 훈련 4

22 I was the only student that found the answer.
23 What he told me was shocking.
24 She saw the note that(which) he left.
25 They live in a house whose roof is red.

01 선행사가 없으므로 선행사를 포함하는 관계대명사 what을 쓴다.
02 주격 관계대명사절의 동사는 선행사(the girl)에 수 일치시키므로 lives로 쓴다.
03 선행사(a writer) 뒤에 오는 관계사절에서 관계대명사가 명사(novel) 앞에 쓰이는 소유격 역할을 해야 하므로 소유격 관계대명사 whose를 쓴다.

04 선행사가 all이므로 관계대명사 that을 쓴다. 목적격 관계대명사는 생략할 수 있다.
05 선행사(an old friend)가 사람이고, 관계사절에서 목적어 역할을 해야 하므로 목적격 관계대명사 who(m) 또는 that을 쓴다. 목적격 관계대명사는 생략할 수 있다.
06 선행사에 the very가 있으므로 관계대명사 that을 쓴다.
07 선행사(the glasses)가 사물이고, 관계사절에서 목적어 역할을 해야 하므로 목적격 관계대명사 that 또는 which를 쓴다. 목적격 관계대명사는 생략할 수 있다.
08 선행사(The cap)가 사물이고, 관계사절에서 목적어 역할을 해야 하므로 목적격 관계대명사 that 또는 which를 쓴다.
09 선행사(a friendly boy) 뒤에 오는 관계사절에서 관계대명사가 소유격 역할을 해야 하므로 명사(dream) 앞에 소유격 관계대명사 whose를 쓴다.
10 '~하는 것'이라는 의미로 선행사를 포함하는 관계대명사 what을 쓴다.
11 선행사(a desk)가 사물이고, 관계사절에서 주어 역할을 해야 하므로 주격 관계대명사 that 또는 which를 쓴다. 주격 관계대명사절의 동사는 선행사에 수 일치시키므로 has로 쓴다.
12 선행사(the girl)가 사람이고, 관계사절에서 주어 역할을 해야 하므로 주격 관계대명사 who 또는 that을 쓴다.
13 선행사에 최상급 표현이 있으므로 관계대명사 that을 쓴다.
14 선행사가 anything이므로 관계대명사 that을 쓴다.
15 선행사에 all이 있으므로 관계대명사 that을 쓴다. 목적격 관계대명사는 생략할 수 있다.
16 선행사(the man)가 사람이고, 관계사절에서 주어 역할을 해야 하므로 주격 관계대명사 who 또는 that을 쓴다.
17 '~하는 것'이라는 의미로 선행사를 포함하는 관계대명사 what을 쓴다.
18 선행사(a beautiful beach) 뒤에 오는 관계사절에서 관계대명사가 소유격 역할을 해야 하므로 명사(sand) 앞에 소유격 관계대명사 whose를 쓴다.
19 선행사에 the same이 있으므로 관계대명사 that을 쓴다. 목적격 관계대명사는 생략할 수 있다.
20 선행사가 everything이므로 관계대명사 that을 쓴다. 목적격 관계대명사는 생략할 수 있다.
21 '~하는 것'이라는 의미로 선행사를 포함하는 관계대명사 what을 쓴다.
22 선행사에 the only가 있으므로 관계대명사 that을 쓴다.
23 '~하는 것'이라는 의미로 선행사를 포함하는 관계대명사 what을 쓴다.
24 선행사(the note)가 사물이고, 관계사절에서 목적어 역할을 해야 하므로 목적격 관계대명사 that 또는 which를 쓴다.
25 선행사(a house) 뒤에 오는 관계사절에서 관계대명사가 소

유격 역할을 해야 하므로 명사(roof) 앞에 소유격 관계대명사 whose를 쓴다.

what을 쓴다. 이때 관계대명사가 관계사절에서 목적어 역할을 하므로 it 등의 목적어는 쓰지 않는다.

1 anything that you need

2 (1) **What** you drew surprised us.
(2) I like singers **whose** voice is powerful.

3 (1) what Kate gave me
(2) who the whole world admires
(3) whose rules are very difficult
(4) that exists on Earth

4 (1) whose name is Jerry
(2) the same runner that won

5 (1) that(which) has over 38,000 works of art
(2) what I want to see most

1 -thing으로 끝나는 대명사가 선행사인 경우에는 관계대명사 that을 쓴다.

2 (1) 선행사가 없으므로 That을 관계대명사 What으로 고쳐 쓴다.
(2) 선행사(singers) 뒤에 오는 관계사절에서 관계대명사가 명사(voice) 앞에 쓰이는 소유격 역할을 해야 하므로 which를 소유격 관계대명사 whose로 고쳐 쓴다.

3 (1) 선행사가 없으므로 선행사를 포함하는 관계대명사 what을 쓴다.
(2) 선행사(a skater)가 사람이고, 관계사절에서 목적어 역할을 해야 하므로 목적격 관계대명사 who를 쓴다.
(3) 선행사(a game) 뒤에 오는 관계사절에서 관계대명사가 소유격 역할을 해야 하므로 명사(rules) 앞에 소유격 관계대명사 whose를 쓴다.
(4) 선행사에 최상급 the biggest가 있으므로 관계대명사 that을 쓴다.

4 (1) 선행사(a dog) 뒤에 오는 관계사절에서 관계대명사가 소유격 역할을 해야 하므로 명사(name) 앞에 소유격 관계대명사 whose를 쓴다.
(2) 선행사에 the same이 있으므로 관계대명사 that을 쓴다.

5 해석 나는 언젠가 루브르 박물관을 방문하고 싶다. 그곳은 38,000점 이상의 예술 작품을 가진 유명한 박물관이다. 그곳에는 위대한 그림들이 많이 있다. 그중에서 내가 가장 보고 싶은 것은 '모나리자'이다.
→ (1) 선행사(a famous museum)가 사물이고, 관계사절에서 주어 역할을 하므로 주격 관계대명사 that 또는 which를 쓴다.
(2) '~하는 것'이라는 의미로 선행사를 포함하는 관계대명사

chapter **8** 관계사 2

1 관계대명사의 생략   p. 100

1 1 that(which) / we chose
2 who(m)(that) / at whom / you are looking at
2 1 The man waiting   2 sent to customers
3 a watch made   4 the people sitting

2 관계대명사의 계속적 용법   p. 101

1 1 which was built in 1753
2 who plays the guitar in our band
3 which disappointed me
2 1 who   2 which   3 who(m)   4 which

영작 기본 훈련   pp. 102~103

STEP 1

1 with whom   2 he painted
3 which surprised me   4 in which my family
5 The movie playing at the theater
6 who is a brave soldier
7 a dog trained by Tim
8 which we love

STEP 2

1 I called Ian, who is a friend
2 Is this the book you are looking for?
3 The woman living on the second floor is a doctor.
4 She went to the gallery, which was closed.
5 The kids I met yesterday are sick now.

STEP 3

1 (that(which)) you wanted to visit
2 Kate, who is kind and cheerful
3 (who(m)(that)) we look up to
4 which worries me

5 The girl (who(that) is) wearing the funny hat

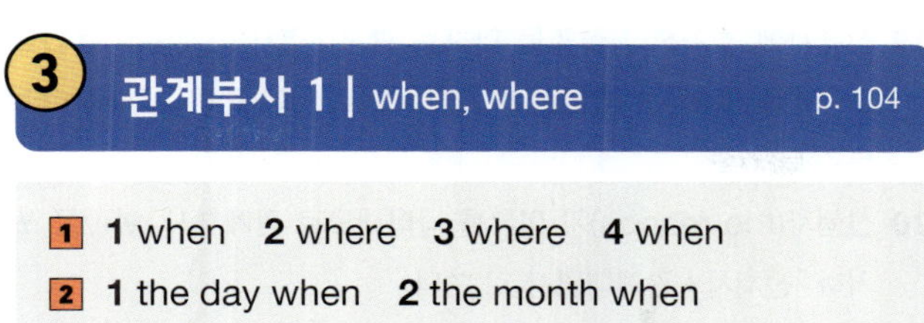

3 관계부사 1 | when, where   p. 104

1   **1** when   **2** where   **3** where   **4** when

2   **1** the day when   **2** the month when
    3 The city where

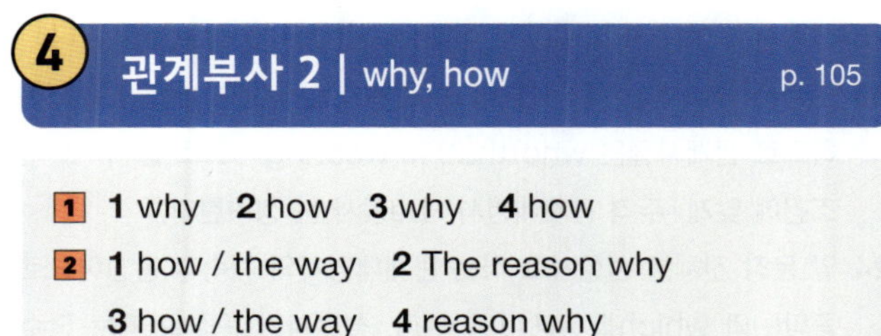

4 관계부사 2 | why, how   p. 105

1   **1** why   **2** how   **3** why   **4** how

2   **1** how / the way   **2** The reason why
    3 how / the way   **4** reason why

영작 기본 훈련   pp. 106~107

STEP 1

1 ⓑ when   ⓒ The day when
2 ⓑ where   ⓒ The village where
3 ⓑ why   ⓒ The reason why
4 ⓑ the way   ⓒ how
5 ⓑ when   ⓒ The date when
6 ⓑ where   ⓒ where we can swim

STEP 2

1 The reason why Tom was late for school
2 This is how I prepared for the test.
3 Thursday is the day when I have a piano lesson.
4 Blogs are spaces where we can share ideas.
5 I don't know the way he made so much money.

STEP 3

1 when she can be alone
2 the reason why you are tired
3 the season when trees become greener
4 the park where he played baseball with his friends
5 know how you made this delicious pizza

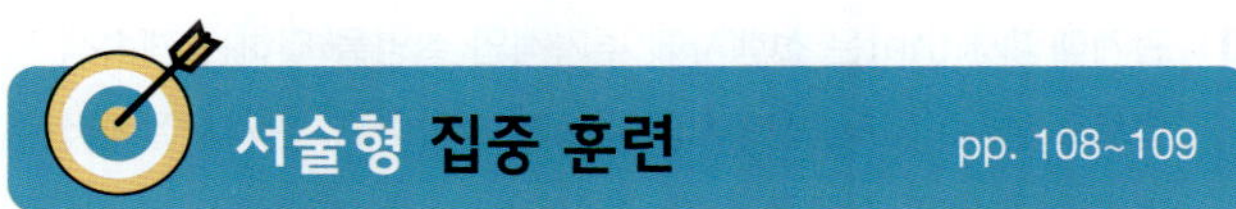

pp. 108~109

집중 훈련 1

01 that → who
02 at that → at which(where)
    (또는 at that I work → (that) I work at)
03 the way how → how 또는 the way
04 to who → to whom
    (또는 to who I'm writing → (who) I'm writing to)
05 how → why 또는 for which
06 that → which
07 that delivered → (that was) delivered

집중 훈련 2

08 The teacher (who(m)(that)) we respect most
09 (that(which)) you are looking at
10 who lives in New Zealand
11 which made her parents upset
12 (who(that) is) dancing on the stage
13 The day when we graduated
14 where we can study

집중 훈련 3

15 That is the car (that(which) was) repaired by John.
16 The room where we stayed was very small.
17 He won the marathon, which was amazing.
18 Sally is reading the magazine (that(which)) she bought yesterday.
19 I found an old ring, which looked expensive.
20 Do you know the reason why(for which) he didn't come?
21 I will never forget the time when(at which) I went there.

집중 훈련 4

22 London is a city where you can visit famous museums.
23 The man wearing big sunglasses is a coach.
24 Kate met her favorite singer, which was a big surprise.
25 This is the way I draw stars.

01 관계대명사 that은 선행사에 추가적인 설명을 더하는 계속적 용법으로 쓸 수 없다. 선행사(Julie)가 사람이고, 관계사절에서 주어 역할을 해야 하므로 주격 관계대명사 who를 쓴다.

02 관계대명사 that은 전치사 뒤에 쓸 수 없으므로 at which로 쓰거나 관계부사 where로 쓴다. 또는 전치사 at을 work 뒤에 쓴다. 이때 관계대명사는 생략할 수 있다.

03 방법을 나타내는 선행사 the way와 관계부사 how는 함께 쓸 수 없고, 둘 중 하나만 써야 한다.

04 관계대명사 who나 that은 전치사 뒤에 쓸 수 없으므로 to whom으로 쓴다. 또는 전치사 to를 writing 뒤에 쓴다. 이때 관계대명사는 생략할 수 있다.

05 선행사(some reasons)가 이유를 나타내므로 관계부사 why를 써야 한다. 관계대명사를 사용하여 for which로도 쓸 수 있다.

06 관계대명사 that은 선행사에 추가적인 설명을 더하는 계속적 용법으로 쓸 수 없다. 선행사(Paris)가 사물이므로 which를 써야 한다.

07 '배달된' 우유이므로 관계사절은 that was delivered ~가 되어야 하고, 이때 「주격 관계대명사+be동사」는 생략할 수 있다.

08 선행사(The teacher)가 사람이고, 관계사절에서 목적어 역할을 해야 하므로 목적격 관계대명사 who(m)〔that〕을 쓴다. 목적격 관계대명사는 생략할 수 있다.

09 선행사(the photos)가 사물이고, 관계사절에서 전치사의 목적어 역할을 해야 하므로 목적격 관계대명사 that〔which〕를 쓴다. 목적격 관계대명사는 생략할 수 있다.

10 선행사(Brian)가 사람이고, 계속적 용법의 관계사절이 이어지므로 콤마(,) 뒤에 주격 관계대명사 who를 써서 나타낸다. 관계사절의 동사는 선행사에 수 일치시키므로 lives로 쓴다.

11 앞 문장 전체를 선행사로 하는 관계대명사의 계속적 용법이므로 which를 써서 나타낸다.

12 선행사(the girl)가 사람이고, 관계사절에서 주어 역할을 해야 하므로 주격 관계대명사 who〔that〕을 쓴다. 「주격 관계대명사 +be동사」는 생략할 수 있다.

13 시간을 나타내는 선행사(the day) 뒤에 관계부사 when을 쓴다.

14 장소를 나타내는 선행사(a quiet place) 뒤에 관계부사 where를 쓴다.

15 선행사(the car)가 사물이고, 관계사절에서 주어 역할을 해야 하므로 주격 관계대명사 that〔which〕를 쓴다. 「주격 관계대명사+be동사」는 생략할 수 있다.

16 장소를 나타내는 선행사(the room) 뒤에 관계부사 where를 쓴다.

17 앞 문장 전체를 선행사로 하는 관계대명사의 계속적 용법이므로 콤마(,)와 which를 써서 나타낸다. 선행사가 문장일 때는 단수 취급하므로 관계사절의 동사는 was로 쓴다.

18 선행사(the magazine)가 사물이고, 관계사절에서 목적어 역할

을 해야 하므로 목적격 관계대명사 that〔which〕를 쓴다. 목적격 관계대명사는 생략할 수 있다.

19 선행사에 추가적인 설명을 더하는 관계대명사의 계속적 용법으로, 선행사(an old ring)가 사물이므로 뒤에 콤마(,)와 which를 쓴다.

20 선행사(the reason)가 이유를 나타내므로 관계부사 why를 쓰거나 「전치사+관계대명사」로 쓴다.

21 선행사(the time)가 시간을 나타내므로 관계부사 when을 쓰거나 「전치사+관계대명사」로 쓴다.

22 선행사(a city)가 장소를 나타내므로 관계부사 where를 쓴다.

23 선행사(The man)가 사람이고, 관계사절에서 주어 역할을 해야 하므로 관계사절은 who〔that〕 is wearing ~으로 쓸 수 있다. 조건에 맞게 「주격 관계대명사+be동사」는 생략한다.

24 앞 문장 전체를 선행사로 하는 관계대명사의 계속적 용법이므로 콤마(,)와 which를 써서 나타낸다. 선행사가 문장일 때는 단수 취급하므로 관계사절의 동사는 was로 쓴다.

25 방법을 나타내는 선행사 the way와 관계부사 how는 함께 쓸 수 없고 둘 중 하나만 써야 한다. 단어 수 조건에 맞게 the way 를 쓴다.

CHAPTER 8
서술형 실전 TEST
p. 110

1 (1) I told you about (2) which is next Saturday
   (3) parked at the gate
2 which made me happy
3 where people can walk their dogs
4 when〔in which〕my family moved to Busan
5 There is a traffic jam caused by a car accident.
6 (1) who(m)〔that〕everybody likes
   (2) how she makes friends easily

1 (1) 목적격 관계대명사 that 또는 which가 생략된 형태이다.
(2) 선행사(my birthday)에 추가적인 설명을 더하는 계속적 용법의 관계대명사절을 쓴다.
(3) 선행사(The bike)를 수식하는 관계대명사절(which〔that〕 is parked ~)에서 「주격 관계대명사+be동사」가 생략된 형태이다.

2 앞 문장 전체를 선행사로 하는 관계대명사의 계속적 용법이므로 which를 써서 나타낸다.

3 선행사(a park)가 장소를 나타내므로 관계부사 where를 쓴다.

4 선행사(the year)가 시간을 나타내므로 관계부사 when을 쓰거나 「전치사+관계대명사」로 쓸 수 있다.

5 선행사(a traffic jam)를 수식하는 관계대명사절(that〔which〕

was caused ~)에서 「주격 관계대명사+be동사」가 생략된 형태의 문장으로 쓴다.

6 해석 Jenny는 모두가 좋아하는 여자아이다. 그녀는 다른 사람들에게 "안녕"이라고 먼저 말하고 모두에게 친절하다. 또한, 그녀는 항상 미소 짓고 있다. 그것이 그녀가 쉽게 친구를 사귀는 방법이다.
→ (1) 선행사(a girl)가 사람이고, 관계사절에서 목적어 역할을 해야 하므로 목적격 관계대명사 who(m) 또는 that을 쓴다.
(2) 방법을 나타내는 관계부사 how를 쓴다.

chapter ❾ 접속사

❶ 시간·이유를 나타내는 접속사　　p. 112

1 **1** while / because(as/since)
　2 when / because(as/since)
　3 since / as(while)
2 **1** When　**2** since　**3** while　**4** as

❷ 조건·양보를 나타내는 접속사　　p. 113

1 **1** 만약 눈이 오면
　2 식당이 붐볐음에도 불구하고
　3 네가 지금 당장 떠나지 않으면
2 **1** unless　**2** If　**3** though

영작 기본 훈련　　pp. 114~115

STEP 1

1 when I went to the shopping mall
2 because(as/since) it was cold
3 Although(Though/Even though) I have little money
4 If you ring the bell
5 since he was 8 years old
6 While(As) I was riding my bike
7 when(as) I sat down
8 unless you have a ticket(if you don't have a ticket)

STEP 2

1 because the road was icy
2 If she arrives on time tomorrow

3 Though it was his mistake
4 As he got off the train
5 unless you go to bed early

STEP 3

1 When I entered the room, people looked at me. / People looked at me when I entered the room.
2 Unless you have other plans, let's eat out together. / Let's eat out together unless you have other plans.
3 Because the room was dark, I turned on the light. / I turned on the light because the room was dark.
4 If the weather is good, we will go to the park. / We will go to the park if the weather is good.
5 Even though the traffic was heavy, we arrived early. / We arrived early even though the traffic was heavy.

❸ 상관접속사　　p. 116

1 **1** not, but　**2** both, and　**3** as well as
　4 neither, nor
2 **1** either stay home or　**2** both math and history
　3 neither interesting nor helpful
　4 not at home but　**5** not only Seoul but also

❹ 기타 접속사　　p. 117

1 **1** Whether　**2** whether(if)　**3** whether, or not
2 **1** 그러지 않으면 너는 기차를 놓칠 것이다.
　2 그러면 신선한 공기가 들어올 것이다.
　3 그러지 않으면 그는 너를 용서하지 않을 것이다.

영작 기본 훈련　　pp. 118~119

STEP 1

1 not only clothing but also accessories
2 either Italy or Germany
3 not today but next Thursday
4 neither tea nor juice　**5** Both Jessica and I
6 Finish your homework, and
7 Get some rest, or
8 whether(if) it will rain or not

1 neither money nor time
2 either by taxi or
3 whether he is a foreigner
4 Not only, but also, is
5 whether (if) my answer is right

STEP 3

1 Both Peter and I are waiting for the school bus.
2 I don't know whether he is telling the truth.
3 She showers not in the morning but at night.
4 We will visit either the museum or the palace.
5 Neither Kate nor I have any plans for tomorrow.

5 의문사가 있는 간접의문문　p. 120

1 　**1** where the subway station is
　2 how you made this cake
　3 how old she is
　4 who stole my wallet
　5 when she called
2 　**1** When do you think you will finish your work?
　2 What do you think the cat ate last night?
　3 Who do you believe will be the next president?

6 의문사가 없는 간접의문문　p. 121

1 　**1** if (whether) he is from Spain
　2 if (whether) she knows my name
　3 if (whether) I can have a seat here
　4 if (whether) he has been to Korea
2 　**1** if (whether) you can come to my birthday party
　2 if (whether) Jane is in the library
　3 if (whether) you sent me these flowers
　4 if (whether) she is angry at us

영작 기본 훈련　pp. 122~123

STEP 1

1 who took my umbrella

2 if (whether) he has a car
3 when she leaves for Australia
4 What, she said to him
5 if (whether) this watch is expensive
6 Where, they will hold the festival
7 how she solved the problem
8 what time the show starts

STEP 2

1 wonder what happened
2 if (whether) we should invite him
3 Who do you believe
4 when he moved to Canada
5 if (whether) this notebook is yours

STEP 3

1 tell me how much this plate is
2 Do you know whether they have met
3 Where do you think she is going
4 I don't know what this word means.
5 I'm not sure if they will hire me.

서술형 집중 훈련　pp. 124~125

집중 훈련 1

01 that → whether (if)
02 if → although (though/even though)
03 was → were
04 are they → they are
05 lives → live
06 and → or
07 Do you think what → What do you think

집중 훈련 2

08 because (as/since) she is always cheerful
09 either walk or take a bus
10 Whether he is married or not
11 while I lived (was living) in Brazil
12 why he is crying
13 Unless it is your bag (If it is not your bag)
14 French as well as English

집중 훈련 3

15 Do you know who that man is?
16 The movie is not only touching but also funny.
17 Have breakfast, or you will have no energy.
18 I wonder if(whether) she is a vegetarian.
19 Neither Tom nor Jane was surprised.
20 If it rains, I will stay home. / I will stay home if it rains.
21 Can you tell me where you live?

집중 훈련 4

22 Even though I was sleepy, I finished my homework.
23 Unless you wear a coat, you may catch a cold. / You may catch a cold unless you wear a coat.
24 Turn left, and you will find the bank.
25 When do you think she will come back?

01 '~인지 아닌지'라는 의미의 명사절을 이끄는 접속사는 whether (if)를 쓴다.

02 '~에도 불구하고'라는 의미의 접속사 although(though/even though)를 쓴다.

03 「not only A but also B」가 주어로 쓰인 경우 B(his kids)에 동사의 수를 일치시키므로 were를 쓴다.

04 동사 know의 목적어로 의문사가 있는 간접의문문이 쓰였으므로 「의문사+주어+동사」의 형태로 써야 한다.

05 「both A and B」가 주어로 쓰인 경우 복수 취급한다.

06 '~해라. 그러지 않으면 …할 것이다'는 「명령문, or …」로 나타낸다.

07 생각이나 추측을 나타내는 think 등이 주절의 동사인 의문문은 간접의문문의 의문사를 문장 맨 앞에 쓴다.

08 '~하기 때문에'라는 의미의 접속사 because(as/since)를 쓴다.

09 'A나 B 둘 중 하나'라는 의미의 「either A or B」를 쓴다.

10 문장의 주어가 되는 명사절을 「whether … or not」을 써서 나타낸다. 이때는 whether 대신 if를 쓸 수 없다.

11 '~하는 동안'이라는 의미의 접속사 while을 쓴다.

12 I'm not sure 뒤에 「의문사+주어+동사」 형태의 간접의문문을 쓴다.

13 '~하지 않으면'이라는 의미의 접속사 unless를 쓴다. unless는 if … not으로 바꿔 쓸 수 있다.

14 'A뿐만 아니라 B도'라는 의미의 「B as well as A」를 쓴다.

15 동사 know의 목적어로 「의문사+주어+동사」 형태의 간접의문문을 쓴다.

16 'A뿐만 아니라 B도'라는 의미의 「not only A but also B」를 쓴다.

17 '~해라. 그러지 않으면 …할 것이다'라는 의미의 「명령문, or …」를 쓴다.

18 동사 wonder의 목적어로 「if(whether)+주어+동사」 형태의 의문사가 없는 간접의문문을 쓴다.

19 'A와 B 둘 다 아닌'이라는 의미의 「neither A nor B」를 주어로 쓴다. 이때 동사의 수는 B에 일치시킨다.

20 조건을 나타내는 접속사 if를 쓴다. 조건을 나타내는 부사절에서는 현재시제로 미래를 나타내므로 will rain이 아닌 rains를 쓴다.

21 동사 tell의 목적어로 「의문사+주어+동사」 형태의 간접의문문을 쓴다.

22 '비록 ~이지만'이라는 의미의 양보를 나타내는 접속사를 쓴다. 단어 수 조건에 맞게 even though를 쓰고, 접속사로 시작하는 문장에서 부사절 끝에는 콤마(,)를 쓴다.

23 not을 쓰지 말라는 조건에 맞게 '~하지 않으면'이라는 의미의 접속사 unless를 쓴다.

24 '~해라. 그러면 …할 것이다'라는 의미의 「명령문, and …」를 쓴다.

25 생각이나 추측을 나타내는 think 등이 주절의 동사인 의문문은 간접의문문의 의문사를 문장 맨 앞에 쓴다.

CHAPTER 9
서술형 실전 TEST

p. 126

1 whether he can help me
2 Although(Though/Even though) they spoke very fast
3 (1) She will try *dalgona* when she **visits** Korea.
(2) We can't start the game unless everyone **is** here(**if** everyone isn't here).
4 (1) not beef but fish
(2) Visit the website, and
(3) when he arrived
5 (1) unless it rains
(2) because I have a sore throat
(3) when I saw my report card
6 (1) neither baseball nor soccer
(2) as well as animals

1 문장의 주어가 되는 명사절을 접속사 whether를 써서 나타낸다. 이때는 whether 대신 if를 쓸 수 없으며, 문장 맨 앞의 It은

whether가 이끄는 명사절을 대신하는 가주어 역할을 한다.

2 '비록 ~이지만'이라는 의미의 접속사 although(though/even though)를 쓴다.

3 (1) 시간을 나타내는 부사절에서는 현재시제로 미래를 나타내므로 visits를 쓴다.
(2) '~하지 않으면'이라는 의미의 접속사 unless에는 부정의 의미가 들어 있으므로 동사에 not을 쓰지 않는다. unless는 if ... not으로 바꿔 쓸 수 있다.

4 (1) not A but B: A가 아니라 B
(2) 명령문, and ... : ~해라. 그러면 …할 것이다
(3) 의문사가 있는 간접의문문: 「의문사＋주어＋동사」

5 (1) '비가 오지 않으면 나는 캠핑하러 갈 것이다'라는 내용이 자연스럽다.
(2) '나는 목이 아프기 때문에 오늘은 노래 부를 수 없다'라는 내용이 자연스럽다.
(3) '내 성적표를 봤을 때 나는 놀랐다'라는 내용이 자연스럽다.

6 (1) neither A nor B: A도 B도 아닌
(2) B as well as A: A뿐만 아니라 B도

chapter ❿ 가정법

① 가정법 과거
p. 128

1　1 had / could visit　2 were / would try
　3 didn't eat / would get　4 weren't / could talk
　5 cleaned / wouldn't be

② 가정법 과거 vs. 직설법 현재
p. 129

1　1 If it were sunny
　2 If you did not(didn't) play games all day
　3 I would go to the movies
　4 they might forgive him
2　1 spoke / could understand
　2 liked / would enjoy　3 weren't / could run

영작 기본 훈련
pp. 130~131

STEP 1

1　weren't, would pick　2　snowed, would build
3　weren't, could play　4　were, might use
5　won, could buy　6　had, wouldn't drink
7　weren't raining, could take
8　didn't have, could go

STEP 2

1　If you knew them
2　wouldn't use my phone
3　were a good drummer
4　might travel around the world
5　didn't have, could go

STEP 3

1　If she kept my secrets
2　I would not(wouldn't) wear glasses
3　studied harder, he might pass
4　you spoke French, you could talk
5　If I were a singer, I would write

3 가정법 과거완료   p. 132

1 **1** had seen / would have been
2 had come / might have found
3 hadn't gone / could have watched
4 had worn / wouldn't have caught
5 had had / might have bought

4 가정법 과거완료 *vs.* 직설법 과거   p. 133

1 **1** If she had been home
2 you would not(wouldn't) have parked your car there
3 If I had had breakfast
4 he would have become our class president
2 **1** hadn't been / would have gone
2 had recognized / could have gotten
3 had gone / would have seen
4 had arrived / could have eaten

영작 기본 훈련   pp. 134~135

STEP 1

1 ⓐ were, would keep
ⓑ had been, would have kept
2 ⓐ were, would go
ⓑ had been, would have gone
3 ⓐ were, might meet
ⓑ had been, might have met
4 ⓐ had, could see
ⓑ had had, could have seen
5 ⓐ remembered, would send
ⓑ had remembered, would have sent
6 ⓐ knew, would introduce
ⓑ had known, would have introduced

STEP 2

1 we would have believed you
2 If she had not lost her cell phone
3 If he had focused in class, he could have passed
4 had left earlier, you might have avoided the traffic
5 had not been icy, the accident would not have happened

STEP 3

1 If you had come to the party
2 I could have bought the album
3 If you had not(hadn't) fought with each other
4 our team would have won the final game
5 had not(hadn't) taken the wrong bus, I would not(wouldn't) have been late

5 I wish 가정법   p. 136

1 **1** were   **2** didn't rain   **3** had
2 **1** hadn't left   **2** had known   **3** had taken

6 as if 가정법   p. 137

1 **1** liked   **2** didn't know   **3** were
2 **1** had seen   **2** had written   **3** hadn't heard

영작 기본 훈련   pp. 138~139

STEP 1

1 ⓐ were   ⓑ had been
2 ⓐ I wish, had   ⓑ I wish, had had
3 ⓐ as if, read   ⓑ as if, had read
4 ⓐ I wish, studied   ⓑ I wish, had studied
5 ⓐ I wish, didn't tell   ⓑ I wish, hadn't told
6 ⓐ I wish, weren't   ⓑ I wish, hadn't been
7 ⓐ as if, didn't want   ⓑ as if, hadn't wanted
8 ⓐ as if, weren't   ⓑ as if, hadn't been

STEP 2

1 the exams had been easy
2 I were a superhero like Iron Man
3 my mom had not(hadn't) turned off my alarm clock
4 as if they had met the actor at the concert
5 as if he did not(didn't) know her

STEP 3

1 I wish we could live on Mars
2 The man looked as if he had not slept well
3 I wish I had ordered a different dish
4 My dad treats me as if I were a child.

5 I wish I had been the main character of the play.

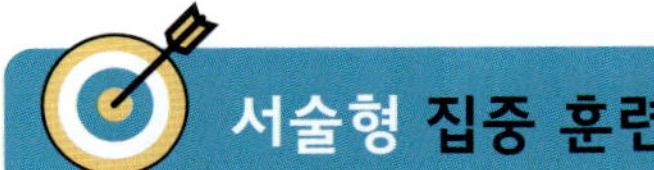

서술형 집중 훈련

pp. 140~141

집중 훈련 **1**

01 is → were
02 won't → wouldn't
03 is → were
04 hasn't → hadn't
05 didn't rain → hadn't rained
06 can → could
07 go → have gone

집중 훈련 **2**

08 If I were not〔weren't〕 busy
09 I were taller
10 I could have a garden
11 as if he knew everything
12 I wish you had not〔hadn't〕 taken
13 as if he had seen the accident
14 had come, we would have played

집중 훈련 **3**

15 If he had a car, he could drive anytime.
16 I wish I had a sister.
17 If it had snowed, we would have gone skiing.
18 People acted as if nothing had happened.
19 I wish I had brought my camera.
20 If I were you, I would go see a doctor.
21 You talk as if you were our team leader.

집중 훈련 **4**

22 If I were rich, I might buy a yacht.
23 If we had had some eggs, we could have made an omelet.
24 He talks as if he hadn't been there.
25 I wish we had stayed longer in Hawaii.

01 현재 사실과 반대되는 일을 가정하는 가정법 과거 문장에서 if절의 be동사는 주어에 관계없이 were를 쓴다.

02 현재 사실과 반대되는 일을 가정하는 가정법 과거 문장에서 주절의 동사는 「조동사의 과거형＋동사원형」으로 쓴다.

03 '마치 ~인 것처럼'이라는 의미는 「as if＋가정법 과거」로 나타내며, as if절의 be동사는 주어에 관계없이 were를 쓴다.

04 '~했다면 좋을 텐데'라는 과거 사실에 대한 소망은 「I wish＋가정법 과거완료」로 나타내며, 동사는 「had＋p.p.」로 쓴다.

05 과거 사실과 반대되는 일을 가정하는 가정법 과거완료 문장에서 if절의 동사는 「had＋p.p.」로 쓴다.

06 '~한다면 좋을 텐데'라는 현재의 실현 불가능한 소망은 「I wish＋가정법 과거」로 나타내므로 조동사 can의 과거형 could로 쓴다.

07 과거 사실과 반대되는 일을 가정하는 가정법 과거완료 문장에서 주절의 동사는 「조동사의 과거형＋have＋p.p.」로 쓴다.

08 현재 사실과 반대되는 일을 가정하는 가정법 과거 문장에서 if절의 be동사는 주어에 관계없이 were를 쓴다.

09 '~한다면 좋을 텐데'라는 현재의 실현 불가능한 소망은 「I wish＋가정법 과거」로 나타내며, be동사는 주어에 관계없이 were를 쓴다.

10 현재 사실과 반대되는 일을 가정하는 가정법 과거 문장에서 주절의 동사는 「조동사의 과거형＋동사원형」으로 쓴다.

11 '마치 ~하는 것처럼'이라는 의미는 「as if＋가정법 과거」로 나타내며, as if절의 동사는 과거형으로 쓴다.

12 '~했다면 좋을 텐데'라는 과거 사실에 대한 소망을 나타내므로 「I wish＋가정법 과거완료」로 나타내며, 부정의 의미이므로 동사는 「had not〔hadn't〕＋p.p.」로 쓴다.

13 '마치 ~했던 것처럼'이라는 의미는 「as if＋가정법 과거완료」로 나타내며, as if절의 동사는 「had＋p.p.」로 쓴다.

14 과거 사실과 반대되는 일을 가정하는 가정법 과거완료 문장은 「If＋주어＋had＋p.p. ~, 주어＋조동사의 과거형＋have＋p.p. ...」로 쓴다.

15 현재 사실과 반대되는 일을 가정하는 가정법 과거 문장은 「If＋주어＋동사의 과거형 ~, 주어＋조동사의 과거형＋동사원형 ...」으로 쓴다.

16 '~한다면 좋을 텐데'라는 현재의 실현 불가능한 소망은 「I wish＋가정법 과거」로 나타내며, 동사는 과거형을 쓴다.

17 과거 사실과 반대되는 일을 가정하는 가정법 과거완료 문장은 「If＋주어＋had＋p.p. ~, 주어＋조동사의 과거형＋have＋p.p. ...」로 쓴다.

18 '마치 ~했던 것처럼'이라는 의미는 「as if＋가정법 과거완료」로 나타내며, as if절의 동사는 「had＋p.p.」로 쓴다.

19 '~했다면 좋을 텐데'라는 과거 사실에 대한 소망은 「I wish＋가정법 과거완료」로 나타내며, 동사는 「had＋p.p.」로 쓴다.

20 현재 사실과 반대되는 일을 가정하는 가정법 과거 문장은 「If＋주어＋동사의 과거형. ~, 주어＋조동사의 과거형＋동사원형 ...」으로 쓴다. 이때 if절의 be동사는 주어에 관계없이 were를 쓴다.

21 '마치 ~인 것처럼'이라는 의미는 「as if＋가정법 과거」로 나타내며, as if절의 be동사는 주어에 관계없이 were를 쓴다.

22 현재 사실과 반대되는 일을 가정하는 가정법 과거 문장은 「If＋주어＋동사의 과거형. ~, 주어＋조동사의 과거형＋동사원형 ...」으로 쓴다. 이때 if절의 be동사는 주어에 관계없이 were를 쓴다.

23 과거 사실과 반대되는 일을 가정하는 가정법 과거완료 문장은 「If+주어+had+p.p. ~, 주어+조동사의 과거형+have+p.p. ...」로 쓴다.

24 '마치 ~했던 것처럼'이라는 의미의 「as if+가정법 과거완료」로 나타내며, 부정의 의미이므로 동사는 「had not〔hadn't〕+p.p.」로 쓴다. 단어 수 조건에 맞게 hadn't로 줄여 쓴다.

25 '~했다면 좋을 텐데'라는 과거 사실에 대한 소망은 「I wish+가정법 과거완료」로 나타내며, 동사는 「had+p.p.」로 쓴다.

1 (1) You talk as if you **had made** the food yourself.
(2) I wish I **were** at the concert.

2 (1) I could speak English fluently
(2) had heard the weather report, I would have brought my umbrella

3 hadn't fallen asleep, would have watched

4 (1) this jacket were smaller
(2) she had visited New York

5 were, would believe in myself

1 (1) '마치 ~했던 것처럼'이라는 의미는 「as if+가정법 과거완료」로 나타내며, as if절의 동사는 「had+p.p.」로 쓴다.
(2) '~한다면 좋을 텐데'라는 현재 사실에 대한 소망은 「I wish+가정법 과거」로 나타내며, be동사는 주어에 관계없이 were를 쓴다.

2 (1) 직설법 문장에서 현재 이룰 수 없는 일에 대한 아쉬움을 나타내고 있으므로 「I wish+가정법 과거」로 쓴다.
(2) 직설법 과거 문장의 내용은 반대 의미의 가정법 과거완료로 나타낸다.

3 해석　A 너는 어젯밤에 그 축구 경기를 봤니?
B 아니, 안 봤어. 잠이 들었어.
　내가 잠들지 않았다면, 그것을 봤을 텐데.
→ 과거 사실과 반대되는 일을 가정하고 있으므로 가정법 과거완료 「If+주어+had+p.p. ~, 주어+조동사의 과거형+have+p.p. ...」로 쓴다.

4 (1) '~한다면 좋을 텐데'라는 현재의 실현 불가능한 소망은 「I wish+가정법 과거」로 나타내며, I wish 뒤에 오는 be동사는 주어에 관계없이 were를 쓴다. (2) '마치 ~했던 것처럼'이라는 의미의 「as if+가정법 과거완료」에서 as if절의 동사는 「had+p.p.」로 쓴다.

5 해석　Lily는 학교 장기자랑에 참가하고 싶어 한다. 문제는 그녀가 수줍음이 많고 다른 사람들 앞에서 공연하는 것에 대해 긴장한다는 것이다. 하지만 그녀는 노래에 대한 열정뿐만 아니라 아름다운 목소리도 가지고 있다.
이 상황에서 너는 그녀에게 뭐라고 말할 것인가?
You Lily, 내가 너라면 나는 내 자신을 믿을 거야. 장기자랑에 (참가) 신청해!
→ 현재 실현 불가능한 일을 가정하고 있으므로 가정법 과거 「If+주어+동사의 과거형 ~, 주어+조동사의 과거형+동사원형 ...」으로 쓴다. 이때 if절의 be동사는 주어에 관계없이 were를 쓴다.

chapter ⑪ 일치 및 특수구문

① 수 일치　p. 144

1 1 knows / know　2 are / is　3 have / has
2 1 is　2 live　3 makes

② 시제 일치　p. 145

1 1 would clean　2 needed　3 had met
2 1 was　2 catches　3 created

영작 기본 훈련　pp. 146~147

STEP 1

1 ⓐ die　ⓑ dies　2 ⓐ is　ⓑ is
3 ⓐ needs　ⓑ need　4 ⓐ enjoy　ⓑ enjoy
5 ⓐ is　ⓑ was
6 ⓐ will quit　ⓑ would quit
7 ⓐ is　ⓑ is　8 ⓐ landed　ⓑ landed

STEP 2

1 Economics is difficult
2 the picnic would be canceled
3 blue whales are mammals
4 A number of people are
5 Skipping classes is

STEP 3

1 All the buildings were damaged
2 that Columbus reached America in 1492
3 People thought that I was lucky.
4 The number of pandas is decreasing.
5 The young need to respect the elderly.

③ 강조 구문　p. 148

1 1 do know　2 did enjoy　3 does like
2 1 at the library　2 is my bike that
　　3 It was Dad that fixed

④ 부정 구문　p. 149

1 1 항상 맞는 것은 아니다
　　2 우리들 중 아무도 듣지 못했다
　　3 그들 둘 다, 가입하지 않을 것이다
　　4 모두가 행복한 것은 아니다.
2 1 Not every song　2 None of the boxes
　　3 don't always walk　4 Not all the clothes

영작 기본 훈련　pp. 150~151

STEP 1

1 It is Tom　2 It was Amy that
3 does look good　4 did do my best
5 Not every worker　6 None of my friends
7 Not all computer games
8 Neither of these books

STEP 2

1 does like kids　2 It is at noon that
3 It is not always hot　4 none of the problems
5 It was my neighbor that made noise

STEP 3

1 Not every K-pop song is popular
2 It was Linda that won the marathon.
3 Neither of her kids enjoys camping.
4 They did finish the project before the due date.
5 It was in the park that I lost my umbrella.

집중 훈련 1

01 shocked → shock　　**02** are → is
03 will → would　　**04** didn't go → went
05 were → was　　**06** are → is
07 was → is

집중 훈련 2

08 It was last summer that
09 She does look like
10 Ten dollars is not(isn't) enough
11 None of the students
12 The young learn new things
13 We did not(didn't) eat all the food
14 the United States is

집중 훈련 3

15 It was Jane that I met at the bookstore.
16 Everybody has different opinions.
17 Helen does not(doesn't) like every kind of music.
18 A number of people are dancing in the square.
19 I thought (that) she might arrive late.
20 I liked neither of them.
21 But we did have fun.

집중 훈련 4

22 We learned that water boils at 100℃.
23 Each class has twenty students.
24 None of them told the truth.
25 It was last Sunday that we took the swimming class.

01 「do/does/did+동사원형」으로 동사를 강조하므로 did 뒤에는 동사원형을 쓴다.

02 거리를 나타내는 말은 단수 취급한다.

03 주절의 시제가 과거이므로 시제에 맞춰 종속절의 조동사도 과거형으로 쓴다.

04 '모든 ~이 …인 것은 아니다'라는 의미의 부분 부정은 「not all+복수명사」를 써서 나타낸다. not이 쓰였으므로 동사에 not을 쓰지 않는다.

05 동명사구 주어는 단수 취급하므로 be동사는 was를 쓴다.

06 '~의 수'를 나타내는 「the number of+복수명사」는 단수 취급하므로 is를 쓴다.

07 과학적 사실은 주절의 시제에 관계없이 항상 현재시제로 쓴다.

08 과거시제이므로 It was와 that 사이에 강조하고자 하는 부사구(last summer)를 쓴다.

09 「do/does/did+동사원형」으로 동사를 강조할 수 있다. 주어가 she이고 현재시제인 문장이므로 「does+동사원형」으로 나타낸다.

10 복수 형태의 금액(ten dollars)은 단수 취급하므로 be동사는 is를 쓴다.

11 '아무도 ~ 않다'라는 의미의 전체 부정이므로 none을 써서 나타낸다. none이 쓰였으므로 동사에 not을 쓰지 않는다.

12 '~한 사람들'이라는 의미의 「the+형용사」는 복수 취급하므로 동사는 learn을 쓴다.

13 '모두 ~인 것은 아니다'라는 의미의 부분 부정이므로 「not ~ all」을 써서 나타낸다.

14 복수 형태의 국가명은 단수 취급하므로 be동사는 is를 쓰며, 일반적 사실은 주절의 시제에 관계없이 항상 현재시제로 쓴다.

15 과거시제이므로 It was와 that 사이에 강조하고자 하는 목적어(Jane)를 쓴다.

16 everybody는 단수 취급하므로 has를 쓴다.

17 '모두 ~인 것은 아니다'라는 의미의 부분 부정이므로 「not ~ every」를 써서 나타낸다.

18 '많은 ~'이라는 의미의 「a number of+복수명사」는 복수 취급한다.

19 주절의 시제를 과거로 쓰고, 시제에 맞춰 종속절의 조동사 may도 과거형 might로 쓴다.

20 '둘 다 ~ 않다'라는 의미의 전체 부정이므로 neither of를 써서 나타낸다. neither가 쓰였으므로 동사에 not을 쓰지 않는다.

21 동사를 강조할 때는 「do/does/did+동사원형」을 쓴다. 과거시제이므로 did를 쓴다.

22 과학적 사실은 주절의 시제에 관계없이 항상 현재시제로 쓴다.

23 each는 단수 취급하므로 has를 쓴다.

24 '아무도 ~ 않다'라는 의미의 전체 부정이므로 none을 써서 나타낸다. none이 쓰였으므로 동사에 not을 쓰지 않는다.

25 It was와 that 사이에 강조하고자 하는 부사구(last Sunday)를 쓴다.

1 (1) David that bought a nice jacket at this store

　(2) a nice jacket that David bought at this store

　(3) at this store that David bought a nice jacket

2 (1) I practice the piano every day

　(2) Tom would win the race

3 (1) None of the students should talk

　(2) don't clean my room every week

4 It was his dog that

5 Technology is not always helpful.

6 (1) Not all the participants won a prize.

　(2) Everybody did enjoy the competition.

---

1 과거시제이므로 It was와 that 사이에 강조하려는 말을 쓰고 나머지를 that 이하에 순서대로 쓴다.

2 (1) 현재의 습관은 주절의 시제에 관계없이 항상 현재시제로 쓴다.

(2) 주절이 과거시제일 때 종속절은 과거 또는 과거완료 시제로 쓴다.

3 (1) none은 '아무도 ~ 않다'라는 의미의 전체 부정을 나타낸다.

(2) every가 부정어와 함께 쓰이면 '모두 ~인 것은 아니다'라는 의미의 부분 부정을 나타낸다.

4 'His dog saved him.'에서 It was와 that 사이에 강조하고자 하는 주어(his dog)를 넣어 쓴다.

5 '항상 ~인 것은 아니다'라는 의미의 부분 부정이므로 not always를 쓴다.

6 해석 우리 학교는 지난주에 특별한 대회를 열었다. 그것은 일종의 노래 대회였지만, 패자는 없었다. 모든 참가자들이 상을 받았다. 모두가 대회를 즐겼다.

→ (1) not all은 '모두 ~인 것은 아니다'라는 의미의 부분 부정을 나타낸다.

(2) 동사를 강조할 때는 「do/does/did+동사원형」을 쓴다. 과거시제이므로 did를 쓴다.

중학 문법＋쓰기

클리어.

Level **3**

Answers

영역 | 브랜드 | 초1~2 | 초3~4 | 초5~6 | 중1 | 중2 | 중3 | 고1 | 고2 | 고3

독해

[중등] 기본서
READING CLEAR

[중등] 수능 대비서
수작 중학 비문학
영어 독해

[고등] 기본서
Supreme
구문독해 / 유형독해

[중·고등] 문장독해
공식으로 통하는 문장독해
기본 완성

듣기

[중등] 듣기모의고사
LISTENING CLEAR
중학영어 듣기모의고사

[고등] 듣기모의고사
Supreme 수능 영어
듣기 모의고사
기본 실전

어휘

[초·중·고등]
영단어, 영숙어
뜯어먹는 시리즈

[중·고등]
영단어
보카클리어

영어 실력과 내신 점수를 함께 높이는
중학 영어 클리어 시리즈

영문법 클리어 | LEVEL 1~3

문법 개념과 내신을 한 번에 끝내다!

- 중등에서 꼭 필요한 핵심 문법만 담아 시각적으로 정리
- 시험에 꼭 나오는 출제 포인트부터 서술형 문제까지 내신 완벽 대비

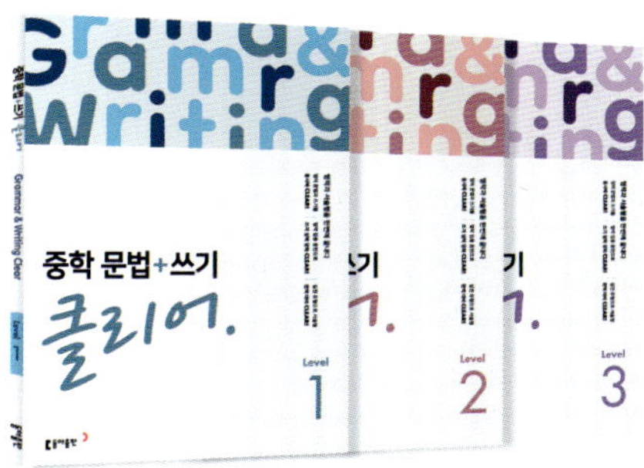

문법+쓰기 클리어 | LEVEL 1~3

영작과 서술형을 한 번에 끝내다!

- 기초 형태 학습부터 문장 영작까지 단계별로 영작 집중 훈련
- 최신 서술형 집중 훈련으로 서술형 실전 준비 완료

READING CLEAR | LEVEL 1~3

문장 해석과 지문 이해를 한 번에 끝내다!

- 핵심 구문 32개로 어려운 문법 구문의 정확한 해석 훈련
- Reading Map으로 글의 핵심 및 구조 파악 훈련

LISTENING CLEAR | LEVEL 1~3

듣기 기본기와 듣기 평가를 한 번에 끝내다!

- 최신 중학 영어듣기능력평가 완벽 반영
- 1.0배속/1.2배속/받아쓰기용 음원 별도 제공으로 학습 편의성 강화